Television: Policy and Culture

Titles of related interest

Television: Policy and Culture

Richard Collins

London
UNWIN HYMAN
Boston   Sydney   Wellington

Published by the Academic Division of

Unwin Hyman Ltd
15/17 Broadwick Street, London W1V 1FP, UK

Unwin Hyman Inc.,
955 Massachusetts Avenue, Cambridge, Mass. 02139, USA

Allen & Unwin (Australia) Ltd,
8 Napier Street, North Sydney, NSW 2060, Australia

Allen & Unwin (New Zealand) Ltd in association with the
Port Nicholson Press Ltd,
Compusales Building, 75 Ghuznee Street, Wellington 1, New Zealand

First published in 1990

British Library Cataloguing in Publication Data

Collins, Richard, 1946–
  Television, Policy and culture
  1. Television
  I. Title
  621.388

  ISBN 0–04–445766–9

Library of Congress Cataloging in Publication Data

Collins, Richard, 1914–
  Television : policy and culture / Richard Collins.
      p.   cm.
  Includes index.
  ISBN 0–04–445765–0 (HB).
  ISBN 0–04–445766–9 (PB)
  1. Television broadcasting policy. I. Title.
  HE8700.4.C65   1990
  384.55'068—dc20   90–39825
                                               CIP

Typeset in 10/12 Times
Printed in Great Britain by Billing and Sons, London and Worcester

Contents

Preface

These essays critically address, with varying degrees of explicitness, the assumptions from which media analysts and communication scholars have customarily approached television. Many of these assumptions are now, I think, ripe for revision. Themes such as the impact of technological and political change on television, the development and limits of the subject of media studies, the internationalization of television and culture, and the extent to which (and the mechanisms through which) television influences viewers' conception of the world are all explored below. Each of the following chapters (except chapters 1 and 2 which are primarily concerned with how media scholars go about their business) are essays in media policy and reflect my interest in television. Television is a medium that promises to remain the dominant mass medium of modern times although the terms of its dominance, and television itself, will change as circumstances change.

Times have changed since these essays were first published. However, although some statistics (such as those concerning the UK's trade in television programmes cited in chapter 7) have now been superseded by more recent data I have not updated the tables I have cited. I have resisted this temptation for two reasons. First any such updating would be selective; although new UK television programme trade statistics have been easily available (in the Department of Trade and Industry's publication *British Business* which has published them annually, generally in September, although official economies have led to the cessation of publication of *British Business*) other data sets are not. Second, and more important, I believe the conclusions I have drawn from the data available at the time of writing continue to be sustainable, even from a contemporary viewpoint which now enjoys 20/20 hindsight.

Of course if rewriting there are places where I would now make different emphases (for example in chapter 6 I would stress that the Thatcher Government's contradictory embrace of 'libertarian' markets and 'repressive' state controls is more pervasive than my discussion of the case of television suggests). But the changes I would have made, had I rewritten these papers for this publication, are ones of emphasis rather than of substance. Moreover I am pleased to republish unchanged articles, such as those on cable and satellite television, which were written at times of pervasive enthusiasm about the prospects for these new media, but which argued that their future was considerably gloomier than was generally supposed. I believe subsequent developments have supported my bearish analyses rather than the more widely touted bullish judgements of other commentators.

Policy research has two very vexing problems; it's difficult to see the wood among the trees, and the trees age rapidly and are supplanted by new growth. To do justice to complex issues all relevant data and the cross impacts of different political, technological, social, economic and cultural forces have to be considered (and each of these forces generates voluminous quantities of data for the researcher to handle), but this undergrowth of data often hides the trees, let alone the shape of the wood. The real task of the researcher – analysis, clarification and identification of the structuring factors at work in a given instance – may either go by default, or the undergrowth of data is cleared only by a crude slash and burn technique out of which comes 'analysis': too often of a normative or prescriptive kind. The Scylla of conjunctural analysis and history of Mark Twain's kind ('one goddam thing after another') is avoided only by crashing onto a Charybdis of assertion of 'universals' which imperfectly capture the complexity and contradictory nature of the 'facts'. Both rocks are littered with wrecked attempts to research broadcasting policy. Such research is further vexed by the perishability of the data with which it deals. The field – especially in the 'hot' areas such as satellite communications – with which these studies deal, is changing very fast, and consequently research, and the conclusions of researchers, sometimes have a short shelf life. Policy research has to find a way between the monitoring performed by the trade press (and UK broadcasting researchers are blessed with excellent trade journals), and the long term structural analysis demanded by the social sciences. To honour both the concreteness and sensitivity to institutional and political changes of short life journalism and the analytical sweep of the best social science, what Gellner calls 'general thinking', is no easy trick to pull. The policy researcher's task is to be a historian of the present without the assistance time affords 'real' historians by winnowing away the chaff of irrelevant data and contingent associations and revealing fundamental structures. But successful integration of information and analysis is far from easy. However there is no escape from policy research. An activity as costly and important as broadcasting requires analysis and comment from academics and other (relatively) disinterested parties. However these essays do not offer a programmatic and internally coherent body of theory or a model(s) of how media policy should be conducted. Rather, they are essays in the original sense of the word, explorations which essay, try out (or, some might argue, try on) ways of making sense of the complex interactions of technological, ideological, political and economic forces which play over contemporary television policy.

The essays collected here are (with three exceptions) reprinted from a variety of journals. From the *British Journal of Canadian Studies* (chapter 8), *Media Culture and Society* (chapters 3, 6, and 10), *Screen* (chapters 5 and 7), and from *Space Policy* (chapter 4). Chapter 11 was previously published in the book *Documentary and the Mass Media* (Corner, 1986). I'm pleased to have this opportunity to acknowledge the contribution the editors of these publications have made to improving my clarity of expression! John Tulloch and John Corner made particularly helpful editorial contributions. Any incomprehensibilities (and nonsenses) which remain are completely my fault. With some minor editorial changes and harmonization of referencing conventions the contents of this book are reprinted here in the form in which they were first published, except for chapters 1, 2, and 9 which are published here for the first time. Chapter 1 is an extended version of the keynote address I gave to the British Film Institute's 1989 conference on *Film and Media Studies in Higher Education*. It also incorporates sections of reviews (of John Fiske's *Television Culture* and Raphael Samuel's edited collection *Patriotism. The Making and Unmaking of British National Identity*) which were published in the *Times Higher Education Supplement* (22 April

1988 and 22 September 1989). Chapter 2 is a revised version of a paper commissioned for the Economic and Social Research Council's Cambridge workshop *Classic Issues in Mass Communication Research* held in 1988. Chapter 8 is a revised and developed version of conference papers presented at the 1988 International Television Studies Conference in London and the 1989 Conference on Communication and Culture in Philadelphia.

Chapter 1 is my view of the 'state of the nation' of media studies. It discusses the invidious condition of media studies, marooned on a remote peninsula of an increasingly depopulated and demoralized academic territory and experiencing the crumbling of the theoretical presuppositions (largely shaped in the 1970s) on which it is founded. These suppositions have been undermined by new trajectories of enquiry (and explicit theoretical challenges) but these new currents, which have undercut the old foundations, have not yet crystallized into a new revisionist paradigm. Although the former foundation and central organizing motif of media studies, the 'dominant ideology thesis' and its pendant notion of a strong media effect, seem no longer capable of bearing the weight of the edifices constructed on it, no new paradigm has been found to replace that which has been lost. Chapter 2 surveys the development of media studies in the UK, its relationship to neighbouring academic subjects (such as cultural studies) and assesses the utility of the subject's established approaches and emphases, and the extent to which it is adequate to meet the challenge posed by the new information and communication technologies (ICTs). Paradoxically I believe media studies' inheritance from literary studies and cultural theory fits it well for these problems and is likely to serve it well in the future. Not least in a new climate for broadcasting regulation where television programme quality (whatever that is) promises to become both a subject for litigation and a condition of corporate survival.

Chapter 3 examines the recent West European history of that paradigm of high tech internationalization of culture: satellite television. It considers Europe's experience of a 'second generation' of satellite television, which used cable to redistribute satellite signals to viewers for final consumption. (The first generation of satellites, such as Telstar, were used to link broadcaster to broadcaster for programme exchanges, the third generation of powerful direct broadcast satellites have established direct to home television services.) The second generation of satellite television was a failure. In particular the hoped for, or feared, development of a transnational European television audience made possible by satellite technology did not take place. The most important reason for the financial failure of the transnational services (and their con- sequential decline) was the absence of a unified taste among West European television viewers. Culture and language presented impermeable cultural 'screens' to the international consumption of satellite television. (Although intervening variables, such as the paucity of transnational brands which could be advertised on satellite television, and thus fund the new services, were important factors which contributed to the medium's lack of success.) Chapter 4 argues that the likely impact of satellite television in the UK has been much exaggerated and that the success or failure of satellite television services (such as Sky television or BSB – if BSB ever begins its oft delayed service), depends principally on the nature of competing terrestrial televi- sion services. Unless these are significantly worsened it is unlikely that satellite television in the UK market will be economically viable. Chapter 5 examines the proposals advanced in the UK government's 1988 White Paper on broadcasting policy. Written (as was this preface) before publication of the long anticipated broadcasting bill which was announced in the Queen's speech opening Parliament in November 1989, chapter 5 argues that the White Paper reveals significant contradictions in HMG's approach to broadcasting policy. And that, in spite of the government's promulgation of disgraceful repressive measures (such as estab- lishment of the Broadcasting Standards Council and prohibition of direct representation of the members and views of lawful pol- itical parties), the White Paper contains many positive elements. Notably its proposals for increases in broadcasting pluralism, replacement of the established expensive, but often ineffective, regulatory system for commercial broadcasting and addition of the criterion of 'popularity' to those of 'diversity' and 'quality' which formerly underpinned UK broadcasting policy. Chapter 6 discusses the nature and power of a system of ideas: the notion of a developing global transition from industrial to information society. Such ideas, associated with Daniel Bell's notion of a post-industrial, knowledge-based society, have been an important motor of contemporary governments' economic policies and their prioritization of the information and communication sectors of their economies. In one sense this chapter is a study of how 'ideas count' but it also, taking cable television in the UK as a case study, examines the relationships between communications hardware and communications software and between information technology and information. In this chapter I argued both that cable television was unlikely to succeed economically in the UK (a judgement that events have so far vindicated) and that there is a crucial, but seldom examined, relationship between communication hardware and software. Because the importance of this relationship has been underestimated by those seduced by high technology and the ideology of the information society (still powerful temptresses as evidenced by the Labour party's 1989 embrace of a fibre optic albatross in its advocacy of a national broadband telecommunication infrastructure) both cable and, (as I have argued in chapters 3 and 4) satellite television have deceived the hopes of their backers.

Chapters 7, 8 and 9 are primarily focused on software and cultural issues (a theme also touched on in chapter 3). Chapter 7 discusses the trade in television programmes between the world's two most important exporters of audio-visual information commodities, the United Kingdom and the United States of America, and the degree to which the conceptual tool customarily applied in media studies to the understanding of such phenomena, the 'media imperialism thesis' is adequate to the task for which it is used. Chapter 8 discusses television in Canada and its role in the development of a national culture. Canada is customarily regarded by advocates of the media imperialism thesis as an exemplary instance of the global condition of subordination of an ostensibly sovereign state to a foreign imperium through television. However, I argue here that television has been less important in the making and unmaking of national identities and political values than has generally been supposed: herein lies the real importance of the Canadian case. Canada suggests that there is a *weak* rather than a *strong* relationship between cultural consumption and political identity and sovereignty. This theme is further discussed in the following chapter, chapter 9, which examines the threat, or promise, of American television in Europe and the extent to which the Canadian case anticipates a likely future European experience. How far do the notions of

decoupled polity and culture advanced by Pierre Trudeau offer a
superior basis for understanding international information flows
and the consequences which follow from them than do those offered
by classic nationalist theory (which has hitherto informed media
studies' discussion of such matters)?

Chapters 10 and 11 are concerned with analysis of television
content and in particular with television news and documentary
programmes. Chapter 10 discusses the theoretical assumptions
which have informed UK studies of television news. Notably
the concept of 'bias', a notion which was so important in UK
news studies of the 1970s and 1980s. I argue that this notion of
bias (and its inverted reflection which presents television news
as impartial and autonomous) is misleading. The relationships
of newsmakers (whether those, such as politicians, who are
depicted in the news or those, such as journalists, who produce
television news) are better understood as negotiations between a
plurality of interests and groups who bargain over what makes
the news rather than as either a conspiracy of a united and
essentially homogenous group (or class) of newsmakers acting in
a common interest or as separate estates. Chapter 11 examines the
practice of the Anglo-American documentary film-maker Roger
Graef who is an exemplary exponent of television's dominant
legitimizing visual representational style of naturalism. Graef's
work, I argue, embodies the purest manifestation of the practice
prescribed for professional news and documentary film-makers.
However the contradictions implicit in Graef's project (and here
he is representative of television journalism in general) both permit
critics of established news practices to argue that television news is
'biased' and journalists to defend their work as 'impartial'.

To Lucy, my mother

Chapter 1

Paradigm Lost?

What is media studies? There is a limited consensus among UK scholars about the content and limits of the subject. In 1988 I circulated a two page questionnaire to 200 'primary definers' in media studies inviting respondents to cite the five most important books or articles for media and film studies published in the last ten years and to make any further comments they thought appropriate. The questionnaire went to those named as contacts for higher education courses in film and television in the directory of courses (Orton, 1987) published by the British Film Institute (BFI), to members of the Council for National Academic Awards (CNAA) Register of Specialist Advisors with media studies expertise, and to colleagues at the Polytechnic of Central London, at the BBC and IBA and in other universities, colleges and polytechnics not reached either through the CNAA or BFI lists and who were known to me to be active media scholars. The 60 respondents who replied nominated 146 different titles. The most cited work was instanced only by 15 respondents and the top 16 titles cited accounted for only 111 citations (out of a possible total of 300 citations). The most cited title was thus instanced by only a quarter of respondents. Thus, assuming that the indicator I chose was appropriate to its purpose, there seems to be little agreement about the nature and limits of media studies. However several respondents commented that the core texts which they thought defined the subject had been produced more than ten years ago and that therefore the last decade had been a rather fallow period. Intuitively that feels right: an important territory and agenda was marked out in the 1970s and has not yet been displaced. Three reflections follow from this observation.

1

First, this absence of development is a symptom of the institutional history of UK higher education in the last decade. There has been very little renewal of personnel in higher education. Many lecturers can testify to the lost generation – generations – of very talented students who have been unable to find academic jobs in the UK. Most of them have been lost to academic life altogether, although a few have found posts in the United States and Australia. Thus a crucial resource for renewal and reworking of paradigms has been lost to the subject. The story goes, perhaps apocryphal but certainly credible, that UK universities have between them only one tenured social scientist aged less than thirty. Most of those media scholars who are fortunate enough to be in jobs have been in post for nearly two decades. Decades in which they have been denied the stimulae brought by new colleagues and new ideas and have worked in steadily worsening material circumstances. Classes have grown in size, there is less time for supervision of individual students, library services and provision of time, resources and institutional legitimacy for research have all eroded. And, most absurd and dysfunctional of all, lecturers paid perhaps £20,000 a year are spending more and more time performing the duties of absent and unreplaced former administrative and technical colleagues who were paid half as much.

Second, key agencies for fostering talent which existed in the 1970s have been lost. There is now nowhere for young academic writers to learn their business. I, and others of my generation, benefited enormously from being able to 'learn how to write'. First by reviewing and writing short articles and then longer and more considered pieces in *Screen Education*. The British Film Institute television monographs performed a similar valuable nursery function. Where now does someone go to write their first article or review or first 40,000 words?

Third, in spite of factors 1 and 2 above there has been an important intellectual migration away from the paradigm articulated in the 1970s and which remains dominant. However, the migration, manifested in criticism of the old dominant paradigm and explorations in a variety of new directions, has not yet been focused in a coherently articulated revisionist thesis. New initiatives remain an unsystematized series of partial antitheses to the 1970s thesis. Here the changed material circumstances which have distinguished the late eighties from the late seventies and, *a fortiori*, the late sixties, have been decisive. The pace of intellectual change and development has slowed, sometimes it seems to a glacial pace. But change there has been. However, the emerging new problematic in media studies needs synthesizing, clearly articulating and quite simply marketing better.

The seventies paradigm of the 'dominant ideology thesis' still, I think, marks the co-ordinates on which our mental map of the media is plotted. Ideology is usefully defined by Lovell as 'the production and dissemination of erroneous beliefs whose inadequacies are socially motivated' (Lovell, 1980, p. 51). The dominant ideology thesis attributes to a unified body of erroneous ideas – ideology – causal status in what is defined as a systematic and pervasive mystification of people's understanding of society and social relations. The mass media are customarily understood to be at least a major agency, and often the decisive agency, in the propagation and reproduction of ideology. Implicit in the dominant ideology thesis is a notion of a strong media effect (despite the lack of satisfactory empirical demonstrations of a strong effect as a *general* phenomenon). The dominant ideology thesis can be seen as a particular instance of a general tendency in twentieth-century political theory to emphasize the role of ideas rather than force in holding society together. It has several characteristics that made it, and still make it, more seductive than other rival theories which also emphasize consent rather than duress as the vital social glue which keeps society together.

First, it was a *grand theory*. It offered comprehensive explanation of the workings of society. It made comprehensible the fantastic complexity of modern social relations by positing a master contradiction, or a few fundamental and related contradictions, from which social structure and social relations were generated. It asserted that fundamental truth(s) was (or were) misrepresented by a false system of ideas (whether or not consciously managed and mobilized by those advantaged by the misrepresentations of the dominant ideology) which served the interests of a few and masked the interests of the many. Second, and consequentially, it had a *moral* dimension. It gave an attractive social role to intellectuals whose task it became to demystify the false image of the world that the dominant ideology constituted as real. We were invested with, and enthusiastically assumed the role which

Brecht prescribed for the dramatist, ushering the audience into 'his [sic] own real world with attentive faculties' (Brecht, 1961, p. 13). The mass media were designated as the principal agency through which the dominant ideology was disseminated. The role of media studies was to strip the legitimizing mask from the media and by revealing them as agents of oppression hasten the day when justice would triumph. We have not lost our taste for such melodramatic morality plays, as examination of the demonization of Rupert Murdoch will show.

Yet the notion that the mass media are crucial sites for the exercise of social power through which ruling groups successfully maintain their rule has, in recent years, been put under considerable pressure. However, an emerging revisionist critique of the dominant ideology thesis has not yet been clearly and systematically articulated and for that reason has not become a new countervailing paradigm. At least within the field of film and media studies it has not. There are, for example, few citations of Abercrombie, Hill and Turner's book *The Dominant Ideology Thesis* (first published in 1980 and reprinted in 1984 and 1985) in the academic literature of film and media studies – none of the respondents to my questionnaire cited it – although Abercrombie, Hill and Turner subject this 'dominant paradigm' in media studies to a powerful and remorseless critique. Indeed they rebut not only a core proposition of the dominant ideology thesis but an axiomatic assumption in media studies. They propose that:

> The evidence of media influence is so thin and subject to so many caveats that our conclusions must be that the media are not significant except in the most isolated instances. (Abercrombie, Hill and Turner, 1985, p. 152)

By and large media scholars have not noticed the sapping of the foundations on which their subject was built. But they have been able to ignore the widening cracks in the structures they inhabit because the walls have not yet fallen; nor has the new structure, which promises a superior vantage point, yet risen above its foundations. The critique of the old dominant paradigm has not yet been followed by a convincing new totalizing vision. Although there have been powerful assaults on the system of ideas on which the UK's orthodoxy in media studies has been founded, and various explorations of alternative lines of argument, there has been no convincing new paradigm articulated. Unless such a revisionist paradigm is systematized it is unlikely to replace the established paradigm (however time-worn and full of holes), because no substitute can so far be offered for one of the most attractive elements in the old paradigm: its claims to comprehensive explanatory power. Any theory which has *general* applicability will be preferred to one that hasn't. For the role of intellectuals is to explain, analyse and systematize, not simply to describe. Letting go of a holistic paradigm which seems to make general sense (however contestable its premises are in particular local instances) of what otherwise appear as contingent, random and inexplicable phenomena in exchange for a sceptical critique, which though making better sense at points A, B and C, doesn't have a 'big picture' analysis to compare with that of the, admittedly, flawed holistic paradigm seems a bad bargain. For without the ability to paint a big picture our pretensions as intellectuals are unsustainable. Any intellectual system that makes comprehensive sense is likely to be more attractive than another which lacks a totalizing power. Herein lies the primary explanation of the continuing dominance of the dominant ideology thesis in our thinking. The second is that our material interests have been served by it. As teachers and researchers concerned with the media, our jobs – not to speak of our cultural capital – have depended on arguing that the media are important. Consequently any decline in the plausibility of the dominant ideology thesis sets us problems. First of finding a new general theory and second a new kind of general theory which will, like the old, maintain our professional *raison d'être*.

What then are the objections to the dominant ideology thesis and its associated notion of a strong media effect? Abercrombie, Hill and Turner (1985) attack the dominant ideology thesis on theoretical and empirical grounds. The core of their case is put forward in an examination of the extent and origins of social coherence at three moments in British (essentially English) medieval and modern history. They argue that the absence of a dominant ideology performing the functions designated for it at these moments (of feudalism, nascent capitalism and post-Second World War capitalism) falsifies the thesis' claims to have general explanatory power. They argue moreover on theoretical grounds, but drawing on their empirical rebuttals, that the dominant ideology thesis is unlikely to have even a limited explanatory power in other historical instances. As Abercrombie, Hill and Turner recognize, their challenge is not only to a Marxist theory but also to 'functionalist theories of common culture in sociology' (Abercrombie, Hill and Turner, 1985, p. 2). To some extent these propositions have been anticipated in an important trajectory in media and cultural studies, which has challenged and qualified the notions of a dominant ideology and an overall social coherence in contemporary capitalist societies. Both feminist scholarship in film and media studies and cultural studies scholarship in general have attested to the authenticity and robustness of contradictory subcultures, persuasively arguing that there is no single dominant ideology but rather that society is animated by a plurality of distinct belief systems. These manifest themselves in a variety of subcultures and worldviews which are differentiated by a number of factors, not least that of gender. However, such studies have characteristically either left unanswered the questions of how large-scale and complex developed societies reproduce themselves and how separate subcultures interrelate. Or they have reiterated the old and unsatisfactory dominant ideology thesis – which is fundamentally inconsistent with the positive recognition in such studies of the plurality of cultures and belief systems in modern societies – anew in terms of a loosely associated but fundamentally compatible unholy alliance of racist, patriarchal and capitalist beliefs. An impressive monument (not least for its bulk) to this trend in scholarship is the more than one thousand page three decker *Patriotism* of the History Workshop (Samuel, 1989).

Patriotism is representative both in its impressive sensitivity to different cultures and traditions in British society and in its lack of a comprehensive integrative intellectual paradigm able to articulate the relationships between the distinct subcultures it surveys. It exemplifies the achievements and limits of a cultural studies approach, here directed towards the understanding of a powerful contemporary social force, nationalism. Thus far its contribution has been productive.

The founding editorial of its journal, *History Workshop Journal*, defined History Workshop's purpose as bringing 'the boundaries of history closer to people's lives' and making 'history a more democratic activity'. It did so by changing those who made history, both by extending the production of history outside the academy (evident in the occupational profile of contributors to the journal, still more so in the participants in workshops, and assisted by the regular sections on archives and sources in the journal) and by redefining the subject of history, epitomized by Raphael Samuel's assertion (which triggered Robert Skidelsky's wrath in the running *Methodenstreit* provoked by The History Working Party's essay in curriculum definition) that the Married Women's Property Act of 1882 is more important than the Battle of Trafalgar. Samuel in his public jousting over the content of the history section of the National Curriculum has effectively broken lances to champion 'history from below' and the study of the private as well as the public sphere. *History Workshop Journal* (HWJ) began (as *History Workshop*) in 1976 as 'a journal of socialist historians' and derived from a decade of History Workshops (which continued in parallel to the journal) held at Ruskin College. Though never edited by a single named editor, Raphael Samuel (the editor and biggest contributor to the *Patriotism* collection) has the most powerful claim to be considered the principal animator of the enterprise: he was a founding editor, joint author (with Gareth Steadman-Jones) of both the first editorial and that which opened the ten year anniversary issue and was named as a member of the four who, in 1982, became the 'inner group' running the journal. In 1982 *History Workshop Journal* metamorphosed into a 'journal of socialist and feminist historians'. It marked this transition from asexual axolotal to mature salamander by stating (in the editorial to Issue 13 of Spring 1982 when 'feminist' first appeared on the masthead):

> socialist history means not merely the history of socialist movements or labour organisations, but the reinterpretation of all dominant social and cultural institutions in terms of a class perspective, so a historical analysis influenced by feminism demands that we ask new questions of the past, challenge old assumptions and become sensitive to the central significance of sexual divisions in the shaping of both past and present.

It is notable how much less clearly defined was the feminist than the socialist project in HWJ; socialist history is clearly and programmatically defined, feminist history is rather an opening to an undefined new subject matter and approach. The first prescriptive, the second permissive. *Patriotism* is in the latter mould, exemplifying an opening of History Workshop to new problematics which lend themselves uncomfortably to analysis in terms of a class perspective. Throughout its decade and a half HWJ has opened up new territories for history and historians. Its fat (more than 200 pages per issue) volumes embrace not only the stuff of academic discourse, the articles and reviews proper to a conventional journal, but also anecdotes (put enough of them together and they become data), obituaries, notices of meetings, scholarly and entertaining gleanings. HWJ is the parish pump around which socialist and feminist historians meet. Diverse, pluralistic, demotic (its notes for authors demand excision of 'foreign, including Latin, words') and democratic. Its strengths have been its heterogeneity, its *parti pris* and openness to new voices and material.

But *Patriotism* reveals vulnerable points in History Workshop's line of battle. An idiosyncratic approach to what can count as evidence, and a disinclination to move from the thickets of particular historical experience to the theoretical high ground. Fine grained concrete particularity is the stuff and strength of History Workshop history, but that strength risks becoming a magpie accumulation of material, and resurrection of what has been hidden from history may shake into creaking life what might better be left unobtrusively interred. There is a consequential underproduction of powerful new generalizations and challenging interpretative paradigms which will make sense of and justify the retrieval of an abundance of empirical material. Such a process demands not simply the addition of new categories to an established system, for example the addition of a feminist to a socialist perspective, but critique of the old organizing principles and synthesis of new. Nowhere more than in the study of nationalism/patriotism is such new theorizing needed. For patriotism is a sentiment attached to an object, the nation, which is opposed to the class perspective espoused by the HWJ. Moreover patriotism, the sentiment in which the ideology of nationalism manifests itself, testifies to the existence of more than one dominant ideology circulating in modern societies. They are neither to be understood in terms of a single master discourse, a dominant ideology which organizes and glues them together, nor in terms of a disconnected plurality of subcultures thrown together in an adventitious proximity.

Nations are communities commonly bound together by ethnicity, language, culture, geography and, yes, history. Such communities, notoriously for socialists, are 'vertically' differentiated from other communities, other nations. Whereas a class perspective, classically manifested in an *international* socialism, asserts horizontal bonds of class which rupture the vertical bonds of nation to bind together workers (and rulers) internationally. History Workshop has rightly paid attention to the history of human attitudes and sentiments, to the ideas which animate and limit human actions. An important part of its expansion of the boundaries of history has been the inclusion of culture within the historian's ambit. Its focus on the local and particular is symptomatic of English Cultural Studies' prioritization of subcultures as an object of study. But reading culture as history too often becomes the substitution of culture for history. Recovering and reporting the sentiments expressed by historical actors (even a writer of fiction's report of the statement of a small child) is potentially productive of insights and new knowledge but it has its dangers. The collection yields examples of the grabbing of a shard of 'evidence' in order to substantiate a proposition. Evidence which may not even attain the status of one of Norman Mailer's factoids (see chapter 2): a real gem (and I have not made it up) is the citation of the behaviour of a vicar in a Richmal Crompton novel in order to demonstrate the social/political role of the clergy in interwar suburbia. And more is required to sustain the judgement that in September 1939 'more attention was paid to the attitude of the Empire than to that of Britain's notional European allies' than a citation from *English Journey* reporting what one of Priestley's small daughters said to him. The judgement made may well be true but the evidence adduced to sustain it is unlikely to convince the sceptical. Here we discover a clue to the limits of History Workshop's work: its characteristic procedure is synecdoche (and here it is representative of a larger intellectual movement), one example sustains a general theory. *Patriotism* testifies to the fine-grained analysis which is often an enormous strength in History Workshop's work and in cultural studies generally. But fascination with the grain means not only that the forest is lost from view but also individual trees. When the absence of these general organizing principles becomes evident, those disorientated by too close an attention to the particularities of the grain grasp at the lodestone of the dominant ideology thesis which promises to organize and orientate all the phenomena in question in terms of a single organizing principle. *Patriotism*, though full of local excellences, lacks a centre. Throughout it iterates the local, minoritarian and particular, but seldom the national, majoritarian and general. Are the relations between the separate elements of England and the English experience evoked in *Patriotism* more than adventitious? If so how? And if not then how and why does the British polity hang together? If we grant the implicit premise of *Patriotism* that one of the peculiarities of the English is diversity, that English culture is extraordinarily atomized and discontinuous, then we have a very challenging paradox. For England and, since the Act of Union, Britain has and does hang together. Yet, if nationalists are to be believed, such an incongruence between a stable state and a diverse polity is inconceivable. Either History Workshop is wrong to propose that Britain is as discontinuous and pluralistic as *Patriotism* implies, or nationalists are wrong in their stipulations about the relationship between culture and polity. Or both. Probably both. The achievement of *Patriotism* is its affirmation of the diversity of experience and identity within the British polity. But its evocation of a plurality of identities does not, except tangentially, address the central questions. Where lies shared national identity? What are the relationships between local and particular and national and general identities? How far do the cases of the United Kingdom, Britain, and England confirm or challenge the central precepts of the contemporary ideology, of nationalism? What holds and has held so plural a Britain together? And how far does the British case challenge the central presuppositions of nationalist theory? The ideology of nationalism demands that polity and culture be congruent, that nations find a political home in their own states. Without such congruence political institutions and national communities are deemed to be vulnerable. Yet, though nationalism is now peculiarly evident as a political force, national identity and the sovereignty of nation-states are more and more difficult to sustain. As the world economy becomes more interdependent, travel and movement of populations more common, and culture internationalized, the stipulations of nationalists become increasingly difficult to realize. More and more we are all, as Salman Rushdie put it (the masculine noun doubtless embracing the feminine) 'translated men'. Our culture is increasingly a borrowed, transposed and synthetic phenomenon, we are everywhere and nowhere at home. Neither subcultural studies nor a notion of a single discourse holding society together provide a satisfactory means of understanding the coherence and variety of modern societies. Subcultural studies, such as those presented in *Patriotism*, demonstrate the society cannot be explained in terms of a single dominant ideology (whether that ideology is nationalism or patriarchy or capitalist ideology). They do not, however, answer the question of how society as a whole works and what, if not a system of shared beliefs, holds it together. Abercrombie, Hill and Turner not only offer a comprehensive and persuasive critique of the dominant idology thesis:

> the importance of ideology has been greatly exaggerated by Marxists and sociologists and that ideologies do not have the consequences which are attributed to them by the dominant ideology thesis. (Abercrombie, Hill and Turner, 1985, p.3)

They also articulate a provocative counter thesis which takes on the problem of explaining social coherence. They argue that far from ideas holding society together social coherence is neither comprehensive nor based either on ideas or on what Althusser named the 'ideological state apparatuses'. Rather social coherence (such as it is) is effected by:

> the dull compulsion of economic relationships, by the integrative effects of the division of labour, by the coercive nature of law and politics. (Abercrombie, Hill and Turner, 1985, p. 6)

By the forces not of 'culture' but of 'structure'. If Abercrombie, Hill and Turner's propositions are true then the media are much less important in social reproduction and social coherence than the dominant ideology thesis and media scholars have hitherto supposed. This is not necessarily to endorse Abercrombie, Hill and Turner's argument; rather to assert that their contentions demand a response which media scholars, and in particular those wishing to argue for a dominant ideology and for a strong media effect, have yet to offer. Seen from Abercrombie, Hill and Turner's point of view the prevailing theory in UK media studies over the last two decades or so is badly flawed. It is reductive (the dark side of its pretensions to a comprehensive explanatory power), it doesn't explain important phenomena and it is a source of significant misrecognitions. Among these misrecognitions is media studies' 'macro thesis' of international media relations: the notion of media imperialism.

Dominance of information flows seems not to directly translate into social power. US domination of world information flows does not guarantee US domination in other spheres. Indeed since the Second World War the military, economic and political power of the USA and UK, which account for more than 90 per cent of world trade in TV programmes, have declined. The waxing power of the 'media imperialists' in the information sphere has been accompanied by their waning economic, political and military force.

Another important misrecognition is the attribution of decisive political influence to the media. Voter behaviour does not readily correlate with media consumption. In what is probably the world's most mediatized political event ever – George Bush becoming President of the United States – barely 50 per cent of American voters turned out to vote. Moreover in the UK marked regional disparities in voting behaviour cannot readily be related to thhe role of the media. Can we explain the return of Labour MPs in Inner London and the north-east of England by proposing that voters there consume different media to that consumed by voters in the south-east of England? And if the media are so poweerful why have regional accents and dialects not disappeared in the wake of national radio and TV?

How does the dominant paradigm explain the establishment of Channel 4 (or the legalization of citizens' band radio) by a Thatcher government, or, in a newspaper industry 'dominated' by transnational capital, the establishment and growth in circulation of *The Independent*? One of my most treasured experiences in 1987 was hearing Jeremy Isaacs speak at the second of the Henry Hetherington lectures (Isaacs, 1987) – organized by a broadly Labour Party group with support from the Transport and General Workers Union (TGWU) – arguing that the British press could plausibly be thought to be in a very healthy condition. Where else in the world, Isaacs pertinently asked, are there five quality newspapers of diverse ownership competing in a single market?

Moreover Isaacs argued that we need not be too worried by the tabloids, which are taken seriously by no one! Obviously demob-happy at the end of his period of office at Channel 4, he turned to Ron Todd, the General Secretary of the TGWU, who was on the platform with other members of the Left establishment and asked him why he'd wasted his members' money on the *News on Sunday* (a Left Sunday newspaper largely financed and supported by trades unions and Labour-controlled local authorities, which produced three issues before folding with a loss of 'at least £2m'. *News on Sunday* is tendentiously and hilariously memorialized in Chippindale and Horrie, 1988.) Instead, Isaacs suggested TGWU policy should be to give members free subscriptions to the *Financial Times*. Unfortunately the chairman permitted no questions from the floor. Todd did not reply to the provocation and Isaacs' interpolation was excised from the printed version of the lecture!

Further questions abound; how do we reconcile the dominant ideology thesis with both the continued re-election of Mrs Thatcher and the declining confidence of viewers and newspaper readers in the veracity of news (see Collins, 1984)? If we posit that the Tory media are crucial agents in the three successive election victories of Mrs Thatcher, how do we deal with indications that during the period of office of the Thatcher government public confidence in that putatively Tory media has declined? Perhaps we can rescue a notion of media effect by suggesting that effects take place at the margin and such marginal changes can be highly influential. For example, the 'first past the post' electoral system common in anglophone states effectively 'amplifies' marginal shifts in voting behaviour into major shifts in party representation in Parliament and thus in government and in policy implementa-tion. But if we have a notion of marginal – albeit significant – effects we have to let go of our notion of dominant ideology.

We have then a crisis in the old dominant paradigm but no coherent revisionist synthesis. Perhaps that's not surprising because it is not only the paradigms in media studies that are in crisis. Many taken for granted categories from other academic fields are also under pressure. There is a global waning of faith in the role of the state. In the field of media studies this shift is reflected most clearly in a waxing concern about and interest in 'deregulation'. However states and peoples east and west are pervasively adopting markets rather than the state, or para-statal institutions, as allocative agencies. Restructuring, *perestroika*, is occurring west and east of the Elbe. Not only is the state withering away and being supplanted by markets but the ground is moving under us in other important respects. Our model of international relations is based on the idea of the normative sovereignty of the nation-state. The conceptual couplet nation-state is the building block from which we construct our understandings of the international political sphere. Yet internationalization of both economy and culture is dissolving the congruences between political institutions, culture and community, and economic activity which we have come to believe to be normal and which have wedded the terms which make up the complete nation-state.

Of course there are counter-indications to the 'decline of the state' hypothesis. In the UK the Broadcasting Standards Council (BSC) and the coronation of Lord Mogg of Video as an electronic Lord Chamberlain can't be understood in these terms. But the flexing of the well developed authoritarian muscles of the UK state and Tory party, though irreconcilable with deregulatory policies, again poses challenges to the dominant ideology thesis. If the mass media are so well adapted to the reproduction of the status quo as the dominant ideology thesis suggests then why do the political agents of the socially dominant forces require a body such as the BSC to check, control and repress the media which are, notionally, so effectively serving their interest?

There is much to think about. Our subject is not alone in feeling the comfortable, familiar rug of well-worn assumptions being pulled from under it. But we should remember that change offers opportunities as well as threats and that we enter troubled times with some very positive inheritances.

The loose field of media studies, without a distinct integrating discipline or heuristic procedures, has, at its best, successfully synthesized insights and modes of analysis from the humanities and social sciences. It has displayed a sensitivity to the content of the mass media and other socially generalized symbolic forms found too seldom in social-scientific content analysis. And it customarily attends to the *social* character of meaning-making which too often goes by default in the humanities. Success in such intellectual bridge-building is not easily won. Media studies demands an intellectual capacity for synthesis and integration that is distinctive and valuable. Here I think is the ground on which we fight when charged by critics from 'proper' academic disciplines that our subject lacks a coherent disciplinary structure. Media studies is not a 'deep' discipline which sports a well developed and coherent body of theory and a stable set of methodologies. But it is a 'wide' discipline, the practice of which demands synthetic habits of mind which are no less valuable than the different mental sets cultivated and demanded by other academic subjects. But at its worst, media studies has sheltered an extraordinary reductivism. Political economists who have read off meaning and effect from ownership and control. Textual critics who have ignored the vexing and contradictory social processes whereby the polysemic potentiality of signs and their combinations are shaped and meaning socially negotiated.

The seductions of reductivism are potent. They offer explanation and security, the ability to order, or seem to order, a baffling heterogeneity of instances. And we must recognize that the dominant paradigm has been advanced with considerable rhetorical power and has revealed important truths, not least in Stuart Hall's work which has probably been the single most important influence on UK media studies in the 1980s (and is enjoying a new public and a fresh influence in the United States). But the limits of Hall's work are identified in John Kelly's excellent review (in the *Times Higher Education Supplement* 9 December 1988, pp. 13 and 15) of Hall's *The Hard Road to Renewal: Thatcherism and the Crisis of the Left* (Hall, 1988) which Kelly mercilessly dissected. Kelly took Hall's grand theory – his overarching analysis about the reasons for the three successive election victories coupled with the largest parliamentary majority since the 1940s achieved by Mrs Thatcher – and comments: 'The question repeatedly begged in these essays is: How does Hall know any of these things?' Not only does Kelly argue that personal judgement and intuition cannot be regarded as sufficient, but adduces a wealth of empirical evidence to challenge Hall's central propositions about the popularity of Thatcherism and the misconceptions which underlie the rhetorical power of Hall's prose. Other instances of rhetorical extravagance imperfectly supported by empirical evidence which were passed over by Kelly could be cited. For example Hall, in an essay written jointly with Crichter, Jefferson, Clarke and Roberts, makes the ridiculous claim that the Heath government's period of office saw UK 'inflation graduated to riproaring Weimar Republic proportions' (Hall, 1988, p. 19). UK inflation has never approached that of Weimar Germany. In Germany in 1923 the mark–dollar parity changed from 7,090 marks to the dollar in January to 190,000 million marks to the dollar in October (McKenzie, 1971, pp. 141 and 150). The UK has simply not experienced, or come close to experiencing, such a trauma.

Media studies has been decisively shaped by Hall's work and by the paradigm of 'cultural studies' which owes so much to his contribution. Kelly's review is a salutory counterblast to well established orthodoxies. Not only for its insistence on evidence for propositions and argument rather than (or at least as well as) polemic, but also for the pointer it offers to the continued importance of a distinction which 'cultural studies' has customarily elided: that between culture and society, symbolization and experience. Cultural studies has characteristically assumed both strong media effects and an absence either of hierarchy between discourses or of different registers in discourse. The category culture (which in English has an ambiguity that makes such elisions easy) needs to be disaggregated and the two distinct referents, which English tends to slide together, require distinguishing, whereas cultural studies à la Birmingham 'read' society as a series of texts and elided the distinction between symbolization and experience. Evidently certain truths were powerfully revealed by so doing but the price paid, of eliding the distinction customarily made by anthropologists between structure and culture under an omnibus rubric culture, has been high. Structure has been read off from culture; symbols constituted as equivalent to experience.

A powerful emergent intellectual current which is steadily eroding territories formerly inhabited by cultural studies – post-modernism – does usefully reintroduce distinctions between different discourse registers which had formerly been eroded. However, though it is in some sense a healthy response to the crisis in the old dominant ideology paradigm, post-modernism is a movement about which we should be cautious.

Post-modernism is a protean phenomenon but at its core it is a refusal of rationalism and explanation. In many ways this has been enormously productive. Post-modernism has decoupled superstructure from base. In doing so it has challenged both the old Left paradigm which asserts that being determines consciousness, that base determines superstructure. And the new Left notion which has similarly identified a strong reciprocal correspondence between superstructure and base but which has argued that superstructural changes will produce changes in consciousness and consequentially political and social changes which will in turn change the base. The first, old Left paradigm of the social equivalence of art has waned considerably in power and respectability but the latter, new, paradigm is ascendent. It valorizes modernist forms because they, it is believed, are an indispensable agency of social change: *vide*, among a plethora of examples, the claim that the film *The Nightcleaners* was 'the most important political film to have been made in this country' (Johnston and Willeman, 1976, p. 104 [see however Willeman, 1978]). The claim for *The Nightcleaners* was made because of its formal characteristics, characteristics which, it was believed, would produce changes of consciousness in viewers and lead them to act. Both old and new Left paradigms affirm a relationship of determination, one asserting the primacy of base, the other of superstructure. Post-modernism has on the contrary reintroduced the category of the aesthetic, of a distinctively non-utilitarian mode of signification. In artistic production, let us say in architecture, it has revalidated invention, decoration and playfulness. Post-modernism scoffs at the brutal Taylorization of humanity implicit in Le Corbusier's notion of the house as a 'machine for living' and the etiolation of architecture's vocabulary implicit in the modern demand for 'truth to materials' and 'form following function'. Instead of modernism's coronation of reason, post-modernism crowns equivalents of the lords of misrule and the boy bishops. Instead of buildings which reveal both their structure and their plan from their symmetrical external appearance, post-modern buildings sometimes appear to be falling over and delight in teasing the spectator's eye so that no internal structure can be imagined from the evidence presented by the building's shell. The tropes and tricks of post-modern architecture signal a general post-modern practice of splitting the Saussurian unity of the sign and emancipating sense from referent. This is liberating as an aesthetic but leaves much to be desired as a system of cognition. A contingent and free relationship between signs, when the signs are signifying, and meaning is attributed to them, denies the essential cognitive principles of causality and rationality. But in an aesthetic rather than cognitive mode such playful combinations give delight.

What is challenging about post-modernism is the contradiction between its potential for witty bricolage, its delight in rummaging through the dressing-up box of art history, its fun, emotion and excess, and the irrationalism and refusal of the principles of causality and rationality which flow from the aesthetic's extension into an organizing principle, disorganizing principle, in discourses which are both representational and heuristic. Discourses to which we apply a truth criterion. The problem posed by post-modernism is the classical problem of the relationship between truth and beauty. Unravelling the truth – beauty conundrum is best essayed by recognizing that a discourse may be both beautiful and untrue, that the aesthetic dimension is simply of a different order from the cognitive and that neither can be reduced to the other. Many of the complex cultural forms which are the object of media studies have an aesthetic dimension, and that dimension has too long been neglected under a reductionist rubric of ideology. Too often media scholars have forgotten both Aristotle's recognition that artistic representation is a mode which enables us not only to learn but also to learn in a very distinctive way, and Kant's notion of aesthetic pleasure residing in the 'disinterested' relationship of the spectator to the artistic discourse. Aristotle states that:

> The instinct of imitation is implanted in man from childhood, one difference between him and other animals being that he is the most imitative of living creatures, and through imitation learns his earliest lessons; and no less universal is the pleasure felt in things imitated . . . Objects which in themselves we view with pain, we delight to contemplate when reproduced with minute fidelity: such as the forms of the most ignoble animals and dead bodies. (Aristotle, 1951, p. 15)

Kant argues that aesthetic pleasure is experienced when certain spectacles and experiences are not 'read' in a utilitarian fashion to derive information or principles for action but perceived 'disinterestedly'. Aesthetic pleasure comes from a distinctive attitude in the human subject which attends to an object or experience without putting it to use. Pleasure derives from a 'disinterested' recognition of the property of 'purposiveness without purpose' in the object contemplated. This property is distinct from (but not necessarily incompatible with) other utilitarian properties of the object or experience in question. A beautiful building may not keep out the rain, a weatherproof building may not be beautiful. A book may stimulate aesthetic delight but make untrue statements. The aesthetic is then a distinct mode of representation and form of discourse. A distinction elided by the reductivism which constitutes all discourses as signifying equivalently (as, for example, 'everything is ideological'). The positive influence of post-modernism has been to emancipate the aesthetic from the chains of the cognitive, but the difficulties which follow such an emancipation are evident. To take a contemporary example, John Fiske's lucid and influential book *Television Culture* suggests that the question of truth can be put to one side in the study of television for, he states: 'Reality is not a matter of any fidelity to an empirical reality but of the discursive conventions' (Fiske, 1987, p. 21). For Fiske television culture is simply a series of discourses within which viewers negotiate meanings. He emphasizes not only the constructed and mediated status of the television text but also the textuality of experience and the constructed nature of reality. But a language may speak the truth or lie. For Fiske veracity is not a question, for reality is not best conceived as an anterior given but as a stage in a continual semiosis and process of meaning-making. The strength of this position is its sensitivity to the culturally constructed nature of experience, its weakness, its assimilation of all structures 'real' or 'imaginary' to equivalence.

Raymond Williams rightly observed that 'culture' is among the most difficult categories in the English language (Williams, 1976, p. 76). But Williams differentiated between distinct clusters of meaning embraced by culture, and notably between what can be named 'symbolic' and 'anthropological' culture (or as anthropologists put it, structure). Fiske does not distinguish between these usages and hence does not pay much attention to the possibility – the reality in a multitude of instances – of a disparity between the anthropological culture of viewers and the symbolic culture of television. Many of the arguments advanced by Fiske are powerful and properly roll back mechanical stimulus–response notions of effects. They rupture the chains that bind cause to effect, break out of the prison-house of sense and referent and unite the estranged couple illusion and reality into a post-modern unity in which a portmanteau category – culture – integrates opposites through homologies, associations and metaphorical equivalences.

Often Fiske's reflections are enlightening, but are customarily made in an aesthetic register (I think of Mayakovsky's distinction between camel words weighed down by burdens of meaning and a chain of argument, and aesthetic usages where words are liberated from such dour responsibilities). Metaphors such as reflection (or Adorno's *Prisms*) evoke the qualities of Fiske's writing. Not of course one to one mimetic reflection but rather a process in which illuminations are split into their component parts and recombined in dazzling combinations through an intricate apparatus of masks and prisms. The lights both shadow and reveal but finally show only what goes on behind the mirror: they show the processes of mediation and recombination of elements; the far side of the mirror, not the real from which the image originates. Characteristic of such elisions is the judgement:

> The difference between news and fiction are only ones of modality. Both are discursive means of making meanings of social relations and it is important that readers treat news texts with the same freedom and irreverence that they do fictional ones. (Fiske, 1987, p. 308)

This is an important truth here but within it another truth is lost. It doesn't matter whether Cagney and Lacey police the 14th Precinct – or whether there is a 14th – whether true or not the meaning is made. But to say Kinnock is Prime Minister, though meaning-making, is untrue and it matters. Fiske establishes the polysemic nature of the television text and its multi-valency, the factors which enable different viewers to make different senses of the same text (itself an insight which powerfully challenges the dominant ideology thesis), but he does not essay a hierarchy of truth nor discussion of the criteria on which truth values might be established and tested. The final chapter of his *Television Culture* explores the homologies between capital and cultural capital, the material economy and what Fiske calls the 'popular economy' between television and the real world. But Fiske doesn't recognize that the real economy is based on scarcity and power to allocate finite resources. Culture is abundant, it is infinitely reproducible and infinitely consumable. Fiske's consumption of *Cagney and Lacey* deprives no one. That is why culture offers pleasure: in it scarcity is abolished. This, though, has little to do with the material world and it is the crucial non-correspondence between appearance and reality, between television culture and the material world, that Fiske and the textual, cultural, tradition of which he is so distinguished an exponent do not confront. The agenda for media studies in the 1990s that follows from the end of the dominant ideology thesis and a return from a diversion with post-modernism should include a probing of the distinction between the anthropological and symbolic notions of culture, or in a less confusing usage, between structure and culture (Gellner, 1987, p. 11).

Formerly media and cultural studies were marked, whether in the dominant ideology thesis or in a latter post-modern playfulness, by a tendency to elide these distinctions between culture and structure. However, this distinction is important and there are grounds for supposing that the linkage between culture – leisure consumption of symbols distributed by broadcasting – and structure – people's political behaviour and assertion of political identity – is weaker than media scholars have customarily supposed. In Canada, a country often taken as an exemplary case by media scholars, the culture/structure distinction is both neglected and important. Though anglophone Canadians have a distinctive structure to their society, which differentiates it from other anglophone societies (most importantly from the USA in its greater social peace, readier acceptance of authority, absent death penalty, parliamentary government, redistributive tax and social policy regime, socialized medicine, etc.), the symbolic culture of English-speaking Canadians, particularly their electronic media, is not radically different from that of other anglophone societies and is particularly close to that of the USA. Indeed in Canada since the 1920s not only have most Canadians consumed US radio, TV and cinema most of the time but much of the Canadian media and communication industries have been owned directly or by proxy by foreigners.

The line of advance for future work in media studies should include a recognition of the importance of the distinction between culture and structure, probing the nature of the links between symbolization and social institutions, and reflection on how, whether and why the social, political and the cultural are articulated. Canada is surely as eloquent a testimony to the robustness of political institutions and identities and the relative lack of influence of symbolic culture (if we take television as a shorthand proxy for culture) on anthropological culture as the reverse. Of course the Canadian case may be highly exceptional, but only further international comparative study will confirm or deny that it is representative.

This paper and those which follow draw their examples principally from television. This emphasis requires no excuse, for the population of the UK's use of television (and in this it is different only in degree and not in kind from the populations of other developed states) makes that medium overwhelmingly the most pervasive contemporary mass medium. If we are interested in the social force of the media it is television which we must first address. The Central Statistical Office's (1989) *Social Trends* states that the average consumption of television by UK citizens amounts to 25 hours and 25 minutes each per week. This contrasts with the lesser time spent on other leisure and media activities. For instance only 8 per cent of the UK population go to the cinema in any four week period. Cinema attendance is less important as a social phenomenon than visiting historic buildings or going dancing (which 9 per cent of the UK population does in any four week period). Over 90 per cent of the UK population watches some television in any week. However only 73 per cent of males and 63 per cent of females read a daily newspaper (Central Statistical Office, 1989, pp. 161–71).

Development of media studies in the 1990s requires crystallization of a new conceptual paradigm in order to displace the tattered but still defiant remnants of the old dominant ideology thesis which still, for want of a clearly articulated alternative, holds sway. Although I was the only primary definer to respond to my questionnaire by naming Gellner's work among my choice of five most important books or articles of the last ten years I believe that there are many provocative and fruitful avenues for exploration in his work. Other intriguing avenues for exploration are signposted above and below. However, renewal and development are not simply matters of intellectual re-orientation. Institutional change is also a necessary condition of a renewal of the subject of media studies and the emergence of new paradigms.

In the late 80s we have very sadly missed the publishing outlets on which my generation cut their teeth, notably *Screen Education* and the BFI TV Monographs. Here the remedy lies principally in the hands of the British Film Institute. A different conception of its own publishing programme and a different funding relationship to UK journals is required. More difficult is the renewal of cadres that should come through higher education. The ESRC's reiterated refusal to establish programme funding for media research is not encouraging. The 1988 application for programme funding for media and communication research was turned down. In 1989 programme funding for research in media education was rejected. Some media research, it is true, squeaks in through personal research grants and at the edges of the PICT (Programme in Information and Communication Technologies) programme both at the Polytechnic of Central London and at Brunel University but not much. Nor of course is the Taylorization of academic labour in the PCFC and UFC sectors helpful to scholarship. In default of action by either the ESRC or the managers of UK Higher Education plc (who seem no more committed to the long term sustainability of their business and the quality of its output than were the managers who ran West Midland Widgets Ltd into the ground), the British Film Institute's role is likely to be decisive again. The Institute has unparalleled primary research materials in its archives and library, a publishing outlet and a number of leading scholars. But no longer is the Institute and its Education Department in particular, as it was in the late sixties and early seventies, the pre-eminent centre of film scholarship and research. In recent years it has rather emphasized – in my view overemphasized – a training and support role for teachers in the primary and secondary sectors. What is needed is a publishing and journal programme, a research orientation and intellectual project which builds from the bottom up and which, once again, will make it possible for new entrants to the field to cut their teeth on small projects. Initiatives which will back the interests, hunches and expertise of those now in place rather than attempt a top-down creation of a new model agenda driven by an expensive guru or gurus parachuted in. Such a bottom-up strategy offers a potential to secure a long term future for media studies and realize in the 1990s for the hitherto enormous quantity of wasted human resources some of the opportunities a different institutional arrangement gave the generation of the 1970s. But to realize this undoubted potentiality it is not only institutions but also the ideas of the 70s that must change.

This chapter is based on the Keynote address th the British Film Institute's 1989 conference on *Film and Media Studies in Higher Education*.

References

Abercrombie, N., Hill, S. and Turner, B. (1985), *The Dominant Ideology Thesis* (London: Allen & Unwin).

Aristotle (1951), *Aristotle's Theory of Poetry and Fine Art*, trans. S. Butcher (New York: Dover).

Brecht, B. (1961), *The Experimental Theatre*, trans. C. Mueller, in *Tulane Drama Review*, Vol. 6, No. 1, Autumn.

Central Statistical Office (1989), *Social Trends 19* (London: HMSO).

Chippindale, P. and Horrie, C. (1988), *Disaster! The Rise and Fall of News on Sunday* (London: Sphere).

Collins, M. (1984), *Perceptions of Bias in Television News* (London: Social and Community Planning Research).

Fiske, J. (1987), *Television Culture* (London: Methuen).

Gellner, E. (1987), *Culture Identity and Politics* (Cambridge: CUP).

Hall, S. (1988), *The Hard Road to Renewal* (London: Verso).

Isaacs, J. (1987), *Second Henry Hetherington Lecture* (London: Henry Hetherington Lectures Association).

Johnston, C. and Willeman, P. (1976), 'Brecht in Britain – The Independent Political Film', *Screen*, Vol. 16, No. 4, Winter 1975/6.

Kelly, J. (1988), 'Iron Lady in a Nanny's Uniform', *Times Higher Education Supplement*, No. 840, December 9th.

Lovell, T. (1980), *Pictures of Reality* (London: British Film Institute).

McKenzie, J. (1971), *Weimar Germany* (London: Blandford).

Orton, L. (1987), *Studying Film and TV. A List of Courses in Higher Education* (London: British Film Institute Education Department).

Samuel, R. ed. (1989), *Patriotism* 3 vols (London: Routledge).

Willeman, P. (1978), 'Notes on Subjectivity. On reading Edward Brannigan's *Subjectivity Under Siege*', *Screen*, Vol. 19, No. 1, pp. 41–69.

Williams, R. (1976), *Keywords* (London: Fontana).

Chapter 2

Media Studies and Research on Information and Communication Technologies in the UK

Media Studies is one of a number of academic subjects that, in Britain in the last two decades, came in out of the cold. A lexicon of topics disdained by academe slipped under the door and found a place in the margins of the higher education system. Youth culture, leisure, women's studies, popular music, sport studies shared the flaky end of the academic hierarchy with cultural, communication and media studies. Most such parvenu subjects have fluid boundaries, none more so than the study of the media, for media studies is a field not a discipline. It lacks (or is blessed by) stable procedures and methods of enquiry and as such attracts the disdain of those dominant in academe who believe their own established subjects possess the distinctive methodology and body of theory which distinguish real academic disciplines. It is distinguished not, as is a 'real' discipline, by a way of studying but only by an object for study. Worse still the object of media studies keeps changing and scholars persist in attempts to extend the boundaries of their domain. Like medieval monarchs they make claims to much whilst ruling, and that not always perfectly, little.

The central object of media studies is the mass media: broadcasting, the newspaper and periodical press and the cinema. The scale of these industries is substantial. A recent estimate (Common Law Institute of Intellectual Property [CLIP], 1985, pp. 10–11) established a contribution of £6 billion to the 1982 UK gross domestic

25

product by copyright industries (not perfectly symmetrical with the mass media). That is 2.6 per cent of total UK GDP. Within the envelope of the copyright industries, the mass media figure as follows:

Table 2.1 Mass media contributions to UK GDP 1982

1982	GVA^a (£m)	GO^b (£m)	EMP^c (thousands)
Printing/publishing of newspapers	1345	2181	95
Printing/publishing of periodicals	649	1498	40
Film production & distribution	114	300	8
Cinemas	38	100	13
Video	181	457	20
Broadcasting	644	1674	53
Total mass media	2971	6210	229
Other copyright industries	3005	6526	399
Total copyright industries	5976	12736	628

$^a GVA$ = Gross Value Added
$^b GO$ = Gross Output
$^c EMP$ = Employment

Source: J. Phillips (1985), *The Economic Importance of Copyright* (London: CLIP).

A more recent study of a narrowly defined UK arts sector found that the arts accounted for 1.28 per cent of UK GDP in 1984 (more than was contributed by the motor vehicle sector). From the mid-seventies to the mid-eighties this sector accounted for a 'fairly constant' 5.4 per cent of UK consumer spending and the arts accounted for 3 per cent of all UK exports in 1984 (BIEC, 1988, p. 13; see also Myerscough, 1988).

But it is not simply the size and economic importance of the mass media that has attracted the attention of scholars. Communications and information have been invested with paradigmatic qualities and are regarded as necessary elements of modern societies. If modernity is constituted in and through mass communications then mass communications must be understood to understand the modern world. Printing is the first of the mechanical brides of Western man and a paradigm of industrialism: Bell (1976) and others have argued that modern developed societies are experiencing a qualitative change and are evolving into 'post-industrial' or information societies. Such societies are distinguished from other, earlier, social structures by the status, quality and accessibility of information within them and by the position ceded to information and communications in the new society. As the cover of a British edition of Bell's seminal *The Coming of the Post Industrial Society* (1976) has it, 'Knowledge rules OK'. And the mass media have been vested with significant power as social and political agents in modern developed societies. The importance of the media as systems of representation has demanded attention beyond that given to industrial sectors of comparable importance. These systems of representation – potent forces through which social organizations of a scale and complexity unable to be known through direct personal experience represent and explain themselves – have developed around communication technologies with a markedly asymmetrical relationship between transmission and reception. One speaks to many and the feedback from receivers to transmitter is either attenuated or non-existent. This structural characteristic of the mass media is customarily assumed to express and reproduce unequal patterns of social power. McQuail (in a paper for an ESRC-sponsored workshop on media and communications, subsequently published in McQuail, 1987) speculates that 'new media seem especially to offer the potential of a shift in the balance of power from sender to receiver' (p. 9). The potential for a change in sender/receiver relationships is certainly there. Videotex systems can be 'tuned' so that any relationship between sender and receiver from 1:1 to 1:infinity can be contrived, but such a spectrum of relationships between transmitter and receiver also exists in the old media of print (letters:newspapers), television (home video:broadcast) and radio media (walkie-talkie:broadcast). The potential for a changed balance of power is not new, and is not a property of a particular new configuration of communication technology. Realization of a new balance of power in the new media will depend (as it did for the old media) on political, social and economic forces rather than on the properties of a particular technology. The new media are unlikely to prove qualitatively different from the old and the practices and procedures of the academic subject developed with the old media as its object are likely to stand up to the demands of the new media.

Because of its imputed economic importance, paradigmatic status in respect of epochal social transitions, and social and political

power, media studies has necessarily been a subject with fluid
boundaries which extend (and contract) as a variety of extrinsic
factors – which putatively bear on the media – are brought within
or expelled from its ambit.

Thus far media studies has been chiefly concerned with media
of *content* (newspapers, cinema films, broadcasting) rather than
media of *carriage* (the mail, telecommunications). But technological change and the convergence of media of content and carriage
are compelling changes in the subject's ambit and procedures. The
established technical/social configurations of the mass media have
created media studies in their own image. Indeed one important
current in the study of the media (that is, empirical study of
audiences and effects) has substituted for the absent or attenuated
feedback between transmitters and receivers, supply and demand
which distinguishes mass communications. This tradition of study,
which has been so important in the USA has been a less powerful
force in the development of studies of the media in the UK.
The model of independent sources of communication transmitting
messages to independent individuals with distinct effects has been
rejected. Far more influential has been a notion of the mass
media as both bearers of and formed by a prevailing dominant
framework of ideas. This 'common sense' is believed to integrate
individuals into a social unity through a shared way of seeing and
experiencing the world. This framework of ideas, whether named
as culture, ideology or central value system, is the glue that both
holds groups together and differentiates them from others. The
importance of the media then, it is argued, is inherent in the
central role they play in articulating and propagating the symbol
systems which aggregate individuals into communities.

How ideology/culture works, its relation to the mass media
and its effects are of course all fiercely contested notions. But
by and large media scholars in the UK have rejected both a
reductivist/derterminist notion of ideology/culture – that is a view
that ideas can be 'read off' from the material existence of their
producers (for example from their class position) – and the oppo-
site view that ideas are autonomous and undetermined by their
material circumstances of production and consumption. However
this second, autonomist, position (which has had a greater cur-
rency in film than in media studies), has in turn generated a
distinctive determinism that, like all notions of determination,

is employed to explain and organize the phenomenal plurality of texts and textual structures. Just as a reductivist version of the idea of material determination seems to explain all phenomena as simply epiphenomena of a master material contradiction, so systems of thought which identify ideology and culture as independent of material forces acquire an explanatory power by constituting ideology and culture as products of, or as determined by, the structure of natural language and/or by the shared formation of the human unconscious. Such determinist notions, though offering great explanatory power, only gain this from a reduction of their objects of study to a state of equivalence. Media studies has clearly been marked by such divergent theoretical tendencies and remains a terrain contested by rival notions. The best work in media studies (and here a value criterion that has been implicit in my description becomes explicit) has recognized the complex and mutually determining interrelationship of production, consumption and content.

The importance of content is 'obvious' and much scholarship has been devoted to its analysis. But paradoxically its importance is often underestimated. Technology-based histories of the mass media mislead because they take for granted the invention of the cultural forms, the specific articulations of content that attract and retain mass audiences and on which the successful or frustrated realization of a technological potential depends. Contemporary enthusiasm or alarm at the frontier abolition promised by cable and satellite television is a case in point. The technological potential (give or take a few lost satellites, burnt-out travelling wave tubes and crashed launchers) for thoroughly international television is in place. What does not yet exist (although American feature films and TV series come closest) is content which can permeate freely through the membranes of national cultures and different languages, and thus sustain the service which technology makes possible. However the information content required to realize the technical potential of communication satellites has yet to be invented. Increasingly the economic viability of new communication technologies rests in the attractiveness and marketability of the information content carried. It is fast becoming a truism that the distinction between media of content and carriage is being abolished (the most striking instance being the convergence of broadcasting and telecommunications). But the high costs of new high tech 'carriage' infrastructures, such as broad band cable networks or powerful broadcasting satellites, can only be paid for if the content services they offer are attractive to consumers in the markets they serve. The commercial failure of the interactive videotex system Prestel (another 'new medium' born of convergence between the content medium of print and the carriage medium of telecommunications), was due to a mistaken conception of the information needs and desires of consumers. They did not, it seems, want the electronic encyclopedia offered by British Telecom and its partners. Indeed Prestel's subscriber base is now predominantly made up of users of time-sensitive information such as travel agents and financial services companies, far from the residential market for which the technology was developed. A similar discovery procedure is taking place in international satellite television services as programme schedules (and the contents of individual programmes) are changed to maximize their attractiveness to audiences within the satellite's footprint. Technological determinism, whether optimistic (see de Sola Pool, 1983) or pessimistic (see *inter alia* Robins and Webster, 1980), has been a powerful current within media studies. Persuasive though its exponents have been (and both de Sola Pool's and Robins and Webster's work repays attention) the Achilles' heel of technology-centred versions of the study of the media is a readiness to pass over matters of content and culture. However there is a dominant and distinctive current in UK media scholarship foregrounding just these matters.

Anderson's (1969) survey of British intellectual life argued that the vacuum left in Britain by the absence of a classical sociology was filled by scholars of English literature. Their ambitious attempt (in *Scrutiny*, published quarterly 1932–53, and reissued in 20 volumes by CUP in 1963) to produce what would elsewhere be called a sociology of culture, embracing discussion of advertising, the cinema and the press, was an important point of departure for British media and cultural studies (see *inter alia* Collins 1977, 1981; Garnham, 1981; Mulhern, 1979). What for Anderson was an unfortunate and deficient peculiarity of the English has lent development of media studies in the UK a remarkable strength. The inheritance from literary studies, and its Leavisian inflection towards cultural history and sociology (though of course not shared by all UK scholars, many of whom brought to media analysis valuable dowries from other academic disciplines) with its orientation to content has been a productive patrimony. An inheritance shared by media studies and its siblings, the closest of which is cultural studies.

Hall refers to cultural studies as 'the whole process by means of which meanings and definitions are socially constructed and historically transformed' (Hall et al., 1960, p. 19). Here he refers specifically to cultural studies' inheritance from Raymond Williams. Williams' work connects the literary cultural tradition of Arnold, Eliot and Leavis to British cultural studies and to the work of the Centre for Contemporary Cultural Studies at Birmingham University in particular. But Hall's remarks about the inheritance from Williams adequately characterize the field as a whole. Here the Siamese twins of media and cultural studies appear most united and the boundaries dividing the two subjects least distinct. Although media studies are centrally concerned with the mass media they have embraced a variety of other phenomena from murals in Northern Ireland to the audience for *Das Wohltemperirte Klavier*. In cases such as these, attempts to draw boundaries between cultural and media study are meaningless. Their shared project is to understand the relation between signs and referents, the meaning of symbols and the processes of mediation involved in representation by word and image. It involves study of the social and historical processes whereby inherently meaningless sounds and markings – whether on paper, celluloid or other media – become intelligible, which in turn demands attention to a wide range of social forces. But the distinctive evolution of British media studies from a root in a tradition of literary/cultural theory and particularly in *Scrutiny* has kept it (and *a fortiori* cultural studies) remarkably sensitive to the content of the mass media, and to the power and problematic nature of the systems of symbolization that are produced and consumed as mass communications. A major point of intersection of the trajectories of cultural and media studies is in audience study – or rather the study of consumption and use of the media (particularly television). Morley (1980 and 1986), Brunsdon and Morley (1978) and Hobson (1982) all came from the Centre for Contemporary Cultural Studies. Their emphasis and approach is not purely a Birmingham ideolect (see for example Ang, 1985), and whilst vulnerable to criticism as anecdotal – based on tiny and imperfect samples and of uncertain reliability (in the sense of producing results that could be not necessarily be replicated by other independent scholars – do promise a salutory reconceptualization of the problem of the effects of the media, from 'what does television do to people?' to 'what do people do with television?' This is a new version of uses and gratifications research. The differences between media and cultural studies (and the third field of communication studies which, though orientated to a different centre in its inclusion of interpersonal communication, is in important respects congruent with media studies, for example, in studies of the two step flow phenomenon in media effects [Katz and Lazarsfeld, 1955]) are not categorical differences in method but rather differences of emphasis in approach.

Where media and cultural studies require to be distinguished is in their application of a broadly shared problematic to different objects for study. Though cultural studies no more than media studies can be given a prescriptive and unitary identity (see Sparks, 1977), the subject has characteristically been concerned with studying (and raising to visibility) a series of distinct subcultures, each governed by its own structures, rules and autonomous practices. It asserts the discontinuities and differentiations presented by different cultures within the social whole. This emphasis, whilst revealing important truths, also poses problems, notably those of explaining social reproduction and continuity. In order to resolve the problem of the evident coherence of British society and its surprising (from a point of view concerned with distinct and often mutually antipathetic subcultures) ability to carry on carrying on, cultural studies has customarily invoked versions of the dominant ideology thesis (Althusser, 1971) to supply the social glue without which its analyses otherwise dissolve. Political theory in the twentieth century has emphasized consent rather than duress – and consequently the role of ideas rather than need or violence – as the glue that holds social organizations together. The media are seen as the pre-eminent source of shared ideas (and therefore of social cohesion) in modern societies, and are the chief source of knowledge and understanding of relations which are not directly experienced face to face. Other agencies also perform this ideological role but are of waning influence (for example, the church) or experienced for a short period (school) and/or selectively (military service). Few such 'ideological state apparatuses' (as Althusser named them) are as pervasive as the mass media and it is their dissemination of ideology which have customarily been invoked to explain the remarkable stability of British and other Western capitalist societies. The notion of ideology, whether used loosely to signify a system of beliefs and values or by Marxists to signify a false consciousness which inhibits peoples' recognition of their real interest (and thus short circuits their impulse to action and the realization of their interests), has been central to media, and to cultural, studies. Clearly any study of symbolization which cannot attend to every utterance on a case-by-case basis will require some such general category: whether naming it culture, ideology, *zeitgeist* or whatever. But it would be misleading to suggest that media studies in the UK has been so pluralistic. Rather, the category of ideology and a broadly Marxist problematic have been central to the subject's definition. To say this hardly clarifies the issue of course, for Marxist notions of ideology range from that of a separate force, decoupled from other 'instances' (notably the separate realms of the economic and the political [Hirst, 1976]), to a highly integrationist version which relegates ideology to the status of a superstructural epiphenomenon of the base, a subset of economic relations or, in a more sophisticated and persuasive version of the base–superstructure thesis, conceiving of ideology as an element in an 'expressive totality' (Lukacs, passim). Communication studies has an ideolect and range of preoccupations that overlap with media study but the two subjects are not synonymous. Communication study embraces (as well as the mass media) interpersonal communication and, rather than tracing its point of origin to literary studies, looks to empirical sociology and psychology and a construction of the subject that took place in the United States. In this more sociological version of the study of mass communications (that attends principally to production and consumption rather than to symbolization and the text) a similarly wide attention to a range of social forces is evident.

Studying the media necessitates attention to forces and processes outside press, cinema and broadcasting and there are broadly two approaches to these. One considers the media as a group of activities and structures demanding attention in much the same way as other powerful institutions such as the army, government or banking, the other attributes a central role to the media as an agency through which ideas governing a *structured* social whole are formed and disseminated. The first pluralistic model of society understands media effects as conditional on the articulation of a range of other social forces in combination with the media. For example Curran characterizes the process thus:

> The integrative nature of the mass media in twentieth century Britain stems from a number of factors – the absence of fundamental tensions between the dominant groups within society, the integration between the hierarchy of power and control over the mass media, the extent of media diffusion and the degree to which other socializing agencies complement the mass media. (Curran, 1977, p. 59)

In the second model there is a hierarchical conception of social institutions which attributes to the media the primary role of production and dissemination of ideas – of the ideology which holds society together and structures it in dominance. Marcuse's statement is representative:

> the irresistible output of the entertainment and information industry carry with them prescribed attitudes and habits, certain intellectual and emotional reactions which bind the consumers more or less pleasantly to the producers and through the latter to the whole. The products indoctrinate and manipulate; they promote a false consciousness which is immune against its falsehood. And as these beneficial products become available to more individuals in more social classes, the indoctrination they carry ceases to be publicity; it becomes a way of life. (Marcuse, 1972, p. 24)

However, both approaches necessarily lead the study of the media outwards into wider social and political issues. Working against this outward 'totalizing' tendency in the definition of the subject (whether in the approaches to the media based on literary studies or on psychology and sociology), is an attempt to limit the promiscuous reach of the subject. The literary element is limited by cohering around formalistic analysis of the internal relations of the symbol systems that constitute texts (a tendency also markedly evident in film study). And the sociological element is limited in empirical studies of audience, effects and content that draw on a research paradigm from the natural sciences. Here researchers have attempted to reduce the variables involved in the social situation studied in order to improve the quality and reliability of their results. However, attempts to do so by applying the paradigms of the natural sciences to analysis of culture and communications have been persuasively criticized by Thomas. She explains the attractiveness of the application of the natural science model to communication research:

> The weight of the mechanical communication model among academics rests most heavily on its seeming scientific character. As previously discussed, the S–R (stimulus–response RC) model lends itself quite conveniently to experimental analysis, high level quantification, and so forth – in short methods of research control and description most notably identified with the physical sciences. To the extent that academic respectability in the study of social behaviour was (and is) seen as coextant with its 'scientific' nature, it apparently seemed only too natural to want to approximate and therefore 'borrow' the tools of already established (physical) sciences. (Thomas, 1980, p. 443)

and rightly observes:

> The application of any model which strips human communications of its social essence, as it were, is not studying the interactional phenomenon which it purports to analyze. (ibid., p. 442)

But although still widely practised, particularly in North America where academic discussion can still turn on such esoteric questions as the best way to attach sensors to heads in order to measure alpha wave activity in subjects exposed to media stimuli, such positivistic reductionism retains no theoretical validity. Although empirical study of audiences, effects and quantitative analysis of content is the received impression of North American work in the eyes of Europeans (and has established a secure foothold in some important currents of European research) American communication research has not been confined to such esoterica. Sponsorship of empirical research was often linked with commercial interest such as market research or advertising companies wishing to improve their performance by changing the behaviour and attitudes of subjects. By and large this research disappointed its sponsors by yielding 'no effect' results or by demonstrating that effects were highly context-dependent. Since the 'no effect' finding was intuitively unsatisfactory (and the finding that effects were context-dependent pointed towards extra-media factors as a research focus) new hypotheses which situated the media within an ensemble of other relevant factors necessarily followed. The definition of the subject widened again. The 'uses and gratifications' approach which followed 'effects' studies reversed the previous paradigm of a passive audience to an active one and research focused on what subjects do *with* the media. But the changed paradigm continued to stress the ensemble of forces at work in the consumption and 'use' of mass communications. However, the 'mechanical communication model' exploded by Thomas does not inform all North American communication scholarship. From its inception North American communication scholars addressed holistic 'big picture' questions such as how 'new societies' (such as the great cities or those established as dispersed agricultural settlements on virgin land) held together and how their communication systems – their media – functioned as integrating forces (see for example Park, 1922, or for a really 'big picture' study, Innis, 1950). Media studies has formulated the relationship between content and context as reciprocal, one in which the processes of representation and symbolization shape, and are shaped by, institutions and relations of production and consumption. However, although it is generally recognized that the shaping process is reciprocal, it remains true that most actual studies have been of the shaping of content by institutional and economic pressures. (But see *inter alia* Collins, 1983, and Silverstone, 1985.) 'Gatekeeper' studies (White, 1950) and those concerned with the concept of bias well exemplify this emphasis. The *locus classicus* is news studies, the rival paladins jousting in the UK to hang the banner of bias on the opponent can be seen clashing most spectacularly in Glasgow University Media Group (1976, 1980) and Harrison (1985).

The fundamental questions about media studies are, 'how systematic can analysis of the media be?' and 'what are the methods of enquiry appropriate to this field of study?' Here we can find few satisfactory answers from a survey of past scholarship. The boundaries of media studies remain exceptionally fluid (as a survey of the contents of journals such as *Media Culture and Society* or the *Journal of Communication* demonstrates). In spite of remaining orientated around the press, broadcasting and cinema and proving slow to adapt to the new media and their actual (or more often potential) recasting of relations between transmitter and receiver, and although a field with its own institutional definitions (media studies is what is done at polytechnics x, y and z and is about the kind of issues discussed in journals a, b and c), the subject lacks a sharply defined ambit and set of paradigms. This lack of definition, and a disposition to promiscuously consort with a range of academic disciplines from econometrics to structural linguistics, has lent media studies an enormous vitality, but at the expense of the subject remaining a field rather than a discipline.

In 1983 the *Journal of Communication* published an issue titled *Ferment in the Field* reviewing the 'discipline'. The first essay in the issue asked of the study of communication: 'Has it produced a central interrelated body of theory on which the practitioners of a discipline can build and unify their thinking?' and answered 'I am afraid that it has not' (Schramm, 1983, p. 14). A similar motif to that in Schramm's essay was common to those of a number of other contributors and the observations of two British scholars exemplify this consensus:

> The mass media or communication would cover a dozen disciplines and raise a thousand problems. When the two are put together the problems are confounded. Even if the field is narrowed to mass media it gets split into many separate disciplines, many separate stages in the flow and quickly you have several hundred subfields. (Tunstall, 1983, pp. 92–3)

and:

> There is no need to apologise for a multi perspective diagnosis in mass communications research; indeed we should seek to promote eclecticism rather than to make excuses for it. (Halloran, 1983, p. 270)

The fluidity (or eclecticism) of media studies and the diversity of research methods within the field are shared with other social sciences. The founding fathers of social science variously used survey research (Mayhew), historical analysis (Weber), statistics

(Durkheim) and ethnographic/participant observations (Evans-Pritchard). There seems therefore no particular reason why media analysis should be performed using a set of normative techniques and procedures; the lesson of Thomas' survey and critique of the 'mechanical bias' (Thomas, 1980, p. 428) of American communication theory is that more may be lost than gained by normative aspirations. However, although there is no established consensus about how the media should be studied, two distinct schools, can be distinguished in anglophone communication scholarship. Some of the character of the distinction can be captured in a set of binary oppositions:

critical	vs	administrative
European	vs	American
theoretical	vs	empirical
macroproblems	vs	microproblems
ill-funded	vs	well-funded
hedgehog	vs	fox
Marxist	vs	pluralist

Terms in the left column neither perfectly fit together nor necessarily perfectly oppose terms in the right column. But the oppositions do capture some of the character of two approaches, within each of which there is a reciprocal shaping of object for study and method of study. A variety of essays explore the kaleidoscopic play of these epistemes (see *inter alia* Curran, Gurevitch and Woollacott, 1982; Lang, 1979; Lazarsfeld, 1941; Melody and Mansell, 1983; Pollock, 1955; Rogers, 1982; Smythe and van Dinh, 1983). In the UK the writings of Blumler and Garnham (see *inter alia* their exchange in *Media Culture and Society* vols 1 and 2, 1979) well exemplify the distinctive character of the two approaches. Berlin's distinction between two kinds of historical knowledge, that of foxes and that of hedgehogs, usefully captures the difference between the approaches of Blumler and Garnham. 'The fox knows many things but the hedgehog knows one big thing' (Berlin, 1953, p. 1). Blumler, arguing for the foxes:

Many effects researchers are undoubtedly sceptical about some of the virtues claimed for so-called 'grand theory'. In their eyes, the accumulation of knowledge is more like a step-by-step venture than the attainment of some comprehensive illuminating *weltanschauung* all at once. It is rather like the process of clearing an awkward piece of ground, which is constantly exposed to successive invasions of numerous varieties of weeds that, however unwelcome, cannot be ignored. You can hope to progress only gradually; sometimes what you have managed to clear will be overrun later and secure gains are more likely to be won by working within the bounds of some carefully delineated territory. (Blumler, 1977, p. 7)

And a particularly Faustian Garnham for the hedgehogs:

Media research . . . allows us to focus upon some of the central concerns of the social sciences, concerns out of which . . . the disciplines of sociology, history and economics . . . have grown. Indeed communication is an area of study along with cultural studies (areas between which I would not wish to make any significant distinction) that gives us a chance to re-integrate those disciplines. (Garnham, 1983, pp. 315–16)

There are evident dangers and potentials in the practices of both hedgehogs and foxes. A grand theory integrationism may lead to a cavalier disregard for contradictory evidence and offer overviews the comprehensiveness of which are achieved only through reductivism. Modest horticultural gradualism may mean a vision that seldom extends beyond a mean, stony and weed-infested territory. The work of both Blumler and Garnham eloquently demonstrates that neither's *parti pris* necessarily inhibits excellent scholarship. And that they, as do most media scholars, appear to be neither pure-bred hedgehogs or foxes but rather to be creatures endowed both with prickles and bushy tails. Berlin argued that Tolstoy's outlook was similarly mixed: 'Tolstoy was by nature a fox but believed in being a hedgehog' (Berlin, 1953, p. 4).

The grand theory which has stuck most persistently to the prickles of media studies' hedgehogs has been Marxism. Its attractions to media scholars have been many but its specifically *intellectual* productivity lay in offering a basis for considering ideas and culture from a historical and sociological perspective. Certainly, there was an indigenous British (and customarily, though not always, *anti-Marxist*) theoretical trajectory in the sociology of culture, marked in the twentieth century principally by the work of Leavis, Eliot, Hoggart and Williams, but not one that systematized relations so compellingly nor which addressed the questions of the relations of culture and ideas so directly to history, social structure, epistemology and power. Within the Marxist problematic there were the same dangers as existed outside it, those of maximizing the explanatory power of an analysis by reducing all phenomena to the epiphenomena of a single cause or maximizing the sensitivity and descriptive powers of an analysis by evacuating any notion of causation from it. Overall, however, the Marxist paradigm was one which promoted an integrative, explanatory analysis attributing effects to causes and surveying a wide range of economic, political, social and cultural forces in the work of its exponents. It has been a fertile hunting ground for the hedgehogs. Foxes remained largely outside (though there are certainly Marxist foxes) and some hedgehogs doubtless roam around looking for an alternative synthesizing and integrative paradigm when they are, for one reason or another, unhappy with Marxism. The ascendant paradigm of the capitalist market (which shares some economistic characteristics with Marxism) appears likely to offer a field in which a new generation of non-Marxist media hedgehogs can snuffle. Market theory is not simply a theory of trade and economics but has a series of fundamental (and contestable) social assumptions built in. Herein lies its attractions and power (its social dimension augments its claims to be comprehensive), and limits and problems. Veljanovski for example is admirably explicit about the assumptions which underpin his critique of an administered broadcasting order and advocacy of a market regime:

> In addressing these questions I take it as axiomatic that individuals are generally self interested and that they pursue their objectives with the minimum outlay of expense and effort. While this may strike one as a cynical view of man it is the appropriate one to adopt when devising a legal regime. (Veljanovski, 1987, p. 3)

Veljanovski's cynicism is echoed, for example, in the Department of Trade and Industry's (DTI) commissioned consultants' report *Deregulation of the Radio Spectrum in the UK* which states:

Government institutions staffed by civil servants cannot be expected to weigh conflicting technical and economic factors as responsively as agents with financial incentives. (DTI, 1987, p. 21)

Clearly there are theories of human action and motivation and the nature of society implied here, theories of considerable power and productivity which can only be reconciled with difficulty to such human activities as the gift relationship (Titmuss, 1970) and are therefore incomplete. My concern here is not to pit one 'grand theory' against another, but rather to show that the paradigms used to understand the mass media have led media studies outwards into general social, historical and political issues and that it is not only Marxist or 'critical' versions which do so. Curiously the ascendant paradigm of neo-classical economics seems less well suited to the tasks posed by mass communications than do those established earlier, for communications and information do not fit the normative assumptions of economic theory. Communication enterprises, such as telecommunication networks, often have the characteristics of natural monopolies while information services, such as broadcasting, have the characteristics of a public good. Neither conform to the normative model of a well-functioning competitive market.

McQuail's 1984 paper 'Is Media Theory Adequate to the Challenge of New Communication Technologies?' poses a central question for the future of media studies. The answer of course depends on two further questions: 'Do the new media differ from the old?' and 'Is media theory adequate to the challenge of the old communication technologies?'. My answers to the pendant questions are no and yes respectively and accordingly think the answer to McQuail's primary question is yes. McQuail in his paper, and more extensively in his book (1987), lays out useful schema for approaching these problems. He identifies three basic values on which media theory turns: freedom, equality and togetherness (or community). No unambiguous impact of the old or the new media on any of these three values can be claimed. Clearly, as they were by the introduction of printing or signalling via Herzian waves, social relations are reconstructed through the agency of the new media. Robins and Webster (1980) and others argue that the new media are re-stratifying the population into 'information rich and information poor'. De Sola Pool (1983) asserts in contrast that the new media are emancipatory 'Technologies of Freedom'. Whichever analysis is found most convincing the nature of enquiry and the theoretical paradigms employed cannot, surely, be very different from those used in consideration of the impact of broadcasting or print. A shift to subscription television from advertising or licence fee finance will constitute 'togetherness' on the basis of ability to pay, in terms of social class. The geographical extension of television signals via satellites (or remote printing of newspapers) reconstruct communities drawn together by shared consumption of information. So too when 'togetherness' or community is considered. Although communities are likely to be changed as a consequence of the new media (perhaps more slowly and less thoroughly than is often assumed), how these processes are to be understood is likely to require few theoretical innovations; the old media studies toolkit should prove adequate. Three things should be noted here. Realization of this potential restructuring is first dependent on the usefulness and desirability of the information transmitted. Here language is a crucial variable; *The Financial Times* and *Wall Street Journal* can aspire to become international newspapers because their target readers – the international financial and political elite – are English speaking. *Le Monde* and *Frankfurter Allgemeine Zeitung* do not have the same opportunities. Nor does *The Sun*, still less *Bild Zeitung*. Second, regulation and the actions of political authorities will foster or inhibit new forms of 'togetherness' or community. Since states, the most powerful political institutions, customarily draw their authority and legitimacy from their claim to represent long established 'national' communities, they are more likely to attempt to inhibit rather than to foster transnationalization of the media and thus, they believe, of communities. Third, perhaps the transnationalization of community and/or culture (whether or not the process is named as media imperialism) does not matter very much. Our implied normative model of political institution is that of a nation-state: economically and culturally self-sufficient, politically sovereign and composed of a coherent national community sharing language, ethnicity, culture, economic interest and history. Few human communities have been like this. Moreover there are important examples which suggest that there is a relatively weak linkage between the strength of political institutions and identities and a shared cultural and communication sovereignty. Canada for example is a bilingual state with little shared symbolic culture. Each of its language communities has long consumed large quantities of information from the United States. Yet Canada's political institutes are secure, and its society comprehends a welfare state, two legal systems each different from that of the USA and a robust differentiation from the USA in spite of pervasive and long established consumption of the US media.

Togetherness is undoubtedly an important value and like freedom and equality is importantly shaped by information and communication flows. By the restratification of societies and re-articulation of these three values under the influence (perhaps over-estimated) of the media is not a new problem for media studies (see *inter alia* Park, 1922). Topics will doubtless rise to the surface and others sink. Nationalism is likely to be among the ascendant topics. For the forces of, among others, technology and political realignment are redrawing the relationship between polity and culture, between the media of mass communication and political institutions and identities. However, the fundamental issues posed by such developments are unlikely to differ much from those posed by, for example, printing with movable type. The central questions for the new media are those that lie behind the old. What is in question is the nature of the reciprocal shaping between symbols and symbolic power, and institutions and social power. The distinctive origins and trajectory of media studies in the UK have productively orientated UK scholars and the UK tradition to these questions.

Within this interdisciplinary field three distinct approaches have evolved, partly as a rational division of labour in a large and complex field, partly in order to crystallize 'schools' and produce more hard-edged and prestigious academic studies. These three modes of media study can be visualized as a triangle:

sociological/social psychological

1

political economic   **2**   **3** aesthetic ideological with the work of different individuals and institutions being plotted in relation to the three points which define the triangle. Individual scholars will doubtless draw the angles of the triangle and the lengths of its sides differently. Self-evidently other spatial metaphors than that of the triangle could be used to map the subject of media studies. McQuail (1984, p. 7, and 1987, p. 59) uses two axes to create four quadrants in which different constellations of media theory may be located. A linear scale bounded by points labelled production and consumption (or supply and demand) could also be used. Or a different triangle could be constructed with its points labelled political, economic and cultural. Each spatial construct would generate different insights and configurations. The linear scale would indicate that most work has been at the production/supply end and the cultural/political/economic triangle would yield a more even distribution of studies in relation to the three points than would either of the two other spatial images.

The first, sociological and social psychological approach has been built around empirical studies of audiences for and effects of the mass media. In the UK (perhaps because of the costs of such studies) it has largely been performed outside academe by the research units of the IBA and BBC, and by market research agencies for commercial sponsors. But the Broadcasting Research Unit (formerly located in London at the British Film Institute and now an independent centre), the group at the University of Aston around Guy Cumberbatch (1986), and the University of Leeds Centre for Television Research (for example, Trenaman and McQuail, 1961; Blumler and McQuail, 1968) have worked in this field. Other studies that fall under the 'sociological/social psychological' heading include studies of professionalism such as Schlesinger's (1978) study of TV news production, Tunstall's (1970 and 1972) studies of journalists and Burns' (1977) study of BBC people.

Political economic analysis has principally been associated with two institutional centres, that at the Polytechnic of Central London which now forms the Centre for Communication and Information Studies (CCIS) and the Centre for Mass Communications Research at the University of Leicester. The core of CCIS's work has been the study of the conditions of existence of cultural production and consumption, the role of 'culture' in modern society, and the 'mediations' in production and consumption that the 'massness' of the mass media enforce. Studies have focused on different media sectors, such as advertising (Garnham, 1980a), the film industry (Garnham, 1980b; Porter, 1981), television (Collins, Garnham and Locksley, 1988), on particular national media formations and comparisons between them, and on the social institutionalization of different systems of ideas.

Research at Leicester has embraced a similarly wide range of topics and has yielded numerous books (such as Halloran, Elliott and Murdock, 1970; Elliott, 1977; Golding and Elliott, 1979; Golding and Middleton, 1982) as well as article-length studies. Elliott's (1972) study of TV documentary production was an early example of what has become a thriving genre of 'production studies' which includes works by non-Leicester scholars such as Alvarado's (with others) studies of television dramas (1978, 1985). Other important work concerning the political economy of the media has been performed by scholars outside the PCL and Leicester centres. For example by Curran in his many studies of the UK press (Curran and Seaton, 1985) and by Robins and Webster who have articulated a distinctive (see, for example, 1980) critique of the unequal possession and exercise of power in the communication and information sectors.

Aesthetic/ideological analysis has been a very strong element in cultural studies, film studies and media studies. Its focus has been a study of the sign systems mobilized in contemporary media artefacts. A powerful tendency in this field has been a formalistic analysis which has primarily attended to the internal relationships and characteristics of sign systems independently of their referents. Another has been to analyse the textual structures as apparatuses of symbolic power that serve to hold in place or disrupt the social order. The latter emphasis (which insists that 'a semiology must also be a sociology', Silverstone, 1986, p. 83) situates texts within an ensemble of relationships through which the text is produced. These concrete material acts of meaning-making are shaped by institutions of consumption and production which the text itself in turn produces.

Many of the distinctive characteristics of the mass media follow from the peculiar nature of information. Information is not exhausted by consumption, it is (potentially at least) imperishable, and cheap to reproduce and distribute. These characteristics provide powerful incentives to extend markets for information products in time and space. New information and communication technologies – printing by movable type, the steam press, radio broadcasting or communication satellites – have restratified information markets. The nature of the communities that consume the information products produced and delivered by these technologies and whose identity is, in part at least, defined in the symbolic systems, the culture, they inhabit, change as information markets change. Linguistic and cultural boundaries, the markers borne by information products, are not the only definers of communities. Economic and political institutions and relations are powerful forces too. But if, as Gellner (1983, p. 125) argues, a nationalist conception underlies the building blocks, nation-states, of the present world order – what he defines as 'the principal of homogenous cultural units as the foundations of political life and . . . the obligatory cultural unity of rules [sic] and ruled' – then the dislocation of the relations of the political and cultural (to say nothing of the economic) that attends the restratification of information markets is likely to be highly significant.

The new Information and Communication Technologies (ICTs) are (as were their antecedents whether initiated by Gutenberg, Marconi or Bell), creating a disequilibrium among the established political, cultural and economic unities in which we live. The UK, for example, is in a European *political* unity, culturally in a transnational (principally North Atlantic) anglophone community and economically moving between a *national* refusal of international/transnational combinations and uncertain and contradictory choices between European and North Atlantic partners. Criteria and imperatives from the political, economic and cultural/linguistic spheres are in play and affecting outcomes in the ICT sectors. Culture is perhaps a curious term to use in the context of information and communication technologies but it is increasingly an explicit policy consideration of governments. They are concerned for the preservation of national culture through resistance to internationalization of communication flows or promotion of certain kinds of production and consumption in order to foster new 'cultures' whether it be an enterprise culture in the UK or a European culture in the EEC. These mental sets (or cultures) possessed by all of us, which are constantly in the process of transformation, bind us to and exclude us from association and community with others. But they are being transformed or (so as not to prejudge the findings of future research) are *potentially* being transformed either directly by the new ICTs or with the ICTs as a catalyst in the processes of change. The cost of reproduction and distribution of information is falling as a consequence of technological change, and accordingly markets are being reconstructed to maximize economic returns or to self-consciously create new cultural and political identities. There is a pervasive, international concern with 'wall to wall *Dallas*' and the anticipated Americanization of hitherto diverse international cultures, a consequence of profit-maximizing behaviour by producers and distributors of information products for which unsatisfied demand exists. This concern seeks to resist the circulation and consumption of such threats to established cultures through regulation and/or the provision of attractive alternative products. But hand-in-hand with resistance to the restratification and internationalization of culture through the imperatives of the market there goes a conscious fostering and creation of new cultural unities by political agencies, by national governments and international organizations such as the European Community (*vide* the European Commission's *Television Without Frontiers* [Commission of the European Communities, 1984] concern to create European unification, a political end through the fostering of European identity, a cultural condition). There is a struggle over the sphere of culture by powerful political and economic agencies which see culture as both a commodity to be sold and as a powerful source of political legitimacy and unity. This is nothing new but the disturbance of long established equilibria has rendered culture, its status as a commodity and as a political force, a particularly important site of contestation and therefore, research. Such questions have been the stuff of media studies. The subject's procedures, various as they are, are orientated towards understanding the interrelationships and cross-impacts of production, consumption and content of the cultural industries. The tradition and its UK practitioners have much to contribute to research into the social cross-impacts in political, economic and cultural spheres of new communication and information technologies. To understand demand, consumption and markets for new (and old) products and services requires attention to culture.

This chapter is based on 'The evolution of media studies and its potential contribution to communication and information research in Britain' which was written for the 1988 ESRC seminar Classic Issues in Mass Communication Research, Madingley Hall, Cambridge.

References

Althusser, L. (1971), *Lenin and Philosophy* (London: New Left Books).

Alvarado, M. and Buscombe, E. (1978), *Hazell* (London: British Film Institute, Latimer).

Alvarado, M. and Stewart, J. (1985), *Made for Television: Euston Films Limited* (London: British Film Institute).

Anderson, P. (1969), 'Components of the National Culture', in A. Cockburn and R. Blackburn (eds), *Student Power* (Harmondsworth: Penguin).

Ang, I. (1985), *Watching Dallas* (London: Methuen).

Bell, D. (1976), *The Coming of the Post Industrial Society* (Harmondsworth: Peregrine).

Berlin, I. (1953), *The Hedgehog and the Fox: Essays on Tolstoy's View of History* (London: Weidenfeld and Nicolson).

BIEC (British Invisible Exports Council)(1988), *Annual Report and Accounts* (London: BIEC).

Blumler, J. (1977), *The Political Effects of Mass Communication* Open University Course Unit DE 3538 (Milton Keynes: Open University Press).

Blumler, J. and McQuail, D. (1968), *Television in Politics* (London: Faber).

Brunsdon, C. and Morley, D. (1978), *Everyday Television: Nationwide* (London: British Film Institute).

Burns, T. (1977), *The BBC: Public Institution and Private World* (London: Macmillan).

CLIP (Common Law Institute of Intellectual Property) (1985), *The Economic Importance of Copyright* (author J. Phillips)(London: Common Law Institute of Intellectual Property).

Collins, R. (1977), 'Revaluations', in *Screen Education* no.22 (London: SEFT).

Collins, R. (1981), 'Media/Film Studies', in C. Gledhill (ed.), *Film and Media Studies in Higher Education* (London: British Film Institute).

Collins, R. (1983), 'Broadband Black Death Cuts Queues: The Information Society and the UK', in *Media Culture and Society* vol. 5 no. 3/4 (London: Academic Press).

Collins, R., Garnham, N. and Locksley, G. (1988), *The Economics of Television: the UK Case* (London: Sage).

Commission of the European Communities (1984), *Television Without Frontiers*, COM (84) 300 Final (Luxembourg: Office for Official Publications of the European Communities).

Cumberbatch, G. et al. (1986), *Television and the Miners' Strike* (London: Broadcasting Research Unit).

Curran, J. (1977), *Mass Communication as a Social Force in History* Open University Course Unit DE3532 (Milton Keynes: Open University Press).

Curran, J., Gurevitch, M. and Woollacott, J. (eds)(1982), 'The study of the media: theoretical approaches', in *Culture Society and the Media* (London: Methuen).

Curran, J. and Seaton, J. (1985), *Power Without Responsibility* (London: Methuen).

de Sola Pool, I. (1983), *Technologies of Freedom* (Boston: Harvard University Press).

DTI, (Department of Trade and Industry)(1987), *Deregulation of the Radio Spectrum in the UK* (London: HMSO).

Elliott, P. (1972), *The Making of a Television Series* (London: Constable).

Elliott, P. (1977), 'Reporting Northern Ireland', in *Ethnicity and the Media* (Paris: UNESCO).

Garnham, N. (1980a), *Developments in British Advertising 1901-1918* a report to the Leverhulme Trust, London.

Garnham, N. (1980b), *The Economics of the US Film Industry* (Brussels: European Commission).

Garnham, N. (1981) 'Film and media studies: reconstructing the subject', in C. Gledhill (ed.) *Film and Media Studies in Higher Education* (London: British Film Institute).

Garnham, N. (1983), 'Towards a theory of cultural materialism', in *Ferment in the Field* issue, *Journal of Communication* vol. 33 no. 3.

Gellner, E. (1983), *Nations and Nationalism* (Oxford: Basil Blackwell).

Glasgow University Media Group (1976), *Bad News* (London: RKP).

Glasgow University Media Group (1980), *More Bad News* (London: RKP).

Golding, P. and Elliott, P. (1979), *Making the News* (London: Longmans).

Golding, P. and Middleton, S. (1982), *Images of Welfare* (Oxford: Martin Robertson).

Hall, S., Hobson, D., Lowe, A. and Willis, P. (1980), *Culture, Media, Language* (London: Hutchinson).

Halloran, J. (1983), 'A case for critical eclecticism', in *Ferment in the Field* issue, *Journal of Communication* vol. 33 no. 3.

Halloran, J., Elliott, P. and Murdock, G. (1970), *Demonstrations and Communication* (Harmondsworth: Penguin).

Harrison, M. (1985), *TV News: Whose Bias?* (Hermitage: Policy Journals).

Hirst, P. (1976), 'Althusser's theory of ideology', in *Economy and Society* no. 5 (London: Routledge and Kegan Paul).

Hobson, D. (1982), *Crossroads* (London: Methuen).

Innis, H.A. (1950), *Empire and Communications* (Oxford: OUP).

Katz, E. and Lazarsfeld, P. (1955), *Personal Influence: The Part Played by People in the Flow of Mass Communications* (Glencoe: The Free Press).

Lang, K. (1979), 'The critical functions of empirical communication research: observations on German–American influences, in *Media Culture and Society* vol. 1 no. 1 (London: Academic Press).

Lazarsfeld, P. (1941), 'Remarks on administrative and critical communications research', in *Studies in Philosophy and Social Sciences* vol. 9 no. 1.

Lukacs, G. (1970), *Writer and Critic* (London: Merlin).

Lukacs, G. (1971), *History and Class Consciousness* (London: Merlin).

Marcuse, H. (1972), *One Dimensional Man* (London: Sphere).

McQuail, D. (1984), 'Is media theory adequate to the challenge of new communication technologies', mimeo and in D. McQuail, *Mass Communication Theory* (London: Sage).

McQuail, D. (1987), *Mass Communication Theory* (London: Sage).

Melody, W. and Mansell, R. (1983), 'The debate over critical vs administrative research: circularity or challenge', in *Ferment in the Field* issue, *Journal of Communication* vol. 33 no. 3.

Morley, D. (1980), *The Nationwide Audience* (London: British Film Institute).

Morley, D. (1986), *Family Television Cultural Power and Domestic Leisure* (London: Comedia).

Mulhern, F. (1979), *The Moment of Scrutiny* (London: New Left Books).

Myerscough, J. (1988), *The Economic Importance of the Arts in Britain* (London: Policy Studies Institute).

Park, R. (1922), *The Immigrant Press and its Control* (New York: Harper).

Pollock, F. (1955), 'Empirical research into public opinion', in P. Connerton (ed.) (1976) *Critical Sociology* (Harmondsworth: Penguin).

Porter, V. (1981), 'Ideology and film culture in the European Community', in *Media Culture and Society* vol. 3 no. 4 (London: Academic Press).

Robins, K. and Webster, F. (1980), 'Information is a social relation', in *Intermedia* vol. 6 no. 4.

Rogers, E. (1982), 'The empirical and critical schools of communicative research', in M. Burgoon (ed.) *Communication Yearbook 5* (New Brunswick: Transaction Books).

Schlesinger, P. (1978), *Putting Reality Together* (London: Constable).

Schramm, W. (1983), 'The unique perspective of communication; a retrospective view', in *Ferment in the Field* issue, *Journal of Communication* vol. 33 no. 3.

Silverstone, R. (1985), *Framing Science: The Making of a BBC Document* (London: British Film Institute).

Silverstone, R. (1986), 'The agnostic narratives of television science', in J. Corner (ed.) *Documentary and the Mass Media* (London: Edward Arnold).

Smith, A. (1971), *Theories of Nationalism* (London: Duckworth).

Smythe, D. and van Dinh, T. (1983), 'On critical and administrative research: a new critical analysis', in *Ferment in the Field* issue, *Journal of Communication* vol. 33 no. 3.

Sparks, C. (1977), 'The evolution of cultural studies', in *Screen Education* no. 22 (London: SEFT).

Titmuss, R. (1970), *The Gift Relationship: From Human Blood to Social Policy* (London: Allen and Unwin).

Thomas, S. (1980), 'Some problems of the paradigm in communication theory', in *Philosophy of the Social Sciences* vol. 10.

Trenaman, J. and McQuail, D. (1961), *Television and the Political Image* (London: Methuen).

Tunstall, J. (1970), *The Westminster Lobby Correspondents* (London: Routledge and Kegan Paul).

Tunstall, J. (1972), *Journalists at Work* (London: Constable).

Tunstall, J. (1983), 'The trouble with US communication research', in *Ferment in the Field* issue, *Journal of Communication* vol. 33, no. 3.

Veljanovski, C. (1987), *Commercial Broadcasting in the UK over Regulation and Misregulation* (London: Centre for Economic Policy Research).

White, D.M. (1950), 'The gatekeeper: a case study in the selection of news', *Journalism Quarterly*, no. 27.

Chapter 3

The Language of Advantage: Satellite Television in Western Europe

'Television is in colour, in stereo and in English'.
Robert Nador at 'Independent Directions' Trade Forum,
1988 Toronto Festival of Festivals.

The integration of the world economy into a single market and the consequential redefinition of communities shaped by a shared culture and information pool is firmly established as what Norman Mailer called a 'factoid'. New distribution technologies threaten, or promise, to restratify international information markets. Communication satellites abolish the relationship between cost and distance in communication and have made usable (for both point-to-point communication – telecoms – and point-to-multi-point communication – broadcasting) radio frequencies that have hitherto been useless. They therefore offer a potential to extend choice and intensify competition in existing communication markets and to create new 'communication spheres' binding together markets and communities that have hitherto been distinct.

Information itself has become a product produced and traded in increasing quantities internationally. Governments attempt to foster the development of their state as an 'information society' and improve their balance of trade by exporting information. Not all societies can have a positive trade balance in information and some are particularly advantaged as international information producers and traders.

English-language publishing accounts for more than half the total world market (*Financial Times [FT]*, 4 January 1989, p. 18). In the important sector of television programmes the OECD estimates that of a world traded volume (1980) of $400 million, $350 million is accounted for by the United States and $22 million by the UK, which is the world's second largest exporter. The importance of information trades for the UK is captured emblematically by the headline 'Arts are earning more than vehicles' (*FT*, 11 October 1988, p. 10) over a report that in 1984 UK overseas earnings from the arts were £4 billion and from vehicles £3.8 billion and the arts accounted for 3 per cent of UK exports – sales to overseas customers accounted for 34 per cent of arts turnover (see BIEC, 1988; Myerscough, 1988).

For the United States, too, information is an important sector. Jack Valenti, President of the Motion Picture Association of America, stated to the US Congress that in one important information sector, film and television programmes, the USA had in 1987 a positive trade balance of $1 billion (Valenti, 1988) and the surplus for the US entertainment industries as a whole was estimated at $4.9 billion in 1986 (Brummer, 1987 cited in Hoskins and Mirus, 1988).

Such positive trade flows for anglophone states are perceived elsewhere to be profoundly threatening. An important motif of Jack Lang's periods of office as Minister of Culture in France has been an attempt to foster a Latin 'audio-visual space' to counter perceived Anglo-Saxon domination. A marked motif of the international symposium on European cultural identity sponsored by the government of France (see SIICE, 1988) was a demand for action to remedy the perceived threat to Europe from anglophone producers of information. André Fontaine (Director of *Le Monde*) stated: 'je me trouvais plus en Europe, à la limite, à Buenos Aires qu'à Paris, parce qu'à Buenos Aires, il n'y pas des enseignes en anglais' (SIICE, 1988, p. 96). A curious comment, implying both that there are no anglophone European states and that Europe is anything but a geographical expression.

But anglophone states also resist international information flows and loss of 'communication sovereignty'. The UK government committed substantial resources to an attempted suppression of Peter Wright's book *Spycatcher* which was published in Australia, Ireland and the United States and read (in English on transmissions directed to listeners outside Denmark including the UK) aloud on Danish radio. The impotence of the UK government to suppress the circulation of *Spycatcher* through print and electronic media inside and outside the UK testifies to the limits of governments' 'communication sovereignty'. Political authorities then may have a schizophrenic attitude to international information flows – promoting them as part of an 'information economy' industrial strategy but resisting them when they are deemed to be damaging to the intellectual, cultural or political health of the governed.

Some linguistic and cultural markets offer producers significant advantages over comparable producers in other markets. The size and wealth of the primary (home) market is an important determinant of the level of investment in information products that is compatible with expectation of a positive return. Hoskins and Mirus (1988) convincingly demonstrate the advantages that accrue to US producers from the large US domestic market. And this undoubtedly contributes to the United States' dominance in international audio-visual trades. But their analysis does not explain the success of UK (and Australian) producers in international information trades. Hoskins and Mirus rightly stress, as advantages of US producers, market size, the comprehensive orientation of the US entertainment industry to business goals and the composition of the US domestic market as a closer approximation to the diversity of the world market than is any other single national market. But they do not comment on the importance of language as a constituent of markets and a factor in determining what they usefully name 'cultural discount'. That is the depreciation in value that information undergoes when exported from its home market.

Wildman and Siwek (1987) have identified the twelve largest language groups in market economies (the two main language groups excluded by such a criterion are Chinese and Russian native speakers who number populations of circa 760 million and 135 million respectively) and the wealth of each language community. They demonstrate that not only is English overwhelmingly the largest language community in market economies (exceeded in size only by the community of Chinese native speakers whose aggregate wealth is less than that of anglophones), but substantially the richest. The linguistic unity of anglophones significantly advantages anglophone producers who are able to count the world's richest market as a home market. They enjoy a classic comparative economic advantage *vis-à-vis* competitors such as that Ricardo identified as attaching to agricultural producers endowed with longer growing seasons and more fertile soils than were their competitors.

It is the advantages enjoyed by anglophone producers within the richest and (of market economies) largest of world language communities that has made their productions the basis of a slowly developing global 'culture'. They are also advantaged by the related status of English as the world's most important second language. Not only are anglophone works thereby available for consumption by a larger population of non-native speakers than exists for any other language but English is the preferred medium for sub-titling, dubbing and translation into the native language of second markets.

A lower 'cultural discount' attaches to work in English in anglophone markets than to works in other languages, and this low cultural discount also attaches to works in English in non-anglophone markets. In non-English-speaking markets works in the dominant language (for example, German in Austria) will have the lowest cultural discount but works in English will have the next lowest cultural discount. For example a work in English

Table 3.1 A comparison of linguistic markets

Language	Native speakers (millions)	1981 GNP (millions US$)
English	409	4,230,375
Hindi/Urdu	352	209,023
Spanish	265	653,958
Arabic	163	328,547
Bengali	160	12,692
Portuguese	157	303,465
Malay/Indonesian	122	237,715
Japanese	121	1,185,861
French	110	812,179
German	101	1,017,528
Punjabi	69	29,575
Italian	62	502,306

Source: World Bank 1985 World Almanac and World Tables, Vol. 1, 3rd edn, p. 29. Cited in Wildman and Siwek (1987).

will be preferred (all other things being equal) in Spain to a work in German. But the advantage of anglophone producers is comparative, not absolute and not all anglophone works will succeed in markets at all times. Though language has been, and will continue to be, an important factor favouring anglophone producers of tradable information in international markets.

Non-anglophones' concern at the less favourable prospects for their information economies (and at the anticipated adverse effects of the Anglicization of international information flows on established cultural, linguistic and national identities) has been amplified by technological change and in particular the establishment of communication satellites.

Satellite communication weakens the ability of political institutions, states, to protect their 'information spheres' from exogenous influences. For the 'footprints' of satellite transmissions cross political boundaries, and the abolition of the relationship between cost and distance of transmission of information that characterizes satellite communications threatens, or promises, to integrate world information markets on an unprecedented scale.

The experience of satellite television in Western Europe offers an interesting case in which (among other things) the importance of the comparative advantage of anglophone producers of information can be assessed. How significant is their comparative advantage? Is it sufficient to justify the alarm voiced by Jack Lang about 'Coca-Cola satellites', or, at the SIICE symposium in January 1988, at the threat of 'la déferlante américaine'?

Satellite Television in Western Europe

The experience of satellite television in Western Europe during the 1980s has been sufficiently extensive to warrant a retrospective survey to assess the extent to which the threats and promises of satellite television have been realized. This is an appropriate moment to do so, for the satellite television regime is about to change radically. The current generation of 'telecommunication' satellites, transmitting weak signals that require final consumers either to access them via cable or through a large and expensive individual TVRO (Television Receive Only antenna), is about to be succeeded by the first of a new generation of 'television', 'heavy' or 'DBS' (Direct Broadcast Satellites) transmitting a more powerful signal accessible to individual viewers through relatively small and cheap receivers.

Services cluster on the four important satellites:

- Eutelsat IFI at 13E is the 'hottest bird' relaying the two most important channels for German-language speakers SatEins and RTL Plus, the most important film channel Filmnet, and the two English-language channels Sky Channel and SuperChannel which attempted to establish a transnational audience and which have achieved access to the highest number of European cable households.
- Intelsat VAF11 at 27.5W is the main carrier of English-language services including Cable News Network, one of two services imported from outside Europe.
- Intelsat VAF12 60E is the main carrier of German-language services. (But not SatEins or RTL Plus).
- Telecom IF2 5W carries the majority of French-language satellite services.

Because reception of signals from more than one satellite requires either a steerable (and expensive) antenna or more than one antenna there is a tendency for services directed at the same (usually defined by language) market to cluster on the same satellite.

It is clear that language is an important factor that shapes the linking of programme offer – the channel – to delivery system – the satellite – and thus to audiences. There is, if not a stratification of audiences on national lines (or more exactly lines of political citizenship drawn by states) a strong tendency for audiences to be stratified on linguistic lines with the main satellite for francophones being Telecom IC, for anglophones Intelsat VAF11, and for German-speakers Intelsat VAF12. The fourth satellite, Eutelsat IFI, carries the only channels which have attempted to build a transnational or, more precisely, mixed language audience: Sky Channel and SuperChannel.

Access

Satellite television is principally accessed via cable rather than directly through a TVRO. And because cable penetration varies greatly among localities in Western Europe so does access to satellite television. Cable penetration (1984) was Belgium 81 per cent, Netherlands 74 per cent, Switzerland 47 per cent, Ireland 25 per cent, Norway 14 per cent, Denmark 10 per cent. In all other West European states penetration was below 10 per cent. Growth in cable subscriptions has been lower than anticipated in the 'undercabled' West European states such as the UK and France.

In the UK (1988) 254,000 homes are cabled though only 32,000 of these are on broadband systems (*New Media Markets [NMM]* 5 May, 1987, p. 11). But few homes (only 18.7 per cent) passed by cable whether broad or narrow band have subscribed to cable services (*Cablegram*, February 1988, p. 8).

In March 1988 the satellite television channel with highest availability on cable, Sky Channel, estimated its potential viewership as 30.5 million across Western Europe (including Hungary and Yugoslavia).

Access to satellite television is a precondition of consumption, and Table 3.2 clearly shows that there is a wide spectrum of differential access to satellite television in Western Europe, shaped principally by the penetration of cable networks in different European states.

The best evidence of actual viewing behaviour by audiences for satellite television comes from the studies of PETAR (Pan European Television Advertising Research). The result of its Spring 1987 diary survey (2651 respondents) is shown in Table 3.3

Whilst satellite television (in particular Sky Channel) achieves reasonable reach (that is attracting viewing at *some* time), within the universe of cable homes what is most striking is how *little* satellite television is watched. And how consumption varies between markets. There does not appear to be a consistent international relationship between access to satellite TV and consumption of satellite television.

Satellite television is watched more in Scandinavia (and West Germany) than it is in other West European localities, though other West European markets (such as the Netherlands) have greater access to satellite television, because more heavily cabled, than do Scandinavia and West Germany.

Sweden combines *low access* to satellite television, 8 per cent of homes (Sveriges Radio estimate, 1988), 11 per cent of TV homes (Sky Channel estimate, 1988) with *high consumption* of satellite

Table 3.2 Access to Sky Channel 1988

Sky Channel penetration as percentage of TV households	Country	Networks (Cable & SMATV)	Households
63	Netherlands	508	3,379,650
11	W. Germany	1039	3,135,040
52	Switzerland	209	1,396,920
31	Belgium	58	1,103,322
11	Sweden	302	420,677
31	Denmark	275	390,669
17	Finland	168	361,471
20	Norway	256	338,789
11	Austria	155	325,661
32	Ireland	22	314,177
1	UK	111	263,341
	Hungary	23	104,694
71	Luxembourg	25	85,713
	France	68	78,960
	Spain	348	72,843
	Portugal	72	28,072
	Greece	5	1017
	Iceland	21	690
	Yugoslavia	1	420
		3666	11,802,126 (30.5 million potential viewers)

Source: Sky Channel (1988).

television by viewers with access to it: 30 per cent share of viewing (Sveriges Radio estimate, 1988), 27 per cent share of viewing (Sky Channel estimate, 1988). But Swedish viewers use television very little (average 13.76 hours per week: Sveriges Radio estimate, 1988; 13.4 hours per week: Sky Channel estimate, 1988) though satellite TV viewers watch more (16.2 hours per week) than do other viewers.

Sweden's low overall consumption of television and high consumption of satellite television suggests dissatisfaction with terrestrial television, and that satellite television provides a welcome additional service. But the Swedish experience is not replicated

Table 3.3 Station share of viewing by country, all cable homes, averages over 4 weeks, 1987

	Scandinavia	Belgium	Switzerland	Netherlands	Germany	Total
Total hours per week of all TV viewing:	13.4	21.3	12.8	16.9	18.2	17.2
% share by station						
RAI	—	2	4	—	—	1
Sky Channel	20	1	2	6	2	5
SuperChannel	7	—	1	2	1	2
SAT 1	—	—	—	—	14	4
RTL Plus	—	—	—	—	13	4
All satellite	27	3	7	8	30	16

Source: PETAR (Pan European Television Advertising Research) Spring 1987 diary survey.

Table 3.4 Percentage share of viewing all individuals aged 2+ in all UK cable homes

ITV	36.7
BBC1	25.1
Premiere	8.8
Sky	7.0
Channel 4	4.8
BBC2	4.4
Children's Channel	4.2
ScreenSport	2.5
MTV	2.4
SuperChannel	1.5
Lifestyle	1.2
TV5	0.4
RAI 1	0.2
Arts Channel	0.2
CNN	0.1
All Terrestrial	71.0
All Satellite	28.5
Non-satellite cable	1.5 (does not add to 100%)

Source: NMM (6 April 1988): 7. Based on two-week diaries of 770 respondents for first two weeks of December 1987.

in other West European markets. The Netherlands and the UK present different pictures.

The Netherlands combines *high access* to satellite television (Bekkers [1987] estimate 50 per cent, Sky estimate 63 per cent) with *low consumption* of satellite television (1988 Sky Channel estimate 8 per cent, Nederlands Oemrep Stichting estimate [1986] 6 per cent) by viewers with access to satellite television. Dutch viewers use television 16.9 hours per week (Sky Channel estimate) and the consumption of satellite television by those with access to it *declined* between 1985 and 1986 (Dutch terrestrial services [1985] 78 per cent, 1986 84 per cent; Satellite TV [1985] 10 per cent, 1986 7 per cent; Bekkers, 1987).

The UK exhibits *low access* to satellite television and *low consumption*. Homes passed by cable were 1.36 million and homes connected 254,508, a penetration of 18.7 per cent of homes passed and 1.2 per cent of TV households (*Cablegram*, February 1988, p. 8).

Sky Channel achieved 7.0 per cent share of viewing in UK homes with access to it (the universe of UK Sky Channel homes is virtually synonymous with cable homes) and SuperChannel 1.5 per cent in its universe.

All satellite TV channels in all UK cable homes achieved a 28.5 per cent viewing share (see Table 3.4).

Though satellite television achieved an impressive share of viewing in UK cable homes (and both the subscription film channels Premiere and Sky Channel achieved higher shares than Channel 4 or BBC2) these achievements should be relativized by recognizing that cable homes are likely to be those favourably disposed towards consumption of satellite television. A locality is cabled *because* entrepreneurs regard it as likely to yield more active cable subscribers than other localities. And subscribers to cable are likely to be more receptive to cable/satellite services than are their neighbours who are passed by, but do not subscribe to, cable. Of homes passed by cable, 81.3 per cent did not subscribe. Therefore only one in five households in areas judged most likely to be receptive to the cable/satellite programme offer actually found the service worth paying for. Even within this population of a quarter of a million TV households (many of which will only be able to receive one satellite TV channel) consumption of cable and satellite television is less than 30 per cent of viewing and has declined from the 46 per cent for cable and satellite channels within the same universe in 1986 (Saatchi and Saatchi Compton, 1987, p. 6).

Programming

The technological potentiality for alternatives to national terrestrial television and for new transnational forms of television now exists but successful establishment of such services is conditional on delivery of programming attractive to the final consumer. The attractiveness of programming is not an absolute, but related to the available alternatives and to the needs and desires of audiences.

West European satellite television has attempted two kinds of programming, thematic and mixed. Channels, whether offering mixed or thematic programme streams, have essayed two marketing strategies: addressing a transnational or a single linguistic/national market. Sky Channel and SuperChannel offered mixed programming to a transnational audience. RTL Plus and SatEins mixed programming to a national (strictly unilingual) audience. Thematic channels such as W.H. Smith's Lifestyle and ScreenSport have been marketed to national audiences, and the theme channel MTV to a transnational audience.

Francis Baron (Managing Director of W.H. Smith Television) sees internationalization of television coming not through delivery of a unified programme stream to a transnational audience but through tailoring services drawing on common programming for individual national markets. Accordingly W.H. Smith's services are being offered in different languages for:

> I have serious reservations about whether pan-European services such as Sky Channel or MTV can ever work financially. We have to accept Europe for what it is – a landmass of different languages and cultures – and work within that framework. (F. Baron quoted in *Daily Telegraph*, 14 August 1988, p. 4)

Baron is not alone in his scepticism about an integrated European television market. Helmut Thoma, the managing director of RTL Plus, echoes Baron's analysis (though discussing advertising rather than programming): 'I have never believed in pan-European advertising. Language will always be a problem', (H. Thoma, *Cable and Satellite Europe*, December 1987, p. 33).

In spite of the bullish predictions of Saatchi and Saatchi Compton that by 1995 'new powerful satellites will have become established with, we estimate, around 35 per cent penetration of UK television households', and that 'satellite broadcasting across national frontiers – Pan European services . . . will predominate and be a key dynamic in our business' (Saatchi and Saatchi Compton, 1987, p. 1) – predictions which were based on straight-line projections of (notoriously optimistic) Cable Authority estimates of cable penetration and the assumption that TVRO penetration will replicate that of VCRs – the difficulties of establishing transEuropean advertising is more striking than its success.

For there are few transnational brands, particularly in the product ranges advertised on television, although a UK industry source (interviewed May 1988) estimated that the transnational European satellite advertising market had grown in five years from zero to £20 million per annum. But the mainstays of transnational TV advertising are the very few well established international products such as Coca-Cola and Pepsi-Cola, and similarly scarce international brands such as Canon, Nikon, Philips and Ford.

There is neither a single European market for advertising (the main funding source for satellite television) nor an integrated audience sharing a taste for similar programming. PETAR (Pan European Television and Audience Research) found that different European satellite television markets favoured different programmes. For example though both Scandinavia and the Netherlands found *The Benny Hill Show* the most attractive of SuperChannel's programmes, their preferences were not echoed by West German, Swiss or Belgian viewers (PETAR survey, Spring 1987).

The United Kingdom and the West European Satellite Television Market

The UK is not only the location from which services (such as Premiere and Lifestyle) addressing UK audiences and the anglophone transnational services Sky and SuperChannel originate; it is also the point of origin for foreign-language services. Why should channels such as Scansat, marketed to Scandinavian audiences, and Canal 10, a Spanish channel, be located in London rather than in their home markets? There are a plurality of reasons. London is the main European centre (and rivals New York and Los Angeles as a world centre) for trade in television programmes rights, facilities, finance and artistic talent. The UK is also the only location in Western Europe where satellite television operators have a choice of telecommunication service providers – Mercury and British Telecom – for uplinking their signal to the satellite. And though satellite television does not fall under the regulatory authority of either the IBA or the Cable Authority, voluntary adherence to their requirements is an important competitive advantage for UK-based satellite television companies. Adherence to the regulatory requirements of a Council of Europe and EEC member, though not guaranteeing access to other European markets, has made other European governments and regulators very cautious about challenging the access of UK-based satellite channels to non-UK markets for fear of reference to a transnational European court. (Though adherence to the requirements of UK regulators has not made UK-based satellite television companies completely fireproof in other markets – the Dutch Media Law has proved troublesome.) UK television advertising regulations are among the most permissive in Europe, allowing interruption of programmes by advertising, and more advertising time per hour than do other regulators. The UK has in such factors important *competitive* advantages as a location for satellite television enterprises, as well as the *comparative* advantage of its anglophone status. And the strength of the UK terrestrial television industry generated profits such that the ITV companies, blessed with a monopoly of selling television advertising (the 'licence to print money' that one of the company owners was indiscreet enough to name), were able to attempt diversification into a new medium which promised to deliver a new, European, market for their services.

The UK-based Sky Channel and SuperChannel, the vehicle of ITV companies in their attempt to capture a European audience, are the two most striking attempts to establish satellite television in Western Europe on a transnational basis. It is they that have achieved the highest level of accessibility in various European markets, have sold advertising on the basis of delivering a transnational audience and have attempted to construct their programme offer to attract and retain a transnational audience. But neither channel has achieved profitability following this strategy. Sky Channel is reorientating its service (maintaining its present programme mix but marketed in the future as one of a 'bundle' of linked programme streams) to UK and Irish audiences following its location on the Astra satellite, which will permit direct to home reception. SuperChannel has an uncertain future under new ownership, which took over an essentially bankrupt enterprise.

SuperChannel began as the music channel 'Music Box' under the ownership of two major ITV companies, Granada and Yorkshire Television (and the UK music and leisure company Virgin). In 1986 it changed its orientation and became a general programme channel, simultaneously expanding its ownership base to include shareholdings from the other ITV companies (with the exception of TVam and the largest, Thames Television, the Managing Director of which, presciently, referred in evidence to the House of Commons Home Affairs Committee on 'The Future of Broadcasting' to satellite television programme services as 'a dubious enterprise' (House of Commons, 1988, p. 113). SuperChannel was launched as a 'best of British' programme stream, intended to draw on the programming archives of its owners (in particular the ITV companies) and the BBC. In the event the requirement to pay high residuals to actors and programme makers forced a shift away from the 'best of British' strategy, and the continuing losses sustained by the channel led to changes in ownership and programming. At the time of writing, the future of SuperChannel is unclear. It is reported to be losing £1 million per month (*New Media Markets* reported revenues of £7 million and expenditure of £19 million in 1986–7 [*NMM*, 5 July 1986, p. 8]) and ownership has now passed to Virgin and Italian interests, Betatelevision, who propose a further format change to relaunch the channel as a music and news service.

SuperChannel's failure demonstrated not only that there was insufficient advertising revenue to sustain transnational satellite television (a problem shared by the loss-making Sky Channel) but also that its programming strategy was unsuccessful. There was insufficient communality of taste in the potential audience for SuperChannel to attract significant audiences in different national

markets for a common programme stream (what was most liked in
one location was not most liked in others). Nor was the 'best of
British' programming strategy successful in attracting and retaining
minorities in different locations that aggregated together would
constitute a viable audience.

Language proved a more resistant 'cultural screen' than Super-
Channel had hoped. The practice in UK programming of separation of sound and vision tracks, characters not speaking to camera
in dramas and documentaries carrying a soundtrack that was not
'motivated' by the images on screen made such programmes hard
to interpret by non-native English-speakers. UK television dramas
were unfavourably compared to US dramas for their emphasis on
dialogue rather than action. Paradoxically UK dramas were also
found to be 'too violent' and 'too realistic'. Police series such as
Taggart were anathematized and compared unfavourably to US
dramas such as *The A Team*; although the amount of violence in
The A Team is quantitatively and qualitatively (shootings rather
than punches and kicks) higher than in UK programmes (such as
Taggart), UK programmes show violence more realistically. UK
TV News was similarly regarded as unacceptably violent by West
European TV viewers. And UK television drama was disliked
for its studio rather than location-based settings (interview with
PETAR source, May 1988).

SuperChannel presented its programme mix as one that recognized the distinctive nature of a transnational audience: 'Super-
Channel takes into account that most viewers are not native English
speakers. Presenters speak clearly, comedies and documentaries
are selected for their visual content while music and sports
programmes have a universal appeal' (SuperChannel Press Pack,
1988). But audience research was to show that few programmes
approached a 'universal appeal' and that on the contrary there was
little in SuperChannel's repertoire of programmes that appealed
widely to distinct European audiences. Rather, audiences in
different countries valued different programmes and there was no
shared West European public taste addressed in SuperChannel's
'best of British' programme mix.

The least unsuccessful of transnational satellite television channels has been Sky Channel. It was the first European satellite TV
channel and began transmission from the UK on Orbital Test
Satellite 2 (OTS2) in April 1982. The company was established

as Satellite Television plc by Brian Haynes (a former employee of Thames TV) backed by Guinness Mahon, Barclays, Ladbrokes, D.C. Thompson and others. In 1983 News International purchased 65 per cent of Satellite Television. News's stake in Satellite TV (renamed Sky in 1984) was by 1988 82 per cent. In the year to June 1987 Sky's losses were variously reported as £14.6 million and £10.2 million (1985–6, £5.69 million). In 1987 Sky raised £22.63 million in a rights issue (in addition to previous rights issues of £5.29 million). Sky's growing losses are attributed to: 'increased competition in a developing marketplace and continued difficulties in obtaining entry and exercising Sky's full market potential, in some key European territories' (*CSE*, November 1987, p. 5).

Sky has also incurred costs in increasing the proportion of original programming in its schedules (purchased programming decreased from 59 per cent in 1985–6 to 56 per cent in 1986–7) and in 'buying' its entry to Dutch and Belgian cable systems. Sky pays 'carriage fees' in kind by agreeing either to purchase an agreed value of programming (£240,000 to gain access to Walloon cable nets) or by establishing production units (Nederlands Instituut voor Lokale Omroep NILO approx. £800,000 [*CSE*, November 1987, p. 30]).

Sky's *Pop Formule* music show (7.35–8.35 a.m., Mondays) is made with the Dutch broadcasting society TROS, and its weekday morning *D.J. Kat Show* is produced by John de Mol Productions in Loosdrecht. Sky has also concluded local production agreements in Paris and West Berlin and claims that the majority of its programming is of EEC origin, with both the UK and the Netherlands contributing at least seven hours per week of original programming to Sky's schedule (interview, Sky Channel, 13 May 1988).

Sky advertising revenues in 1986–7 were £9 million (£7.5 million in 1985–6). As well as conventional spot advertising (limited to IBA seven minutes per clock hour standards) Sky also has sponsored programmes including the Uniroyal weather report, golf sponsored by the Spanish tourist board, and a morning home shopping show.

Sky is now carried on nearly all European cable networks and is close to achieving maximum possible availability for a satellite TV channel with 11 million homes and a 10 million weekly viewer reach (with a 13.7 million viewer reach over four

weeks).But wide accessibility of Sky has guaranteed neither
audiences nor advertisers, and Sky Channel's current business
strategy is to retreat from Europe and, using a higher-powered
satellite, attempt to establish a UK audience.

There are potent instabilities in West European satellite television, not least the unprofitability of all current services. These
instabilities occasion changes in the satellite television environment on, almost, a day-to-day basis. Predictions and firm conclusions are correspondingly hard to make. But some provisional
observations can be ventured.

First, there is a marked characteristic for services to be addressed
to a single-language community, and those that have essayed creation of a transnational audience have not fared well. Second, the
configuration of individual services and clusters of services is shaped
by the still dominant force of terrestrial television in all markets.
Third, the development of a multi-channel environment, 'external
pluralism', leads to a decline in 'internal pluralism', of what was
known in the BBC as 'mixed programming', as channels develop
a strong identity that differentiates them from rival products. This
'branding' can take the form either of specialization in programme
type (film channel, 24-hour news, children's programmes) or, in
channels such as Sky Channel or RTL Plus, an overall style and
mode of address across the channel's output. Scheduling also tends
to change so that programme junctions become regular (on the hour
and half hour) and schedules recur cyclically (every Thursday at 7
p.m.) in order to reduce viewers' search time.

The only channels that seem to approach profitability (and such
judgements must be highly tentative because of the sensitivity
of such data and the consequential difficulties of collecting it)
are those addressing a single-language community. Notably RTL
Plus and SatEins which enjoy competition from West German
terrestrial broadcasters offering neither a satisfactory medium to
advertisers nor an entertaining programme mix to audiences.

The major international channels Sky and SuperChannel are
loss-makers. What differentiates these two channels is (prior to the
October 1988 Virgin/Betatelevision buyout of ITV shareholdings)
the diversity of ownership of SuperChannel and reluctance of some
of its owners to continue to capitalize its losses, the absence of a clear
programming strategy and 'brand' image for SuperChannel, and the
presence in Sky Channel of a capable management and vigorous

pursuit of advertising revenue (including opening a Japanese office from where a third of its advertising revenue now originates).

A new period of satellite television is about to open. Higher-powered satellites will, it is believed, increase audiences for satellite television as viewers unable to access satellite television by cable (and unwilling to pursue TVROs of the size and cost necessary to receive signals from existing telecommunication satellites) find the cost of access to satellite television lowered. The anticipated consequential growth of audience size will, it is threatened or promised, make satellite television a viable medium in markets where its presence has hitherto been invisible (notably the UK). Larger audiences will attract advertisers and will thus permit the funding of attractive programming, which will in turn promote growth in audience size and initiate a self-sustaining enterprise. Proposed services on the new generation of satellites suggest that there has been a significant retreat from earlier notions of transnational European programme services. Sky Channel now looks to the UK (and Ireland) for its audiences; its Executive Chairman, Andrew Neil, stated: 'We see Sky as a British popular entertainment channel.' Sky has closed its European sales offices (*FT*, 6 January 1989, p. 5). SuperChannel proposes similarly to reorientate itself to national rather than international viewing; and to delivery of news and music to Italy (circumventing the established monopoly of television news now enjoyed by RAI).

DBS (Direct Broadcasting Satellites) in Western Europe

The difficulties in establishing direct to home service by high-powered television satellites should not be underestimated. The 'telecommunications' satellites currently transmitting television signals in Western Europe are relatively low-powered (Intelsat VAF11 and VAF12, 10 watts, Telecom IC, 20 watts, Eutelsat IFI, 20 watts). True DBS transmit at much higher powers. The two states, Japan and West Germany, that have launched DBS have experienced difficulties in making the satellites work. The problems centre on the Travelling Wave Tubes (TWTs) which are key components in signal transmission. In all satellites the power output from the TWTs tends to decline as components age, but the Japanese and West German DBS are both thought to have experienced problems of component reliability in TWTs designed to transmit at more than 100 watts.

The West German DBS launched in November 1987 was written off ostensibly because its power arrays did not deploy properly, but industry gossip also suggests that the TWTs, with a designed output of 230 watts, greatly scaled up from those on 'telecommunication' satellites, also failed. The Japanese Yuri DBS series has also experienced recurrent TWT failures. DBS are also, of course, subject to the same risks of aborted launches and losses in establishing satellites in orbit that apply to lower-powered satellites (in January 1988 the French PTT's Telecom IB went out of control and was written off, launcher failures have occasioned a rise in insurance rates to premiums of around 30 per cent of insured value, and insurers refuse to underwrite more than $100 million per launch).

France launched a DBS in 1988 and the UK plans to launch its DBS in 1989. Luxembourg has launched its medium-powered Astra satellite (1988) which, though not a true DBS, will, nonetheless, offer direct-to-home reception with relatively small and cheap TVROs. The French TDFI is nearly identical to the failed West German TV Sat (though with TWTs of even higher-designed power) whereas the UK BSB (manufactured by Hughes in the USA) has a 'modest' designed output of 100 watts. Luxembourg's Astra has a designed power output of 47 watts and though industry sources see this scaling up of TWTs to be less risky than those of TV Sat, TDFI and BSB, Astra has no back-up satellite or launcher and, though technically more conservative than the true DBSs, is therefore vulnerable to technical failure.

However, although the difficulties of establishing a working DBS in geostationary orbit are not negligible, a working DBS will not be sufficient to establish a viable satellite television channel. DBS, whether BSB, Astra or TDFI, offer viewers the possibility of television reception with smaller and cheaper TVROs than has been necessary for existing services. UK manufacturers (Cambridge and Amstrad) are retailing receiving equipment at prices of below £200. The hope of service providers is that the decline in cost of reception will provoke sufficient growth in numbers of viewers to make possible establishment of profitable new service.

It is beyond the scope of this paper to speculate on the financial viability of the proposed DBS services, but whether financed by advertising or subscription their success will depend on the attractiveness of their programme offer relative to competitive services (in particular those delivered by terrestrial television) and the cost of service.

At the time of writing programming on France's TDFI is limited to a high-culture channel, La Sept.

The anglophone services on Astra and proposed on BSB are firmly orientated to UK audiences. All operators have recognized that hopes of profitability on a multinational audience – whether for thematic or mixed-programme channels – are currently unrealizable.

The future success or failure of Direct Broadcast Satellite television in Western Europe will depend on the balance of costs and benefits to audiences offered by satellite television and competing services. The prognosis for DBS varies from national (linguistic) market to market; for the strength of the competition offered by established terrestrial services differs from market to market.

Satellite television has undoubtedly provoked changes in viewing behaviour, but these are best understood within the terms of national or, strictly, linguistic, markets. The transnationalization of television, dissolution of national identities, and loss of the power of states and para-statal bodies (such as the public broadcasters) anticipated as a consequence of technological change have yet to be realized.

The future of satellite television is conditional on the nature of national (or unilingual) markets rather than a transnational European market. The success of satellite television will depend on the nature of the terrestrial television regime in various national markets and the degree to which costs of service can be amortized by revenues won in competition with terrestrial broadcasters advantaged by a more favourable cost structure than satellite broadcasters. Since neither the costs nor the revenues of Direct Broadcast Satellite television are known, predictions are dangerous.

The first generation of European satellite television has convincingly demonstrated that neither the threats nor the promises of the transnationalization of European television are likely to be realized in the proximate future. But the powerful comparative advantage enjoyed by anglophone producers, and the competitive advantages of London as a location both for production and distribution, will continue to influence the development of broadcasting in Western Europe.

Language (and culture) is a very important factor in the shaping of television markets; some producers are significantly advantaged and others disadvantaged by language. But the ability to create an integrated television market in Western Europe is not one of the undoubted peculiarities of English. The dismal failure of SuperChannel's 'best of British' strategy eloquently testifies to the imperfect permeability of the cultural and linguistic membranes that separate satellite television viewers in Western Europe.

This chapter draws on research conducted at the Centre for Communication and Information Studies, Polytechnic of Central London. It was first published in *Media, Culture and Society*, vol. 11, no. 3, 1989.

References

Bekkers, W. (1987), 'The Dutch Public Broadcasting Service in a multi-channel landscape', *European Broadcasting Union Review* (Programmes, Administration, Law) 38 no. 6 Vol. XXXVIII. November, pp. 32–8).

BIEC (British Invisible Exports Council) (1988), *Annual Report and Accounts 1987-88* (London: BIEC).

Cablegram Monthly (Newsletter of the Cable Television Association). London.

CSE (Cable and Satellite Europe). Monthly: London.

Daily Telegraph. Six days a week: London.

(FT) Financial Times. Six days a week: London.

Hoskins, C. and Mirus, R. (1988), 'Reasons for the US domination of the international trade in television programmes', *Media, Culture and Society*, vol. 10 no. 4 pp. 499-515.

Myerscough, J. (1988), *The Economic Importance of the Arts in Britain*, (London:Policy Studies Institute)..

NMM (New Media Markets). Fortnightly: London.

PETAR (Pan European Television and Audience Research)(1987), *Survey*, March–April 1987.

Saatchi and Saatchi Compton (1987) 'The media landscape now to 1995' (Report), London.

SIICE (Symposium International de l'identité culturelle européenne) (1988), *Europe sans rivage*, (Paris: Albin Michel).

Sky Channel (1988) Press Pack.

SuperChannel (1988) Press Pack.

Sveriges Radio (1988) (by A. Gahlin and B. Nordstrom), 'Access to and use of Video and Foreign TV Channels in Sweden' Fall 1987, (Stockholm: Audience and Programme Research Dept.).

Valenti, J. (1988), 'The US film industry's trade crisis in Canada', *Cinema Canada*, no. 152 (May).

Wildman, S and Siwek, S. (1987), 'The economics of trade in recorded media products in a multilingual world', paper presented at the conference on the International Market in Film and Television Programs, Centre for Telecommunications and Information Studies, Graduate School of Business, Columbia University, New York City, 1987.

Chapter 4

The Prognosis for Satellite Television in the UK

Satellite television has attracted attention for two reasons. First, it abolishes the relationship between cost and distance of transmission and potentially offers new market stratifications. If signals are propagated over Europe, for example, an integrated advertising market and an information or cultural community is potentially available. This potentiality is attractive to interests such as the European Commission charged with the creation of a single EEC market by 1992. Equally, it is threatening to those who fear the erosion of existing communities and cultures.

Second, by using super high frequencies (SHF), hitherto without practical usefulness for television broadcasting, satellite television promises to abolish the spectrum scarcity that has been thought to constrain development of additional television services competing with the one, two, three, four or five terrestrially broadcast channels established in West European states. Satellite television therefore offers hope to those wishing to introduce more competition and more choice in television.

These potentialities undoubtedly exist. But what is most striking is not the ease but the difficulty of realizing them. The differences of language (and to a lesser extent culture) in Western Europe have slowed consumption of transnational television. Helmut Thoma, Managing Director of RTL Plus, the most successful satellite television channel in West Germany, has stated: 'I have never believed in pan-European advertising. Language will always be a problem.' (Cited in *Cable and Satellite Europe*, No. 12, 1987, p. 33.) Few transnational brands exist (particularly in the product ranges most frequently advertised on television, such as domestic cleaning products), and the establishment of an integrated European market is proving slow and difficult to achieve.

Frequency planning authorities such as the Deutsche Bundespost and the Department of Trade and Industry are proving successful in 'finding' additional frequencies for terrestrial broadcasting which promise to expand the supply of television to final consumers at lower cost than satellite television. However, there is undoubtedly a limit to this process: at some point either frequencies outside the UHF/VHF range will have to be exploited using satellites or a microwave video distribution system (MVDS) or cable networks will have to be established, if more television is to be supplied.

The costs and difficulties of establishing cable networks are well known. But existing satellite television services are delivered by low-powered 'telecommunication' satellites which *complement* cable rather than compete with it. It is only successful launches of high-powered direct broadcast satellites (DBS) that will extend television services at lower cost and over wider areas than competing delivery systems such as cable. But DBS, once established (and the existing DBS satellites in orbit, launched by West Germany and Japan, do not work satisfactorily), will face competition from an emerging and potentially cheaper technology, MVDS.

The success, or failure, of satellite television will depend on its delivery to final consumers of programming with equal and preferably superior benefits in relation to costs.

Costs

The existing four UK broadcast television channels provide information, education and entertainment to final consumers at very low cost, estimated at 1.5p per hour for ITV and 2p per hour for the BBC (Ehrenberg and Barwise, 1982). To receive existing satellite television final consumers must either subscribe to a cable network (Westminster Cable's 'price slashed' basic service costs £9.95 per month) or purchase a TVRO (Television Receive Only Earth Station) or 'dish' (say £600 for a 90 cm dish and associated electronics). Viewers using a TVRO incur additional costs (for additional dishes, steerable dish, decoders, etc) if they wish to receive signals from more than one satellite and/or scrambled signals available only on a pay-per-channel basis. DBS promises to reduce dish and receiving electronics costs to final consumers: receiving apparatus for News International's proposed services on the medium-powered Astra satellite is promised at less than £200 before installation. British Satellite Broadcasting (BSB) promises a similar price for its receiver, though descramblers for encrypted signals such as 'premium' film or sports programmes will cost a further 30 to 40 per cent.

Accounts of the recent Touche Ross report for the Department of Trade and Industry suggest that 'MVDS using existing technology is less expensive in total system terms than either cable television or direct broadcast satellite services'. MVDS is admittedly an unproven technology in Western European conditions but in the core Western European markets – not least the UK with increasing hours of transmission of terrestrial services and a likely establishment of a new terrestrial Channel 5 – more competition and more choice between television services are being established through lower-cost media.

If further terrestrial broadcast channels (using bandwidth compression techniques, unused VHF or UHF frequencies, or both) and/or MVDS services are established then the existing poor outlook for satellite television is likely to worsen. Though costs (for aerials and converters) will be incurred by final consumers wishing to receive such new services, these costs are likely to be lower than for either satellite or cable distribution of new television channels. Unless therefore satellite television can deliver programming more attractive to final consumers than that available via competing distribution media the uptake of satellite services is likely to be low.

The Audience

Terrestrial television, though cheap in relation to competing systems, delivers to advertisers and programmers largely national audiences. It is possible that the wide 'footprints' of satellite television may offer advertisers and programmers opportunities to restratify European audiences (now largely national) in new ways. Programmers have seen opportunities to agglomerate audiences across Europe to create a sufficiently large and prosperous audience for programme services that are uneconomic on a national basis.

France has led development of a high culture channel, 'La Sept', in the hope that a Europe-wide scope, hoping to reach either the European mass audience (though there are few Europe-wide 'mass' brands) or a particular audience segment ('Yuppies' or international business, financial and political elites) that can only imperfectly and wastefully be addressed by mass national television services.

To these potential 'horizontal' groups in the European public should be added potential 'vertical' groups of audiences dissatisfied with existing national television services. But whether programming is directed to 'horizontal' or 'vertical' audience groups, it has to be paid for, either through advertising (where advertisers buy access to viewers) or by final consumers.

Advertising Finance

Satellite television has proved attractive to advertisers wishing to reach audiences in West European markets with an undersupply of terrestrial television advertising time. Belgium and Denmark have, as yet no advertising on terrestrial services and in other markets – most importantly West Germany – terrestrial broadcasting provides a poor service to advertisers. In West Germany the satellite channels RTL Plus and SatEins deliver more entertaining programming than their terrestrial public service competitors and thus attract and retain audiences. These audiences can then be sold to advertisers since satellite television not only attracts audiences but offers a much more effective advertising medium than the terrestrial ZDF and ARD networks. But other West European television markets offer more competitive television advertising regimes. Although in the UK there is a monopoly seller of TV advertising time and, probably, an undersupply of time, satellite television has not proved an attractive medium for advertisers. DBS (whether 'medium' power such as Astra or 'high' power such as BSB) will lower the cost of reception of satellite television but at the same time competition for advertising revenues is likely to increase through establishment of other new advertising media. In the UK there will be three national commercial radio channels and, very likely, an advertising-financed fifth terrestrial television channel. Nor is there yet a sufficient repertoire of transnational brands to establish a European television advertising market. Satellite television programmers also encounter advertiser resistance to buying time in some classes of programme. Sky's highest-rated programme *Wrestlemania* attracts little advertising because advertisers do not wish their products to be associated with a 'downmarket' programme.

Advertising finance offers a means of funding satellite television such that final consumers may enjoy the service at low cost. However, the experience of European satellite television to date suggests that:

- no transnational advertising market exists;
- there is advertiser resistance to funding some programming popular with final consumers;
- even in large and prosperous markets undersupplied with television advertising and popular programming, sufficient advertising revenues are not yet available to cover costs, still less to yield profits for satellite television.

Subscription Finance and State Funding

The principal alternative sources of funding to advertising revenue are subscription and state funding.

Subscription funding involves significant transaction costs; the Peacock Committee reported that the transaction costs of the French Canal Plus service were about £7 per year and in the USA for a multichannel service $33 per subscriber per year. If receiving signals are scrambled to reduce piracy, final consumers also incur the costs of purchase or rental of a decoder (and if subscribing to a number of scrambled pay channels, the costs of *several* decoders). Subscription services are also by no means cheat-proof: Peacock cites an estimate for the USA of between 10 per cent and 25 per cent of consumers evading payment (Peacock, 1986).

Subscription channels therefore need to deliver to final consumers programmes offering benefits sufficient to outweigh not only costs of programming equal to or superior to those available through competitive distribution media but significant transaction costs as well. Canal Plus (a large terrestrial service) has done so and the UK-based satellite-to-cable film channel 'Premiere' is close to financial viability. But the prognosis for subscription television in the UK advanced in the Home Office's 1987 *Subscription Television* study is not encouraging.

State-funded services such as Italy's RAI and the television channels of the USSR and Iran are available to European satellite television viewers who wish to consume these unscrambled signals. As with radio services there is little that governments can do to regulate the consumption of foreign signals by their citizens. There is no evidence that such services have had a significant impact on UK viewers, but if the Government wishes to restrict access of UK viewers to such programmes bilateral discussion between governments offers a possible means to this end.

Programme Services

Given the higher costs to final consumers of satellite television *vis-à-vis* terrestrial television (the costs of cable, TVRO or MVDS for advertising and subscription-funded services and additional transaction costs for subscription-funded services), satellite television must deliver programming superior to terrestrial services if it is to be successful.

Satellite television has the potential to deliver high-definition television (HDTV) more effectively and economically than terrestrial broadcasting. HDTV will, *ceteris paribus*, require a wider bandwidth than conventional services, and there is unlikely to be space for this in the frequency range used for terrestrial broadcasting. If, as predictions suggest, final consumers desire HDTV they may be willing to pay additional reception and transaction costs in order to secure it. However, HDTV can be delivered by cable or MVDS and it seems likely that MVDS can supply HDTV at a lower cost than can satellite transmission. Though the relative prosperity of consumers in the 1960s and 1980s was sufficiently different to inhibit a firm conclusion, the slow diffusion of colour television receivers relative to the rapid penetration of VCR suggests audiences are prepared to pay more, earlier, for choice in programming than for improvement in image quality.

HDTV offers a possible scenario for the successful development of satellite television services, but in default of satellite
TV offering picture quality of a higher *technical* standard than
terrestrial services success will be conditional on the supply either
of programming superior to that available at equivalent costs by
other means or programming unavailable through other means.

The relative attractiveness of satellite TV programming *vis-à-vis*
terrestrial (or other) TV programming depends on the nature
of both services. I do not discuss all actual (still less possible)
combinations but confine observations to general principles and
to the UK situation.

Programming Unavailable via Terrestrial or Other Services

Certain categories of programming are undersupplied for reasons
of public policy: pornography, violence, material affecting the
security of the state. There is a spectrum of judgement as to
whether individual works fall into any or all of these categories
but I believe that satellite television is unlikely to pose serious
problems in any of these fields. If satellite television is to be
provided by profit-making organizations programming must be
financed by either advertising (including sponsorship) or subscription. Advertisers have shown themselves unwilling to associate
the products they promote with programming that they regard
as offensive even though such programming attracts substantial
audiences. The withdrawal of advertising by Tesco Stores from the
Daily Star and the difficulties Sky CChannel experiences in securing
advertising for *Wrestlemania* suggest that advertising finance may
not be forthcoming for violent, or pornographic, programming.
In default of advertising finance such programming can only
be financed from subscription; to collect subscription revenue
programme providers need to control access to programming.
This they can do only via cable distribution and/or scrambled
transmissions and sale or rental of decoders.

Both cable distribution and sale/rental of decoders are sus-
ceptible to control by government should Parliament so decide.
The Cable Authority (likely to be replaced by the proposed
new television authority, the ITC) is empowered to regulate the
content of cable TV; sale or rental of decoders could be confined

to licensed sex shops (in the same way that R18 videotapes are sold or rented).

Doubtless there will be unauthorized reception of services but the regulation of cable redistribution and decoders should deny revenues to operators sufficiently to render programming services judged undesirable in the UK impossible to run profitably on revenue flows from the UK. A possibility remains that UK viewers may 'eavesdrop' on unscrambled services established overseas for overseas consumption funded either by advertising or by government but I judge that advertisers will not fund offensive television programming, though there may be foreign markets which will sustain programming (and advertising finance) that some in the UK will deplore.

The French Canal Plus service is a case in point (though its erotic programming is currently scrambled). In such cases the UK government has the possibility of recourse to bilateral diplomacy but the presumption should usually be that what another EEC government regards as unlikely to deprave and corrupt its citizens should not be prohibited to UK citizens. Satellite television may deliver to UK audiences access to more erotic television than has hitherto been available, but it is very unlikely to deliver such programming as *Driller Killer* or even such non-violent erotica as *Deep Throat*.

The Home Office *Subscription Television* study established that there is an undersupply in the UK of 'premium' programming – high-budget drama, feature films and sports programmes. But the establishment of new services seems unlikely to increase the supply of such programming (the Home Office study was not optimistic about the future for subscription services). The existing UK supply of premium programming is relatively high due to the concentration of resources (only one hand in the advertising pot and a different single hand in the licence fee pot) and the absence of competitive bidding for programming. The first instance of competition between terrestrial and satellite broadcasters for premium programming (BBC/ITV/BSB for soccer) has not increased supply but has driven up the price. In a future of hot competition for premium programming long-term advantage will lie with well-funded organizations with low distribution costs – that is, with terrestrial broadcasters (particularly the BBC).

Programming Competitive with Terrestrial Services

Terrestrial broadcast television is significantly advantaged in competition for audiences with satellite TV. Its distribution costs are
low, it has long been established and in many cases – notably the
BBC – transmits advertising-free programming. In large European
countries broadcasters have enjoyed funding sufficient to finance
a range of high-cost programmes. Satellite television has not
yet generated revenues sufficient to cover its costs anywhere in
Western Europe. However, there are two environments in which
it has enjoyed some success.

Small countries offer promising opportunities to satellite television (because national terrestrial services do not dispose of
sufficient revenues to fund high-budget national programming in
sufficiently large quantities to offer viewers a range of choices),
but what is most striking is the low consumption of satellite TV
in the small European countries.

Sweden and the Netherlands

In Sweden in February 1988 only 8 per cent of viewers had access
to satellite television, and satellite TV had a 3 per cent share of
overall viewing.

In the Netherlands in 1986 50 per cent of television viewers had access to Sky (and from February 1987 40 per cent to
SuperChannel). This population spent 5 per cent of its viewing
time on Sky and a further 2 per cent on other satellite channels.
The viewing of Sky and other satellite channels declined from the
1985 total of 9 per cent for Sky. A 1987 survey of cable subscribers
in Amsterdam showed that there was more interest in receiving
foreign terrestrial signals than satellite services (very interested in
BBC1 45.8 per cent, BBC2 40.6 per cent, BRT2 37.8 per cent,
ARD 31.9 per cent, ZDF 29.8 per cent, BRT1 29.8 per cent, Sky
satellite TV 26.2 per cent, WDR 25.2 per cent, SuperChannel
satellite TV 21.2 per cent).

Both Sweden and the Netherlands have undersupplied advertising and entertainment on television. Both countries are taking
steps to close these windows of vulnerability which have offered
opportunities to satellite television services. As Wim Bekkers
(Head of Audience Research, NOS Netherlands) put it: 'The most

important challenge for public broadcasting in the commercial satellite era is to compete and survive with entertaining, education, cultural and news programmes' (Bekkers, 1987).

The United Kingdom

In the UK consumption of satellite television is derisory. Although it is only the UK, France and Scandinavia in which the viewing of satelllite television (where available) rises above 10 per cent (and France's total includes Canal Plus which is available to most viewers through terrestrial broadcasting) the UK satellite-receiving population is tiny. Satellite TV has a 28 per cent share of viewing in UK cabled homes but only 16 per cent of homes passed by cable subscribe. The proportion of satellite television viewers in the UK population to which satellite television is available via cable is not, as is sometimes claimed, 28 per cent but rather approximately 4.5 per cent.

Audience response to UK terrestrial television is difficult to evaluate. The Peacock report and other commentators have demonstrated that there is a poor market in broadcasting services, that service providers get poor and possibly misleading signals from consumers and that audience behaviour is not necessarily indicative of audience wants. High (or low) consumption of existing programming is indicative only of preferences between existing alternatives and not necessarily of an optimal matching of supply to either actual or latent demand. Peacock pertinently cited the findings of the National Consumer Council that 'it would not be wise for broadcasters to assume that consumers think that everything is wonderful in the world of British broadcasting' and that the 46 per cent of television viewers who expressed satisfaction with UK television was 'a very low figure'.

But there has been little enthusiasm for either cable or satellite television in the UK: the cost–benefit analysis performed by viewers have resoundingly favoured the existing terrestrial services. Of cable homes the two main English-language satellite TV channels, Sky and SuperChannel, secure only 7.1 per cent and 3.8 per cent of viewing respectively. Though UK terrestrial channels do not provide an optimal service to viewers it is unmistakably clear that viewers' cost–benefit analysis is that terrestrial services are to be preferred to cable and satellite alternatives and that, even among the small proportion of the television audience that is prepared to pay for cable, satellite television is little consumed.

West Germany

The Federal Republic of Germany provides an exception to the general rule that satellite television has had little impact on viewing habits or advertising markets. The success of the two commercial satellite channels transmitted to West Germany, RTL Plus and SatEins, is due to the distinctive character of terrestrial broadcasting in West Germany.

The three channels of public-service terrestrial broadcasting in West Germany offer a poor medium for advertisers. Advertising is confined to 'blocks' separated from programmes and transmitted between 6 and 8 p.m. (and not on Sundays or religious holidays). Advertising is sold by an organization at 'arm's length' from programmers so advertisers are unable to locate advertisements next to particular desired programmes. Moreover, programming on West German television is not designed to maximize ratings and the exposure of audiences to advertisements. Satellite television offering popular programming (12 minutes of spot advertising per hour and an audience-maximizing orientation) is attractive to advertisers. Feature films and TV series are the mainstay of the schedules but in at least one area of West Germany in which satellite TV is widely available satellite news achieves higher ratings than either of the main news programmes of the terrestrial services. In the Saarland RTL Plus's *7 vor 7* achieves a 42.6 per cent rating, the ARD *Tagesschau* 26.4 per cent and ZDF's *Heute* 26.9 per cent.

In 1987 RTL Plus reached an estimated 10 million West German homes (via cable, terrestrial broadcasting and re-broadcasting, SMATV and TVROs) and an estimated advertising revenue of DM45-50 million. SatEins is estimated to reach 11 million viewers and to have achieved advertising revenues of DM35 million in 1987. Each channel is likely to reach in excess of 20 per cent of the West German population in early 1988 (and perhaps an additional half million viewers in Austria and Switzerland). In November 1987 viewers with access to RTL Plus and SatEins watched respectively an estimated 13 minutes and 28 minutes of satellite television daily.

West German terrestrial television has long had the character of a secular church and the success of RTL Plus and SatEins in attracting advertising revenue and a growing proportion of audience attention testifies to the vulnerability to commercial competition of public-sector broadcasters who have lost contact with popular taste. But even in West Germany, though satellite TV is close to economic viability, it reaches less than a fifth of the population and accounts for a small proportion of total viewing.

Factors determining the success of non-terrestrial TV

International comparisons suggest four reasons for the success of non-terrestrial television services, none of which currently applies to the UK:

Access to television services relayed from a neighbouring country with a comprehensible language and better-funded (thus permitting more expensive programming) television. The highest penetration of cable is in countries such as Belgium, the Netherlands, Canada and Switzerland. In these countries cable delivers at low cost access to well-funded terrestrial broadcast television from neighbouring countries in a comprehensible language.

Underdelivery of entertaining programming by national terrestrial broadcasters. The BBC's past loss of audiences to Radio Luxembourg and Normandy in the 1930s, to ITV in the 1950s and to pirate radio in the 1960s and 1980s was due principally to its patrician, improving and boring programming. The loss of Canadian viewers to American television has been, in part, for this reason: even francophone Canadians, to some extent insulated by language from the attractions of American television, compare French Canadian television – *'une télévision vieillissante'* – to American television – *'une télévision véhiculant la richesse, le rêve et l'éspoir'*. The most successful of European satellite TV channels, SatEins and RTL Plus in West Germany, offer much more entertainment than public-service television to West German viewers.

Underdelivery of a satisfactory medium for television advertising (though the attractiveness of a channel to advertisers depends most importantly on the attractiveness of its programming to final consumers). But where advertising is intrusive audiences may avoid advertising-financed television even if the advertising-free alternative is available only at higher cost.

Underdelivery of a technically satisfactory sound and image quality and/or programming free of intrusive advertising. Cable television (and direct-to-home reception of satellite television) in the USA is attractive to final consumers for these reasons. US broadcast television has 12 (and sometimes more) minutes of advertising each hour – the advertisements are intrusive and are not (as UK advertisements are supposed to be) at 'natural breaks' in programmes. Many US television viewers are unable to receive broadcast signals of a quality comparable to that taken for granted in the UK, and cable television in the US began as a medium to rectify the technical deficiencies in broadcast signal quality. The introduction of HDTV as a non-terrestrial broadcast service may offer a similar scenario in which UK consumers find non-terrestrial, notably satellite television, attractive.

In default of HDTV the success, or failure, of satellite television depends on its programming offer. Satellite television revenues are low in comparison to those of terrestrial broadcasters. Recent estimates suggest that UK satellite television will command revenues sufficient to fund programming at the rate of £4000 to £5000 per hour. *TV World* (1987) estimates the average price paid by Sky Channel and SuperChannel for an hour's programming as $2500. The BBC states its average cost of purchased programmes as £30,000 per hour and the cost of cheap programming such as golf as £24,000 per hour and snooker as £10,000 per hour. BBC costs may be higher than satellite TV costs and the price the BBC pays for acquired programming will reflect the BBC's larger audiences, but the disparities are sufficient to suggest that:

- satellite TV will be able to make little programming and then only in low-cost genres;
- most satellite TV programming will be acquired on the international programme market or 'cascaded' from the archives of owners.

Satellite television is, and is likely to continue to be, a vehicle for recycling existing programming to audiences not yet exposed to it. Much of this programming will originate from the USA and, secondly, from the UK where large archives of entertainment programmes exist.

Satellite television, though attracting only a fraction of the total television audience, may have important cross-impacts on other services. In advertising-funded systems competition in the supply of advertising will tend to lower advertisement time prices and the subtraction of the fraction of audience viewing satellite television from the audience pool consuming competitive services will make competitive channels less attractive to advertisers. In theory a spiral of decline in exisiting services could be established. But this is an unlikely scenario for the UK.

The Future

If and when powerful television satellites are successfully launched (and their success cannot be taken for granted – the German and Japanese Direct Broadcast Services do not work satisfactorily and Astra has no back-up satellite), the costs of reception of satellite television will decline. But this decline in costs may not be sufficient to render satellite television attractive to viewers where terrestrial television already delivers acceptable, if not optimal, programming. Advocates of satellite television argue that even if audiences are not dissatisfied with terrestrial television they welcome the extension of choice; but choice may be extended by additional terrestrial channels or MVDS at lower cost than by satellite. And, however low the cost of extension of choice, service providers must draw on the revenue streams of either subscription or advertising to defray costs. No one has yet done so sufficiently to return profits.

In present European conditions satellite television is unlikely to be a serious presence in the UK broadcasting market. The existing 'successes' of satellite television (though insufficient to cover operators' costs) are very vulnerable to changed policies and practices of terrestrial broadcasters. The existence of a plurality of low-powered (and projected high-powered) satellites testifies more to the lobbying power of the European aerospace and electronics industries than to demand for new television services. Astra and BSB, to be sure, fit this scenario imperfectly but the viability of their programme services remains very doubtful. One of Astra's shareholders (Richard Dunn, Managing Director of Thames Television) commented to the House of Commons Committee on the Future of Broadcasting that satellite programme services were a 'dubious enterprise'.

There seems small likelihood of a genuinely transnational European audience, programming and advertising market evolving in the foreseeable future. Rather television viewers will remain primarily orientated to national services (assuming that these services meet audience demand for entertainment, since television is used primarily for leisure and relaxation) and secondly to foreign national services in a comprehensible language. Where national terrestrial services underdeliver either television advertising or entertainment (or both) they will, as West Germany exemplifies, remain vulnerable to competition from new services.

It is unlikely that pornographic satellite programming channels will be established. It is inconceivable that they will be advertising-funded. If subscription-funded services develop, revenue flows from UK audiences to programme providers could be controlled by government by providing that decoders be available only from licensed sex shops. No prior restraint of programming should be attempted, such as that proposed through the Broadcasting Standards Council, but if programme providers persistently transmit programming judged by the authority to be undesirable then the authority would have the power, after due warning, to curtail revenue flows to the programmers by withdrawing permission to sell or rent decoders.

Should unscrambled advertising-funded services be established in other West European countries TVRO owners in the UK will be able to 'eavesdrop' on such services. However, it is unlikely that public policy will demand UK audiences be denied access to programming deemed acceptable by another European government for its own citizens.

The key to the future of satellite television is the terrestrial television regime. If the present UK terrestrial services are maintained (still more so if expanded) satellite television, a higher-cost, lower-funded medium with difficulties of establishing a place in the market, is unlikely to make a serious impact on UK viewing.

It is often suggested that the rapid establishment of a high level of VCR penetration in the UK offers hope to satellite television operators. The 55 per cent of UK homes with VCRs is particularly high in comparison to other developed Western states. But the low proportion of VCR households that rent pre-recorded tapes (30 per cent of VCR households rent one or more pre-recorded tapes a week, i.e., less than 20 per cent of UK TV households) suggests that VCRs are used to optimize consumption of terrestrial television and that the high UK VCR population does not demonstrate demand for an alternative to terrestrial television but rather a desire to restructure and improve control of its scheduling by viewers.

The UK television market is too small to sustain the additional services projected. BSB and Astra will treble the supply of television to which UK audiences now have access. The Peacock Committee's view was that the UK advertising market is too small to finance additional television services and they were sceptical of claims (such as by BSB) that subscription revenues will prove substantial. Accordingly a future of intense competition between television broadcasters can be anticipated, in which those with lowest costs and high capitalization will survive. The cost structure of terrestrial broadcasters will favour them in this competition. Their distribution systems are cheaper than those of satellite (and cable) operators and they enjoy large stocks of programming the costs of which have already been written off. Moreover, among satellite television operators those using unscrambled signals from Astra (which promise to be available to final consumers at lower cost than either those from BSB or encrypted signals from Astra) are likely to be advantaged. Satellite programmers will increasingly be forced to programme their services with material acquired 'off the shelf' on the international programme market. There may therefore be a decline in funding for original programming, but this is not an inevitable outcome. The television market in the USA has evolved so that well-funded strata (Home Box Office from subscription and the ABC, CBS and NBC advertising-financed networks) produce original programming and the syndication/independent television stratum programmes repeats. However, the US market is bigger and richer than that of the UK.

A possible but not inevitable scenario is that of destructive competition between satellite and terrestrial commercial broadcasters, in which competitors seek to lower their costs as competition for a limited revenue pool intensifies. Original programming will decline outside the BBC, which will continue to receive an assured revenue flow from licence fees, but advertising-financed services, terrestrial and satellite, will compete (with new radio services) for, at best, a slowly growing advertising pool. The ability of advertising-financed services to fund premium programming will decline, thus possibly opening a window of opportunity for subscription services. However, subscription services will suffer high transaction costs and will be unlikely to generate revenues sufficient to fund large quantities of new premium programming on which assured flows of revenue from subscribers will depend. The cost–benefit analysis performed, explicitly or implicitly, by viewers that has in the past favoured terrestrial broadcast television over competing delivery systems seems likely to continue to do so. Doubtless there will be niches in which new services establish themselves. Sky Channel, though trebling its losses in the year 1986/7 (the most recent period for which accounts are publicly available) relative to 1985/6, requires only an estimated 7 per cent of the UK TV audience for profitability. But Sky's 7 per cent reach is more likely to come from its projected terrestrial transmitter on the Isle of Man than from its satellite services.

The future of UK television is one of greatly expanded supply of channels and very hot competition (except for the BBC) for revenue sources. In this new environment many advantages reside with terrestrial services and few with satellite. Unless the regulatory environment favours satellite television (and the French government created a playing field tilted heavily in favour of Canal Plus) its prognosis is poor.

This chapter was first published in 1989 in *Space Policy*. An earlier version was submitted as evidence to the House of Commons Home Affairs Committee on the Future of Broadcasting and is printed in the minutes of Evidence and Appendices which form Volume II of the Committee's report. (262-II HMSO London 1988).

References

Bekkers, W. (1987), 'The Dutch Public Broadcasting Service in a multi-channel landscape', in *European Broadcasting Union Review* (Programmes Administration Law) Geneva V XXXVIII no. 6 November.

Ehrenberg, A. and Barwise, P. (1982), *How Much Does UK Television Cost?* (London: London Business School).

Home Office (1987), *Subscription Television: A Study for the Home Office* (London: HMSO).

Peacock, A. (1986), *Report of the Committee on Financing the BBC* (The Peacock Report), Cmnd 9824 (London: HMSO).

Chapter 5

White and Green and Not Much Re(a)d: The 1988 White Paper on Broadcasting Policy

> In putting forward the idea of a free broadcasting market without censorship, Peacock exposed many of the contradictions in the Thatcherite espousal of market forces. In principle, Mrs Thatcher and her supporters are all in favour of de-regulation, competition and consumer choice. But they are also even more distrustful than traditionalist Tories such as Douglas Hurd of plans to allow people to listen to and watch what they like, subject only to the law of the land. They espouse the market system but dislike the libertarian value judgements involved in its operation. (Brittan, 1987, p.4)

Broadcasting policy in the UK has seldom been a hotter issue. There has been an accelerating flow of official documents of which the Home Office's White Paper *Broadcasting in the 90s: Competition Choice And Quality* (Home Office, 1988) is probably the penultimate statement, to be followed by a new Broadcasting Act in 1989.

But it is not just the structural issues of broadcasting policy, concerning the finance and organization of broadcasting institutions (addressed in numerous official documents, see *inter alia* DTI, 1988; Home Office, 1987a; Home Office, 1987b; Peacock, 1986) which have been the object of official attention for the government has made explicit use of its powers (in the BBC Licence and the 1981 Broadcasting Act) to prohibit transmission of particular messages.

The banning of broadcast actuality coverage of statements by speakers on behalf of or in support of two lawful political organizations, Sinn Fein and the Ulster Defence Association, is unprecedented. The rationale offered for his act by the Home Secretary is contradictory. Statements by the UDA and Sinn Fein are deemed by the Home Secretary to be both so repugnant to UK audiences for radio and television as to require the audience to be protected from them, and persuasive enough to attract audiences' support for illegal terrorism and thus to require their suppression. The ban follows an assumption that terrorists must be denied (in the Prime Minister's words) 'the oxygen of publicity'.

It is questionable whether the presence or absence of actuality coverage of statements of support for the UDA or Sinn Fein affect terrorism in the UK and Ireland, particularly since twenty years of broadcasters' coverage of events in Northern Ireland has followed Lord Hill's precept (when Chairman of the Governors of the BBC) that 'as between the British Army and the gunman the BBC is not and cannot be impartial'. It is more likely that curtailment of direct representation of the views of an elected Westminster MP, sixty elected local councillors in Northern Ireland (and more in the Republic) and a party that attracts 35 per cent of the nationalist vote in Northern Ireland will have an effect that is the reverse of that intended by the UK government. Rather than reducing support for Sinn Fein (and the UDA) the government's measures may reduce Northern Ireland nationalists' tolerance of the UK political order which denies parity of representation to lawful political organizations.

A principal aim of counter-terrorism is to win the support, or at least acquiescence, of the 'floaters' who have no firm commitment to either state or terrorist organizations. The state's reduction of civil liberties for legal organizations may lead to loss of popular support and/or acquiescence for the state and a corresponding shift by 'floaters' towards organizations opposed to the state and its institutions. Unless the UK state guarantees formal political rights (including access to representation in broadcasting equal to that enjoyed by other lawful political organizations) for all lawful political organizations, its legitimacy declines and the pragmatic effect of measures such as those imposed by the government is likely to be, from the government's point of view, negative. The increased use of the repressive powers of the UK government in broadcasting is not confined to suppression of representation of lawful political organizations, but also extends to suppression of representation of sex and violence by a new censorship body, the Broadcasting Standards Council (to be given statutory authority in the forthcoming Broadcasting Act). The White Paper's stated *raison d'être* is extension of viewer (and listener) choice and augmentation of consumer sovereignty. To this end it proposes substantial changes in organization and regulation of broadcast television (and radio).

> The Government places the viewer and listener at the centre of broadcasting policy. Because of technological, international and other developments, change is inevitable. It is also desirable; only through change will the individual be able to exercise the much wider choice which will soon become possible. The Government's aim is to open the door so that individuals can choose for themselves from a much wider range of programmes and types of broadcasting. (Home Office, 1988, para 1.2)

Yet this profession of liberalization and devolution of authority is impossible to reconcile with the new repressive powers and augmented repressive actions of government. The central question therefore posed by the White Paper is this: is government broadcasting policy internally incoherent, in which case professions of liberal intent such as that cited above must be judged mendacious, or contradictory, asserting simultaneously stricter control by government and structural change in order to give 'viewer and listener a greater choice and a greater say' (ibid.).

Diversity, Quality and Popularity?

Discussion of the White Paper has largely been hostile (here there is room for a fascinating sociology of who speaks, the agenda-setting function of interested parties particularly the broadcasters, and of the belief system and interests of the UK media elite) and has mobilized two categories in defence of the status quo: diversity (range) and quality in television programming. The White Paper deploys these categories and adds a welcome third: popularity. These important notions are difficult to operationalize and have tended in the UK to be assigned as an exclusive property of public service systems.

Diversity is relatively easy to research and empirically test *post hoc* (whether a particular institutional form for broadcasting offers more or less diversity than another). But it is hard to predict whether a new institutional arrangement will, *propter hoc*, deliver more or less diversity than its predecessor. In a single-channel broadcasting environment diversity can only come via 'internal diversity' (mixed programming) but as channels proliferate 'internal diversity' tends to decline and to be supplanted by 'external diversity' as individual channels become less mixed in their programming and differentiate themselves from each other with a strong and consistent 'brand' image.. (So that viewers', and listeners', search time for a particular kind of programming is reduced). Changes in UK broadcasting (independent of the White Paper) are leading to a decline in internal diversity, but not necessarily to reduction in diversity realized through different means, externally. There are undoubtedly institutional arrangements in which neither internal nor external programme diversity exists. (And programme diversity does not map exactly onto diversity of programme producers and suppliers, another important kind of diversity.)

US network television, for example neither offers internal diversity, types of programmes scheduled, nor external diversity – channels have a similar mix and tend to schedule similar programmes at the same time, for example news programmes at 10 pm – reducing viewer choice. But such conditions may also apply in public service conditions (for example, in Italy before 1976 and arguably in contemporary West Germany) and may be absent in commercial-for-profit broadcasting environments (US radio and cable television). The absence or presence of diversity (internal or external) cannot be attributed to a single factor whether it is public or private ownership, mode of finance or number of channels, though all of these factors are important. Decline in 'internal diversity' in UK broadcasting may, or may not, be paralleled by an increase in 'external diversity'. However, diversity in the present (pre-White Paper) arrangements for public broadcasting in the UK should not be too readily assumed. Though Blumler, Nossiter and Brynin (1986) – in a well researched attempt to grapple with the difficult questions of diversity and quality – claim that:

> the range of programming available to all the population in the UK is among the most extensive, if not actually the most extensive, provided by the major broadcasting systems studied. (Blumler, Nossiter and Brynin, 1986, p.167).

Stephen Hearst, a leading guru of public service broadcasting (formerly the BBC's Controller of Radio 3, Controller of the BBC Future Policy Group and Special Assistant to the Director General) suggests that the role of broadcasting is to promote social integration and assimilation of minority ethnic groups into the dominant culture, thus reducing diversity. Accordingly he criticizes the growth of community radio and its challenge to the BBC for institutionalizing cultural difference and for maintaining diversity:

> We need to ask what the likely social and educational effects of community radio might be if local sets are largely, if not permanently, switched onto its new wavelengths. Over the centuries immigration has been of immense benefit to Britain . . . Social integration has nearly always been successfully accomplished. Now we are about to license an electronic medium which uncontrolled, could have the unintended effect of delaying such integration. (Hearst, 1988)

If the role of broadcasting is to reduce diversity in the population of viewers and listeners then it is not surprising that audiences have refused the BBC's invitation to assimilate along the lines it prescribes. And that BBC and ILR radio services have been supplemented by hundreds of unlicensed 'pirate' radio stations which have substantially extended the diversity of programming delivered by authorized public service radio. But, whether or not diversity is best realized through a maintained status quo or in changed arrangements for broadcasting, a problem remains. Internal or external diversity, whether delivered by public service or by

'for profit' broadcasters, has still to be matched to the demand for
diversity from audiences. How are we to know whether too little
or too much diversity is offered? Or whether diversity of one kind
(A, B, C, D) is preferred, or not, to diversity of another kind (1,
2, 3, 4)?

Blumler, Nossiter and Brynin's study is the most serious attempt
to grapple with the intractable notions of diversity (range is the
category they use) and quality. As has been seen, diversity is
by no means an easy category but quality is even more difficult.
How is a proposition such as, *'Brideshead Revisited* is quality
television' to be tested and either confirmed or refuted? The
problem is intractable. The valiant attempt by Blumler *et al.*
to address it by canvasing the views of professional broadcasters (unsurprisingly concluding that, whatever quality is, there's
certainly lots of it in UK broadcasting) is open to the summary
refutation offered by the Peacock Committee. That broadcasters'
judgement on each other's work is not a reliable guide to audience
judgements.

> It is entirely understandable that so much attention is paid in
> the Annual Reports of both the BBC and IBA to the most
> important professional symbols of success – EMMY or BAFTA
> awards . . . However the award of professional accolades can
> only be at most an indirect guide to what will promote the
> interests of those for whom the system is ultimately designed.
> (Peacock, 1986, para. 198)

Diversity and quality, categories mobilized in the broadcasting
policy debate largely by defenders of the status quo are difficult
to implement (though this difficulty does not mean the values
to which they refer are unimportant, only that one should be
cautious about attributing the qualities) and are, it seems, insufficiently present within the present UK broadcasting system to
satisfy audiences. Peacock cited a MORI survey for the National
Consumer Council which found that 46 per cent of television
viewers said they were 'very or fairly satisfied with the quality
of television against 45% who were very or fairly dissatisfied' and
added 'all our experience of measuring consumers' attitudes show
that you can normally expect 75–80% to say they are satisfied
with a service whatever it is. 46% satisfaction is a very low

figure,' (Peacock, 1986, para. 198). The evaluation of current government policy, and of the White Paper in particular, is further complicated because *Broadcasting in the 90s*, although a 'White Paper', has many 'green edges'. That is, it represents an agenda for discussion as well as a declaration of official intent. On balance the White Paper (and government policy) is better understood as the unstable resultant of contradictory ideas and conflicting interests, rather than as a coherent and consistently repressive policy which nakedly reveals itself in new censorship policies but veils its emasculation of 'intermediate institutions' – those between the state and civil society – under a rhetorical assertion of public choice and devolved power. But because there are a lot of green edges to the White Paper judgements must be provisional. The White Paper signals both the continuing conflicts within government over broadcasting policy, the principles that should inform it, and the difficulties of implementing agreed principles in new conditions. While its specific recommendations are not always firm, some evident general principles underpin the White Paper which reflect responses to important shifts in the broadcasting environment, and new ideas that have entered the policy discourse between the last sustained period of government reflection on broadcasting policy (from publication of the Report of the Committee on the Future of Broadcasting in 1977 – the Annan Report – and the Broadcasting Act of 1981) and the present.

National Broadcasting and Internal Diversity: Waning Powers?

Governments, including the UK government, do not now control their own communication destiny and must make history on terms less of their own choosing than heretofore. For example, the White Paper's proposals for radio include establishment (following the Green Paper *Radio: Choices and Opportunities* [Home Office, 1987a]) of the UK's first national advertising-financed radio channels. Were the UK not to launch national advertising-financed radio it would be vulnerable to a leakage of advertising revenue to Ireland, where a medium wave commercial radio station (variously known as Radio Tara and Radio 252), receivable in the UK, is to be established. For the UK not to be economically disadvantaged it must establish its own national advertising financed radio channel(s). It must respond to an agenda set by others.

Changes in UK broadcasting policy reflect the global phenomenon of 'deregulation', a waning of confidence in state and parastatal agencies and waxing confidence in competition and the market as allocative agencies. Such changes are symptoms of the growing assumption of power by a new class. The emergent radical middle class, best represented by Mrs Thatcher, has an image of society as an agglomeration of atomized individuals (or families). Such a conception, married to political power (particularly in the UK system of 'elected dictatorship'), is a powerful solvent of traditional notions of community. Accordingly it, and the social forces it mobilizes, are resisted by the two long established, but waning, classes with a strong communitarian vision: the traditional dominant class, in England the Tory wets with a paternalist model of community, and the traditional working class with its conservative egalitarian vision of community.

The new social forces and the social vision they mobilize are genuinely radical and their exercise of power is unleashing 'gales of creative destruction'; breaking familiar social structures and making new. Consider 'deregulation' of broadcasting in Italy. Before the Italian Constitutional Courts judgement 202 in 1976, broadcasting was the monopoly of the state agency RAI. In turn the three television channels of RAI were the property of the three main Italian political parties, the Christian Democrats (RAI *Uno*), the Socialists (RAI *Due*) and the Communist party (RAI *Tre*) which installed their political clients in the offices of broadcaster. The commercial wave that flooded over Italian broadcasting rapidly located established powerful Italian media corporations as broadcasters. The established publishing houses Rizzoli, Rosconi and Mondadori each ran television stations, although their interests have now declined and have been eclipsed by Silvio Berlusconi and his *Fininvest* holdings. Berlusconi was (and is) a builder, financier and property developer, not an intellectual, not a client of a major political party nor a member of an established Italian media elite (though there are suggestions that he was close to the notorious P2 Freemasons' lodge). His presence, now dominant in Italy's for-profit broadcasting, has added a new voice to the Italian media chorus. It is usually argued that Berlusconi is saying nothing new and that what he says in objectionable.

However the hypocrisy of the most prominent of Berlusconi's UK critics is worth comment. In September 1988 the UK commercial television company TVS ran a display advertisement showing a partly dressed woman, purporting to be an Italian housewife, stripping on television and exemplifying the debasement of Italian television by unregulated commercial interests. TVS used the titillating image to attract attention whilst censuring Italian television for the same technique. It transpired that the woman shown in TVS's advertisement was neither Italian nor a housewife (though defined by TVS as both). Moreover TVS is a co-production partner of the Berlusconi company *ReteItalia* and advertisements in the broadcasting trade press for its production *The Endless Game* distributed jointly by TVS's daughter company Telso and Berlusconi's *ReteItalia* juxtapose image and title of *The Endless Game* with another advertisement showing image and title of *Valentina: The Sexy Heroine of the 80s*. The Valentina advertisement shows a nubile woman semi-dressed in similar black underwear to that sported by the model in TVS's UK advertisements. That is TVS, a business partner of Berlusconi, associates its products with just the kind of imagery and programming it purports to deplore.

One salutary lesson to be drawn from this example and from UK media coverage of the White Paper (and broadcasting policy in recent years) is the extent to which vested interests (few major UK newspapers do not have an actual or potential financial interest in broadcasting, and broadcasters by definition have an interest) will use their command of the media to serve their institutional or personal interests. Whether this entails the BBC and the ITV companies defending the status quo or the press conglomerates attacking it. Too often there is a selective appropriation of evidence to support an interested *parti pris* rather than an attempt to elucidate changing structural conditions.

The rise of Berlusconi television has increased the *external* pluralism of the Italian media and exemplifies a structural change (which may be evaluated negatively or positively) from a broadcasting order nominally delivering *internal* pluralism (a range of diverse programmes within a single channel or a few channels managed by state or para-statal organization) to *external* pluralism where a multitude of channels each deliver a strongly 'branded' single type of programming drawn from and transmitted by an augmented number of producers and broadcasters.

To judge whether the change from internal pluralism delivered by state or para-statal vertically integrated broadcasters (transmitting programmes largely made in house) to external pluralism delivered by broadcasters not owned, or not exclusively owned, and controlled by the state (transmitting programmes made out of house) is positive or negative requires an evaluation of broadcasting before (and after) the change. My iconoclastic advocacy of Berlusconi is of course polemical but the case of Italian television does suggest that 'deregulation', even in the national instance usually cited to disparage it, has not been an unqualified disaster. The rampant clientism in RAI, its disdain for popular taste and the absence of external pluralism in Italian broadcasting have all been challenged and changed by Berlusconi's rise.

In the UK the benefits and losses that attend the dissolution of the old forces by the new (as Brecht observed the good old things are not always preferable to the bad new ones) are not as clear-cut as in Italy. But something of the same calculus is required. I was once privy to the railing of a former very senior official of the BBC against 'the Poujadist woman' and reflected that anyone who can make successful old Wykehamists fearful must have something to be said for them. The BBC has pre-eminently represented the good old things in the UK broadcasting but the negative side of its communitarianism is more and more evident. Burns (1977) and a decade of vicarious experience of the difficulty of talented polytechnic students in being accepted for jobs in the BBC testify to the weight the Corporation places on the intangible qualities possessed by members (even the rebel members) of the UK's traditional elites. Similarly Arthurs (1988 and 1989) convincingly shows the absence of external pluralism in the UK broadcasters' (including the BBC) under-representation of women in their personnel profiles. Though independent television programme producers are by no means perfectly representative of the social composition of the UK, there is no doubt that the erosion of the boundary between broadcasting 'insiders' and 'outsiders' that has followed the government's encouragement of independent production (first for Channel 4 and latterly through the requirement that 25 per cent of ITV and BBC programmes be independently produced) has augmented external pluralism in programme supply and entry to employment in broadcasting and internal pluralism in TV programmes representation of previously excluded and invisble social groups. Here the government's forced dissolution of the unitary, vertically integrated system exemplified by the BBC and the ITV companies has been very positive. The White Paper promises to continue this process.

The communitarian ethos for which public broadcasting in the UK has stood excluded sections of the UK population from representation. In contrast the new class social model of atomized individuals does not assert so forcefully a normative and exclusive definition of community as that which has animated the discourses of the old paternalistic and egalitarian classes. Rather its central notion of 'choice' asserts difference and advocates competition as an agency through which ossified norms may be dissolved. (This is not to deny that the new model mobilizes its own systems of exclusion nor that the old had its instances of openness.) Examination of the history of broadcasting in the UK testifies to the productive influence of competition and the laggard pace of change and renewal of the established broadcasters. Whether protected by what Reith (1952) called the 'brute force of monopoly' or in the 'comfortable duopoly' identified by Peacock. In the 1930s the Reithian Sunday held in place by the 'brute force of monopoly' was challenged by commercial radio from Luxembourg and France. Radio programming shifted as audiences were lost to the American Forces Network (AFN) in the 1940s. The introduction of ITV in the 50s, though eloquently anathematized by Reith (the echoes resound in many of the responses to *Broadcasting in the 90s*):

> Somebody introduced Christianity and printing and the uses of electricity. And somebody introduced smallpox, bubonic plague and the Black Death. Somebody is minded now to introduce sponsored broadcasting into this country. (Reith, 1952)

had a very productive influence. Reith's alarm testifies to UK broadcasters' endemic fear of competition, a fear to which commercial television, the beneficiary of competition in the 1950s, now appeals by cloaking its monopoly perogative to sell advertising in the costume of public service.

UK broadcasting's fear of competition is rationalized in terms of a conception of the audience (particularly for television) as uniquely vulnerable. The Pilkington Report commented that 'the television audience is vulnerable to influence in a way that readers of newspapers and cinema audiences are not'. (Sitting at home people are relaxed, less consciously critical and therefore more exposed. [Pilkington, 1968, para.41.]) From this notion of the audience follows the need for a protector, a platonic 'Guardian' required to regulate broadcasting in the audience's interest because the audience is incompetent to identify its own interests unaided. It is fascinating that the rationale for the British Board of Film Classification's (BBFC)'s stricter censorship of videocassettes is that the video audience in the home has more control over its viewing experience than does the cinema audience (for example, replaying the naughty bits).

Whether the television audience is deemed to be active or passive and vulnerable there is a consistent thread in the UK broadcasting policy discourse before 1986 that demands its viewing experience be controlled and directed. This tendency continues into the late 1980s as the establishment of a new censorship body, the Broadcasting Standards Council and the prohibition of actuality coverage of the UDA and Sinn Fein demonstrate. But the discourse of authoritarian control and platonic guardianship is no longer articulated alone and important elements in the White Paper and the government's agenda for change stem from a new conception of the audience.

Peacock and the Robust Consumer

In 1986 the Report of the Committee on Financing the BBC, the Peacock Report (1986), was published. Peacock's conception of broadcasting is based on a robust consumer, better able to identify and act in her and his own interests than are the 'guardians', who are charged with protecting the public and its interests and who have controlled broadcasting policy in the UK to date. Indeed Peacock views the established broadcasting authorities not only as less competent guarantors of viewers' and listeners' interests, but as having been 'captured' by producers' (broadcasters) interests which the authorities tend to serve more than they do those of the consumers. (In the UK broadcasting system there are only very fine distinctions between producers and authorities.)

The regulation of UK broadcasting is a process of preferring producer interests over those of consumers, of broadcasters over the public as taxpayers and as listeners and viewers. The 'comfortable duopoly' of the BBC and IBA/ITV system exemplifies (as one of the leading members of the Peacock Committee, Samuel Brittan, stated) a class stratified UK society divided into insiders and outsiders (see *The Financial Times* 20 November, 1986). Accordingly for the Peacock Committee the goal of broadcasting policy (and social policy generally) is to break up the blocs of privilege, open institutions to entry by outsiders and make them more responsive to the general will of a public able to identify and act in its own interests and which has scant need of authorities. Peacock has been a powerful influence on the drafting of *Broadcasting in the 90s*, as the White Paper itself acknowledges. In particular, Peacock's advocacy of consumer sovereignty and the creation of a competitive market in broadcasting as the agency through which the interests of viewers and listeners are to be realized underpins recommendations such as regulation with a 'lighter touch' through an Independent Television Commission (ITC), the break up of vertical integration in television, and the promotion of competition wherever possible. Yet Peacock is clearly not the only influence on the White Paper, the repressive elements of which cannot be reconciled with Peacock's advocacy of consumer sovereignty and his recognition that if governments are not to threaten free circulation of information, bodies such as the BBC need to be strong enough to challenge government. Rather the White Paper is the result of a number of conflicting forces and will itself become the site on which struggles between the opposed forces will continue.

The struggle itself has all the characteristics of modern war: the forces are protean, alliances shift, the order of battle changes, flexibly articulating different arms in new combinations of offence and defence; above all, the fronts are fluid. In part the war is a range war between the Home Office and Department of Trade and Industry for jurisdiction; in part it is a conflict of differing material interests; and in part the battle is one of ideas – the White Paper constitutes quality, diversity and popularity as the central values for broadcasting in the 1990s instead of the time honoured 'inform, educate and entertain', the new values being no less difficult to recognize and implement than the old. The institutional, material and ideological forces are not precisely congruent, so analysis of the course of the battle will vary depending on which force is most closely observed. But the general character

of the campaign reflects both the advantages of well established
defensive positions and the offensive power of new ideas. Thus
the White Paper can be read as plausibly as a defence of public
service broadcasting, preserving the BBC and Channel 4 as it can
be seen as a proposal for comprehensive change dedicated to the
destruction of the public service element in UK broadcasting.

Important innovations canvassed in the White Paper are subscription finance for funding television (pay-per-view and/or pay-
per-channel), and changes in regulation of commercial television
in order to foster competition and replace regulated monopoly by
a better functioning market. The proposal for subscription finance
follows suggestions made in the Peacock Report – Peacock was
attracted to subscription finance for the potential improvement
in information flows between consumers (viewers) and producers
(broadcasters) – and the successful establishment of the French
'Canal Plus' service. Subscription finance, if possible pay-per-view,
offered the opportunity of using price as a signalling system to
express the desires, and intensity of desires of consumers for
particular programmes or bundles of programmes. Other funding
mechanisms, whether advertising, licence fee or state-budget,
offer inferior signalling systems, whatever their merits as funding
systems. In advertising-financed broadcasting, the broadcaster
responds to signals from advertisers not from audiences, and
licence fee or state-budget finance for broadcasting has broadcasters responding to signals from the funding source, ultimately
government, and similarly estranges final consumers, viewers and
listeners, from broadcasters. Accordingly the White Paper states:

> The Government looks forward to the eventual replacement of
> the licence fee . . . The Government intends to encourage the
> progressive introduction of subscription on the BBC's television
> services. (para. 3.10)

However the White Paper also notes that the subscription television
study commissioned by the Home Office (1987b) observed that subscription funding, though potentially offering a programme menu
better tuned to consumer demand than the existing producer-driven
menu – Peacock commented acerbicly that 'the viewer's or listener's
main function is to react to a set of choices determined by the
broadcasting institutions' (Peacock, 1986, para. 577) – would also

reduce consumer welfare by excluding existing viewers who paid the licence fee and used the BBC's services but would not be able or willing to pay subscription fees. The study observed: 'Even BBC2 is only viable at price levels which result in a large part of the audience being excluded from the market,' (Home Office, 1987b, p. 128). In fact the study goes further and points out that licence-fee funding is an efficient means of financing broadcasting and that: 'there is no price level (and corresponding audience size) for which either BBC1 or BBC2 can recoup enough revenue from the market to finance the channel at the current expenditure level' (Home Office, 1987b, p.126). As Professor Peacock himself has observed (Peacock, 1986a), a 'table d'hôte' programme menu may be preferred to an 'à la carte' menu for its lower cost in spite of its inferior sensitivity to consumer demand. The subscription funding proposal for the BBC exemplifies a number of characteristics of the White Paper: accurate diagnosis of a neglected problem but prescription of a cure that may well be worse than the disease. Consequently there is uncertainty not only about the colour of the edges of *Broadcasting in the 90s* (white or green) and about the level of commitment of political centres (the Home Office, the Department of Trade and Industry and Downing Street) to particular regimes of treatment but, most important, therefore uncertainty about the prognosis: remission, cure or decline.

It is quite possible that Government will seek reduction of the 'insulation of the BBC from its customers and from market disciplines' (Home Office, 1988, para. 3.13) by means other than subscription finance because of the welfare losses that are entailed by subscription finance. But whether or not subscription finance is chosen as the instrument through which efficiency and responsiveness to audiences and the extent to which the arguments of the study 'subscription television' are rehearsed rather than its recommendations. For the latter follow more the authors' sense of their client's political agenda rather than the logic of their analysis.

The White Paper proposes more changes to the profit-making sector of UK broadcasting than to the non-profit sector. The three non-profit TV channels of the BBC and Channel 4 are to experience changes in funding (though even that is not certain for the BBC) but the BBC's radio services, though challenged for the first time by domestic national commercial competition, will remain substantially unchanged. BBC Television will be pressured to increase the efficiency of its resource utilization and to increase external pluralism, the proportion of programmes screened that are made out of house. However, with the exception of the proposals for subscription finance, which are by no means certain to be implemented, BBC Television remains otherwise substantially unchanged. Channel 4 is fulsomely praised but, in one of the sections of *Broadcasting in the 90s* with greenest edges, new proposals for its funding are canvassed including one suggested by Channel 4's chairman for the channel to sell its own advertising. The requirement for a new funding mechanism for Channel 4 is a consequence of the White Paper's abolition of the channel's current owner, the IBA, and dramatic changes to its funder, the ITV system.

The most important changes proposed in the White Paper are focused on profit-making broadcasting, on the ITV companies and their regulator, the IBA. Here the aims to augment consumer sovereignty and improve the signalling system between consumers and producers, through creation of a market between broadcasters and viewers and listeners, are joined by concern about the cost and wastefulness of UK commercial television and its regulation. The changes proposed for commercial broadcasting will do little to improve its responsiveness to audience demand or to augment 'consumer sovereignty'. But the creation of an efficient signalling system between audience and broadcasters, whether through prices in a market or through new political institutions and systems of accountability, is a highly intractable problem. Terrestrial broadcasting is very cheap but its low cost goes hand in hand with absent feedback from consumers to producers. To improve feedback raises costs, thus an inescapable dilemma in broadcasting policy is a choice between cheap 'table d'hôte' or expensive 'à la carte' programme diets. The broad framework of the government's choice is clear: cheap service provision at the expense of imperfect responsiveness to consumers.

The Role of Advertising

The White Paper's proposed changes to commercial broadcasting and its regulation address the Peacock Committee's concerns about the absence of competitive markets for advertising, for programme supply and for access to radio frequency spectrum. The proposals are directed to improving (or establishing) competition in those markets in the belief that efficiency gains will follow. In programme production, supply of advertising and access to spectrum, the agenda established in the White Paper is the augmentation of competition, a challenge to established monopolies, with a particular concern to reduce broadcasting costs. *Prima facie* there is cause for concern about ITV's cost structure. Industry sources estimate that the costs of producing a television programme in Australia is *ceteris paribus*, 60 per cent of the cost of UK production. The Australian cost advantage is amplified by the Australian government's programme of production subsidy ($170 million per annum from 1989–90 spread between feature films, TV drama and documentaries). If UK costs of production remain higher than those in Australia, programme production will tend to leak away from the UK to Australia. Cost of production is not the only factor affecting location decisions (US production costs are higher than UK costs) but is significant and a legitimate concern of public policy. The concern to drive down production costs and erode barriers between insiders and outsiders underlie government's consistent support for independent producers.

The White Paper's proposed elimination of the ITV companies monopoly of supply of television advertising reflects the successful lobbying of the advertising industry. Establishment of a terrestrially broadcast Channel 5 (and perhaps Channel 6), decoupling of the sale of advertising on Channel 4 from Channel 3, and establishment of satellite television channels will give advertisers alternative suppliers of television advertising time, although advertisers will not necessarily enjoy a decline in costs due to their audience being spread a over a greater plurality of channels. Advertisers are likely to have to purchase more advertising time, albeit at a lower cost per minute, in order to reach the desired population of viewers.

The core of the White Paper's proposals is monopoly busting in commercial television through creation of markets and the use of competition. Hitherto commercial television policy in the UK has granted profit-making companies monopoly rights in the exploitation of a public asset – the radio spectrum – and have exacted from franchisees' benefits that putatively accrue to the public in exchange for a monopoly to sell television advertising. The return to the public is of two kinds: programmes of a range and quality that the public would not otherwise enjoy, and a financial return to the Treasury as payment for monopoly privileges not ordinarily enjoyed by capitalists. The Independent Broadcasting Authority is the trustee for the public, charged with ensuring that an equitable bargain is struck and that the public receives a proper return in exchange for the monopoly it grants to the ITV companies.

Evaluation of the changes in the organization and regulation of for-profit television proposed in the White Paper first demands assessment of the existing institutions and their performance. How far have those benefits, in cash and in kind, that the IBA is charged to realize for the public been delivered? We must consider not only whether a new set of principles is worse, or better, in the abstract, whether deregulation is to be preferred to regulation, but also the concrete practice of regulation. A good theory of regulation will beat an imperfect actual market any time just as a good, internally coherent, theory of markets will beat an actual imperfect practice of regulation.

Markets, political control and the middle term between them, regulation, are all dangerously imperfect. The broadcasting market, because of the peculiar economic characteristics of broadcasting and its 'public good' characteristics, is particularly imperfect (see *inter alia* the Peacock Committee's discussion of 'free riding' [Peacock, 1986, p.29]). But so too are political systems. First-past-the-post voting systems are imperfect representations of citizens' preferences, but even these are far more sensitive to public preferences than the modes of control and allocation that distinguish broadcasting in Britain. Public sector institutions of the type that characterize European public broadcasting are very vulnerable to political clientism, elite capture and to being run by insiders to express their own values and interests rather than those of the public (or 'publics') that consumes the broadcasters' output. Regulatory institutions (and regulators) are prone to 'capture' by the industries and interests which they are to regulate, that is, with coming to identify the interests of the regulated sector with those of the public as a whole (and also exemplifying the phenomenon of elite capture).

I have indicated above some of the difficulties in identifying programme quality (and diversity). I propose therefore to consider the financial benefits realized by the IBA for the public, for whom it acts as trustee, in exchange for the monopoly granted to the ITV companies. Cash is always easier to discuss than value. Discussion of finance has been neglected in the past (and pre-White Paper) debate: the financial return to the public is only one of the bases on which the UK broadcasting system and its regulation should be evaluated. The most obvious characteristic of broadcasting regulation in the UK is its cost. The IBA is very expensive. In 1987/8 it employed 1,378 staff of which 956 were engineers. If the engineers are removed from consideration we are left with 422 regulators who

1   Select ITV and ILR contractors
2   Supervise programmes
3   Control advertising

If engineering and transmission costs are removed from consideration, 422 people discharging these three functions cost £27.4 million per year for television and £2.0 million for radio (but note these calculations are far from perfect: the IBA annual report, on which I have drawn for data, states that some costs and revenues are not readily apportionable [Independent Broadcasting Authority, 1988, p.10]). That is, the IBA's annual expenditure on regulation is £29.4 million. The IBA generates £2.6 million in revenue (other than from ITV and ILR) of which £1m is for facilities. Let us assume that regulators earn £1.6 million and that that portion of revenue should be deducted from the £29.4 million cost of regulation, leaving a net cost of regulation of £27.8 million for the year 1987/8. In terms of international comparison the IBA seems costly, but because there are few regulators which occupy the IBA's intermediate position between government and industry, and those that do (concentrated in anglophone states) are charged with a different repertoire of tasks from those discharged by the IBA, comparisons are imperfect. Nonetheless there are significant cost disparities.

The Canadian Radio-television and Telecommunications Commission regulates telecommunications and cable as well as broadcasting. It holds public hearings across Canada and, apart from its telecommunications responsibilities, regulates 4,983 cable and broadcasting undertakings. It costs (1987/8 converting $ Canadian at 2.16:£1) £13.5 million per annum. The Australian Broadcasting

Tribunal (1985/6) regulates 205 radio stations and 50 commercial television stations and costs £3.38 million ($Australian $2.16:£1). The United States Federal Communications Commission (1985) was almost twice as costly as the IBA (£54.23 million at $US1.76:£1) but, like the Canadian CRTC, it regulates telecommunications as well as broadcasting and exercises authority over 12,258 radio and television broadcasters. Such comparisons have indicative value (though it is important to recognize that like is not being compared with like) and establish only that the IBA is a relatively expensive regulator. It still remains to be assessed whether the IBA is worth it. Does it deliver benefits that would not otherwise be enjoyed sufficient to compensate for its costs?

The UK public receives a financial return from ITV for its exploitation of the radio spectrum via the Exchequer Levy. The Levy (as the 'additional payments' referred to in Section 33(4) of the Broadcasting Act 1981 is usually known) is paid to the IBA and levied on the ITV companies profits. In 1986/7 and 1987/8 the return to the Exchequer from the Levy declined by £19m per annum from the level achieved in 1985/6 following a change in the basis on which levy was calculated. The change (from 66.7 per cent of profits that exceeded £650,000, or 2.8 per cent of net advertising revenue (NAR), to 45 per cent on NAR and 22.5 per cent on profits from overseas programme sales) was designed to capture benefits that were escaping the Exchequer because of the way in which the ITV companies were organising their financial affairs. The Levy on profits from NAR gave ITV companies an incentive to load costs (and thus reduce profits and liability to levy) on their UK operations, including programme production. By doing so ITV companies were able to reduce or avoid their liability to Levy. In 1982/3 Thames Television paid no Levy but made (unleviable) profits of £5.7 million in overseas programme sales. In the same year Granada Television with a lower NAR than Thames (and overseas programme sales profit of £282,000) paid £5.8 million in Levy.

The incentives in such a taxation regime to load costs onto domestic activities and take profits in overseas programme sales are obvious. In subsequent years Granada embarked on a very costly programme of drama production and successfully reduced its liability to levy. In order to capture the revenue lost to the

Exchequer by such strategies the basis of assessment of Levy was recalculated (following the advice of the IBA) but the recalculation resulted in a *reduction* of revenue of £19 million per annum.

The House of Commons Public Accounts Committee (in early 1988) took the IBA to task for a loss of £38 million to the Consolidated Fund that followed the changed basis of Levy calculation which in turn was based on the IBA's expert advice. The Director General of the IBA regretted the shortfall and argued that the IBA had expected the result of the Levy recalculations to be broadly neutral and revealed that the Authority had reached its conclusion after consultation with the ITV companies! The Levy debacle clearly influenced MPs on the Public Accounts Committee (the most important and influential of parliamentary committees) and doubtless fuelled parliamentary sentiment that was already hostile to the IBA. In December 1988 the government announced a further recalculation of Levy which from January 1990 will be calculated on a basis of 75 per cent of advertising revenue and 25 per cent of profits. The new Levy is likely to cut ITV profits by 20 per cent.

Granada's changed financial strategy after 1982/3 demonstrates clearly the dynamics of UK commercial television, which either delivers a financial return to the Exchequer or programme quality (to assume that *Brideshead Revisited*, *The Adventures of Sherlock Holmes* and *Jewel in the Crown* constitute quality programmes) but not both. Why then pay more than £27 million per annum for the IBA, a regulator that cannot contrive a broadcasting regime that delivers both quality and a financial return (and the advice of which has led to a loss of £38 million to the Consolidated Fund)? The proposals in the White Paper to allocate commercial television franchises to the highest bidder promise to realize a financial return to the Exchequer more cheaply than has the IBA. A regulator is only worth financing if it can deliver benefits otherwise unattainable (in this case both programme quality and a financial return for monopoly rights). The IBA has not done so. Not only has its advice and administration resulted in decline in revenue (though the benefit in kind of *Brideshead Revisited* does need to be weighed against the losses in cash), but it has not established a common basis for attributing costs and hence establishing leviable profits among the television companies it regulates. Quick research examining the accounts of the ITV companies reveals that some companies depreciate freehold land, others do not. It is questionable whether freehold land does depreciate and therefore whether it is a properly allowable cost, but if it is assumed to be a legitimate cost why do some ITV companies account for it and others not? (LWT and Yorkshire TV depreciate freehold land at 2 per cent per year, Anglia, Granada and Border not at all, Scottish Television over 11 to 50 years).

The 'deregulatory' proposal canvassed in the White Paper to allocate commercial television franchises to the highest bidder (and to reregulate by abolishing the IBA and the Cable Authority and establish an ITC) follows the demonstrated failure of the IBA to realize for the public both benefits in cash and in kind (and to establish a common basis of cost allocation among the television companies it regulates). The franchise auction promises to realize a financial return more effectively and at lower cost than has the IBA. To be sure there are good grounds for doubt about the auction's ability to deliver programme quality (whatever that is) but the IBA does not have an unassailable record on that score.

Conclusion

Comprehensive evaluation of the White Paper is premature. It is best perceived as setting an agenda for discussion with, in some areas, very firm government proposals, in others a more tentative approach. Assessment of the government's agenda entails evaluation of the established broadcasting order and in particular the ITV system and its regulation. For it is on the for-profit sector of television that proposed changes are focused. In my judgement there are good reasons for change to this sector.

The prospect of cheaper regulation, and an end to monopoly in supply of television advertising, an increase in external pluralism (through establishment of Channel 5 and programme sourcing from independent producers) are as welcome as the reduction of ITV's costs is necessary. Justification for the existing ITV/IBA system comes from its imputed delivery of programme diversity and quality. These are very difficult categories to implement but my judgement is that insufficient diversity and quality have been delivered by ITV to justify continuation of the present commercial television regime. Whether the new regime that will follow the Broadcasting Act will do better remains to be seen. It seems quite clear that there will be an increase in external diversity, but less clear whether internal diversity and/or programme quality will change, whether for better or for worse. The agenda set by the White Paper presents considerable opportunities for improvement in UK broadcasting. Many of these will go by default if the green edges of the White Paper are misconceived as black edges and are seen to result from a coherent government broadcasting policy aimed at weakening or eliminating 'intermediate institutions' and augmenting the repressive powers of the state. Certainly the repressive powers of the state *are* being augmented (if only the agenda were deregulation and not creation of more onerous regulation) and certainly the reintroduction of the censorious inquisition of a new and ridiculous Lord Chamberlain in the guise of Lord Mogg of Video and the prohibition of representation of lawful political organizations is iniquitous. But these are not policy changes that flow from Peacock and the fundamental shift in the theoretical basis from which broadcasting policy discourse proceeds that Peacock performed.

The terms of the debate are now set by a conception of the audience as robust rather than vulnerable, able to recognize its own interests rather than requiring protection for its weakness and vulnerability. The problem of inventing institutional forms through which the audience can exercise sovereignty has not been solved in *Broadcasting in the 90s* (nor will it be through the welfare reducing instrument of subscription television). But the opportunities presented for realizing audience sovereignty through new political institutions and mechanisms of accountability should not be foregone because of a justifiable alarm at growth in government powers of censorship and the less justifiable desire to see the conspiratorial hand of the puppeteer of Downing Street exercising its subtle sway in a coherent broadcasting policy. There is no coherence in *Broadcasting in the 90s*. For that reason it contains promises as well as threats. The benefits of a salutary change in regulation of commercial broadcasting, increase in external pluralism, pressure on the 'comfortable duopoly' and a change in the basis on which broadcasting policy is discussed should not be foregone because the good old things are preferred to the bad new ones.

I owe much of my knowledge of Italian television policy to discussions with Philip Schlesinger and Jay Stuart, I am grateful to them both for telling me many things I did not formerly know. They are not responsible for my interpretation of the information which they generously provided.

This chapter was first published in *Screen*, 1989, vol. 30, no. 2/3.

References

Annan, Lord N. (Chairman) (1977), *Report of the Committee on the Future of Broadcasting*, Cmnd 6753 (London: HMSO).

Arthurs, J. (1988), 'Technology and Television Production' Paper presented to the International Television Studies Conference, London.

Arthurs, J. (1989), 'Women, Technology and Gender', in *Screen* vol. 30, no. 2/3.

Blumler, J. Nossiter, T. and Brynin, M. (1986), *Research on the Range and Quality of Broadcasting Services* (West Yorkshire Media in Politics Group for the Committee on Financing the BBC) (London: Home Office, HMSO).

Brittan, S. (1987), 'The fight for freedom in broadcasting', in *Political Quarterly* vol. 58, no. 1, January/March.

Burns, T. (1977), *The BBC: Public Institution and Private World* (London: Macmillan).

DTI (Department of Trade and Industry) (1988), *Report on the Potential for Microwave Video Distribution Systems in the UK* (London: HMSO).

Hearst, S. (1988), 'Neighbourhood watch', in *The Guardian* 4 July, 1988, p. 23.

Home Office (1987a), *Radio: Choices and Opportunities*, Cmnd 92 (London: HMSO).

Home Office (1987b), *Subscription Television* (London: HMSO).

Home Office (1988), *Broadcasting in the '90s: Competition, Choice and Quality*, Cm 517 (London: HMSO).

Independent Broadcasting Authority (IBA) (1988), *Annual Report 1987–8* (London: IBA).

Peacock, A. (Chairman) (1986), *Report of the Committee on Financing the BBC*, Cmnd 9824 (London: HMSO).

Peacock, A. (1986a), 'Television Tomorrow'. Paper at the International Institute of Communication Conference, Edinburgh, 1986. Revised version in *Intermedia*, vol. 14, no. 6, 1986, pp. 35–7.

Pilkington, H. (Chairman) (1962), *Report of the Committee on Broadcasting* (1960), Cmnd 1753 (London: HMSO).

Reith, Lord J. (1952), House of Lords *Hansard* 22 May 1952. Cited in A. Smith (ed.) (1974) *British Broadcasting* (Newton Abbot: David & Charles).

Chapter 6

Broadband Black Death Cuts Queues: The Information Society and the UK

The Government are on record to scuttle – a betrayal and a surrender; that is what is so shocking and serious; so unnecessary and wrong. Somebody introduced dog-racing into England, we know who, for he is proud of it, and proclaims it *urbi et orbi* in the columns of Who's Who. And somebody introduced Christianity and printing and the uses of electricity. And somebody introduced smallpox, bubonic plague and the Black Death. Somebody is minded now to introduce sponsored broadcasting into this country. (Lord Reith, House of Lords *Hansard*, 22 May 1952)

Another concern that has been voiced has drawn attention to the extent to which the new information technology will encourage the individual to withdraw into his home. There will be no need to go shopping in person, to cash a cheque at the bank, to place a bet at the bookmakers, or, that most sacred of British passions, standing in queues to buy theatre tickets, train tickets, etc. The possible social effects of information technology have hardly begun to be counted. (Lord Thompson, Chairman of the IBA at Bath University, 3 March 1983)

Fifty million television sets in America; and now the coaxial cable! (Tom Ewell [in extremis], *The Seven Year Itch*, 1955)

The messiah has foretold the coming of the post-industrial society and his disciples in Canada, Britain, France and Germany are locked in competition to induce the earliest birth of a viable infant. The spectacle of governments of diverse political colours across the world throwing money up in the air or into holes in the ground should give pause to those sceptical of the power of ideas.

The Information Society

Bell's (1976) thesis of the information society has been embraced as a doctrine that will lead industrial societies currently locked into a cycle of beggar my neighbour protectionism, declining rates of profit and mass unemployment into a new promised land. In the UK, 1982 was designated Information Technology Year (1983 World Communication Year), in which government promulgated a number of initiatives to advance the labour of the old industrial society: the telecommunications monopoly of the state-owned British Telecom was terminated with the licensing of a competitive privately owned network, Mercury, the supply of terminal equipment was opened to competition, Direct Broadcasting by satellite commencing in 1986 was authorized (hardware by Unistat, a consortium owned equally by British Aerospace, British Telecom and General Electric Company – Marconi, software in two TV channels by the BBC), and the 'wired society' – a broadband and cable network delivering entertainment television and a cornucopia of other services, including interactive security systems, remote banking, shopping and polling encouraged in the report commissioned by the Cabinet Office (the Prime Minister's department), *The Cabling of Britain*. Nowhere in this sustained performance of prestidigitation by the government and its allies in the 'information society' industries has there been any acknowledgement of the trail of aborted foetuses that have attended previous initiatives, the effects on the existing 'information society' industries, and the possibility of providing most of the notional benefits and services that will flow promiscuously from the IT society's horn of plenty through modest development of existing facilities (for example, all the interactive cable services can be carried by the existing narrow band telephone system – including, using slow scan TV, security and, using a new GEC gizmo, video telephony).

The information society thesis (or 'forecast' as Bell calls it) distinguishes post-industrial societies thus:

> The first and simplest characteristic of a post industrial society is that the majority of the labour force is no longer engaged in agriculture or manufacturing but in services, which are defined residually, as trade, finance, transport, health, recreation, research, education and government. (Bell, 1976, p. 15)

Bell offers a triadic division of the labour force into agricultural, industrial and service sectors and cites OECD figures of 1969 for Britain (presumably meaning the UK) showing the percentage of workforce in each sector:

agriculture	3.1%
industry	47.2%
services	49.7%

Figures derived by Wall (1977) are based on – for Bell's thesis better – a quadripartite division and come from the decennial general censuses taken in the UK for the years 1961 and 1971:

	1961(%)	1971(%)
agriculture	3.9	3.0
industry	36.2	33.7
services	26.9	26.7
information	33.0	36.6

Crude though Bell and Wall's categorization is (as they recognize) and open obvious objections such as only counting paid work (doing one's own washing does not count as work, buying a washing machine boosts the industry statistics, taking washing to a laundry boosts the service sector, and presumably the displacement of electro-mechanical controls for washing machines by micro-processor controls boosts the information sector) and constituting definitions of information work extremely widely – including occupations such as typewriter mechanic, bookbinder and clergyman as information workers – there seems no reason to doubt that some kind of shift is going on. Whether it is to a post-industrial society or merely a development in the international division of labour or perhaps a reversion to pre-industrial forms of organization (one could, if clergy are to be counted as information workers, count the whole monastic and ecclesiastic structures of the European Middle Ages as a burgeoning information sector) is another question. But the seduction of Bell's thesis does not inhere alone in its 'explanation' of shifts between employment sectors and the hope he offers of jam for all tomorrow, he also explains – as have a variety of other social theories of twentieth century (for example, the general shift in Marxist theory whether Hegelian or anti-Hegelian, in the Frankfurt School or in Gramsci or Althusser to emphasizing the importance of ideology rather than repression as the crucial agency in reproducing capitalist society) – the non-realization of the supersession of bourgeois hegemony by proletarian hegemony anticipated by Marx by referring to the crucial agency of the information sector. For Bell the shift is not towards proletarian hegemony but to the hegemony of the 'Angestellten', to an emergent white-collar salariat charged with complex, technocratic control and information functions in a society in which knowledge is power – or where, as the graffiti reproduced on the cover of the British edition of *The Coming of the Post Industrial Society* (Bell, 1976) has it, 'Knowledge rules O.K.'.

Every modern society now lives by innovation and the social control of change and tries to anticipate the future in order to plan ahead. This commitment to social control introduces the need for planning and forecasting into society. (Bell, 1976, p. 20)

For Bell the information society is distinguished by its reliance on planning and control functions and thus the social groups charged with these functions dispossess the industrial proletariat of the power vested in them by Marx. The development of novel procedures and technologies for information processing enhance the efficiency of the traditional economy (notably manufacturing but also primary production and services) and call into existence new forms of production – the information industries – and constitute information itself as a commodity. Other commentators though are sceptical:

When I am weary or nasty, I sometimes remark that the post industrial society was a period of 2 or 3 years in the mid 60s when GNP, social policy programmes and social research and universities were flourishing. Things have certainly changed. (S. Michael quoted in Kumar, 1978, p. 185)

Kumar points out that there is no empirical evidence to support Bell's thesis that prosperity attends the infant information society. Bell is careful to buttress his arguments with prudent knee dips to the diseconomies of scale of the large organizations that modern information transmission techniques make possible and acknowledgements of the false dawns of earlier communication revolutions but overall his message is bullish and the *Coming of the Post Industrial Society* is larded with references to the productivity and wealth gains that have followed the application of knowledge to the problems of pre-post-industrial societies. But Kumar's *Prophecy and Progress* argues against the central elements of the Bell thesis and in particular its positive correlation of expenditure on knowledge (for example, industrial research and development) and economic growth or as Bell says, 'the inexorable influence of science on productive methods' (Bell, 1976, p. 378). Rather Kumar states:

It appears that, as in the past, market forces and political goals (need pull) are far more important in determining the nature and rate of technological innovation than the ideas and inventions springing from pure research (idea push). Post war Japan demonstrates this conclusively with one of the lowest levels of research and development expenditures of all industrialized nations, it has had the highest economic growth rate in the post war period. (Kumar, 1978, p. 226)

One can in turn challenge the conclusiveness of Kumar's demonstration for more recent statistics suggest that Japanese research and development expenditure is not out of line with that of other advanced countries (see Table 6.1).

But neither do these statistics support Bell's propositions that 'The roots of the post-industrial society lie in the inexorable influence of science on productive methods' (Bell, 1976, p. 378).

And whilst there is clearly not a perfect fit between the information/service sector and invisibles or the manufacturing/agricultural sector and visibles, the trade balances between the UK and Japan

Table 6.1 R&D expenditure as a percentage of GNP, 1980 (Japan, 1979)

Italy	Japan	FRG	UK	USA
0.84	2.04	3.39	2.20	2.41

Source: Conselio Nazionale delle Richerche, Italy and OECD, quoted in the *Financial Times*, 28 March 1983, p. xi.

in visibles and invisibles are hard to reconcile with Bell's overall thrust and suggest that knowledge does not necessarily rule OK and that there is no necessary correspondence between wealth and a post industrial society:

Table 6.2 Trade balance UK/Japan, $US Millions (+ / −) expressed in terms of UK economy

Year	Visible	Invisible
1966	− 58	+ 241
1971	− 102	+ 490
1976	− 616	+ 1498
1981	− 2398	+ 4398

Source: Bank of Japan, 'Balance of payments monthly', cited in J. Bartlett letter, *Financial Times*, 13 April 1983.

Kumar's argument that need pull is more important than idea push can be supported by examination of Videotex (a linchpin of the information society and selected by Nora and Minc (1980) in their report 'The Computerisation of Society' as one of five crucial foci for French national information society policy). Videotex has been developed as an 'idea push' technology by state organizations in Canada (Telidon fostered by the Department of Communications), France (Télétel/Antiope) by the PTT), and the UK (Prestel by British Telecom). Nowhere has it achieved significant market penetration still less profitability. Prestel for example has received *circa* £50 million in development funds and has achieved a penetration of *circa* 23,000 terminals in early 1983. Contrast the market pulled penetration of videotape recorders in the UK (manufacture of which has recently commenced on a small scale in the UK under Japanese licence). In 1982, 2,351,000 machines were imported at a cost of £519.2 million (*Broadcast*, 18 April 1983). To some extent of course the distinction between 'idea push' and 'need pull' is theological – every product or service combines 'idea push' and 'need pull' and the policy question is not of choosing between 'idea push' and 'need pull' but of correctly assessing and articulating the two forces. In the UK though government policy oscillates contradictorily between commitment to need pull and the market (for example, introducing competition in the provision of telecommunication services) and idea push and the central role of the government (for example, the insistence on establishing a broadband cable infrastructure – an election manifesto commitment of Mrs Thatcher and the funding of 'fifth generation' computer research under the Alvey £200 million program). But a constant element in Conservative government policy is commitment to advancing the birth of the post-industrial society in the UK and force feeding the infant UK information economy. Elsewhere the information society thesis has been embraced and consciously promulgated as state policy but nowhere has national policy considered and successfully articulated the hardware and software elements of the information industries.

The International Lemming Race

The case of Canada is well known and exemplifies the contradictions of national policy directed to securing an advantageous position in the international communications hardware business (Spar Aerospace, Mitel, Northern Telecom are among the major winners) but which in using the domestic information economy as a base for hardware manufacturers from which international markets may be colonized opens the domestic software market to very serious international competition. To be sure the penetration of foreign software into the Canadian market is by no means wholly a consequence of Canadian hardware policy but the Canadian government's hardware policies have done nothing to inhibit the penetration of foreign software.

Canada embraced the information society thesis early – the historical importance of communications in establishing and holding together the Canadian nation, the continuing importance of the political as an agency for engineering Canadian national solidarity in a country held together by few cultural, geographical or economical ties perhaps disposed Canada to its early involvement in the development of 'leading edge' communication industries, for example communication satellites and Telidon. But the cost has been high – Melody (1979) has described satellites as 'well on their way to becoming 20th century pyramids'. And cultural and information sovereignty has not been protected by legislation, whether by requiring broadcasters to use 'predominantly Canadian creative and other resources' (Section 3d, Broadcasting Act, 1968), or the Bank Act (1980 amended) requiring that client information be stored in Canada. Defensive action on the software front is also extremely costly and attended by no great success; support for Canadian public service broadcasting from federal and provincial budgets is currently in excess of $500 million per annum. Hoskins and McFadyen (1982) state that Canadian television broadcasters obtained in 1975 an average margin per half hour of $21,000 from foreign (i.e. largely US) programmes compared with $55 (fifty-five dollars) from Canadian programmes. The disincentives to using Canadian software are evident.

Four paragraphs in the 1983 Canadian government publication *Towards a New National Broadcasting Policy* will exemplify three central themes of the race towards the information society. First, that there is a race on, whether or not domestic needs lead government to support information industries, international considerations make it imperative. If the French, British and German lemmings are running, a Canadian lemming should be in the race too. Second, wealth and employment will accrue to the national hardware industries of the competitors. Third, the double think, software industries will benefit too but in order to benefit they will need financial support from government.

In France, 27 major cities are soon to be cabled, while West Germany will shortly commence large-scale cabling projects in 11 major cities. Australia too is about to begin wiring all its major population centres. Meanwhile, Belgium is rapidly moving ahead of Canada as the world's most heavily cabled country on a per capita basis, while in the United Kingdom the recently released report of the Hunt inquiry advocates a concerted move to cable.

Canadian high technology industries should benefit directly as cable operators retool their plants to carry these new programming and non-programming services. Cable companies will require significant amounts of new capital equipment – such as earth stations, scrambling and descrambling equipment and a variety of other types of cable hardware. Canadian high technology industries manufacture much of this equipment, and jobs should be created as a result.

The new technological environment can be shaped to create opportunities from which the entire program production industry can benefit. The Government of Canada will establish a special Canadian Broadcast Program Development Fund to assist private production companies and independent producers. The fund will be administered by the Canadian Film Development Corporation and will rise from a total of $35 million in the first full year of operation to $60 million in the fifth year.

The need for such funding arises from the continuing metamorphosis of the environment in which programs are produced. The new technology is bringing about a proliferation of programming services, not just in Canada but around the world. This transformation of the global broadcasting environment will result in a continually growing and voracious demand for new programming to fill the multiplicity of channels soon to be available. This hunger for new content represents an enormous opportunity for Canadian program producers.

But, in order to compete effectively in these new markets and in our own domestic market, Canadian program producers must have the resources to produce attractive, high-quality Canadian programming in both official languages and of international calibre – Canadian programming that people will choose to watch. (Government of Canada, 1983)

Canada perhaps best exemplifies an enduring contradiction in government policies for an information society. Investment in national communications infrastructure, that is a distribution system, simply creates demand for information products which can be met much more cheaply by importing product from large producers and the controllers of archives. For many information goods are imperishable (*I Love Lucy*, *The Munsters* and *Sergeant Bilko* are currently scheduled in the UK) and once first copy costs have been amortized then costs of further copies are low and sale is very profitable. The size of the US market is such that US producers are able to amortize very high programme budgets by domestic market exploitation. A well-funded product exhibiting high production values is therefore available for sale in other markets at low cost. The UK Government Cable White Paper (HMSO, 1983, p. 51) gives representative figures:

> An hour of original material can range from around £20,000 for a current affairs programme to £200,000 for drama (or even more in the case of prestige projects). Bought in material from the USA, where the production costs have already been largely if not wholly recovered on the domestic market, can be obtained by the broadcasters for as little as £2,000 an hour.

Quotas restricting imports of foreign products can provide some protection for the domestic industries of small nations but once distribution capacity is expanded beyond a certain level then the system can no longer be fed from domestic resources. Foreign product is purchased and consumed, audiences for domestic material decline (not as a consequence of superior quality of the foreign programming but necessarily as the audience is fragmented), revenues for domestic production decline and a spiral develops in which the system as it expands sucks in more and depends more on foreign material. As Melody (1982) points out the effective national policy of Canada has been to 'rather sell satellite hardware in international markets than produce programming content for domestic consumption'. The good intentions of the 1968 Broadcasting Act, the CRTC, Uncle John Meisel and all notwithstanding.

In France the government commissioned two senior officials Simon Nora and Alain Minc to report (Nora and Minc, 1980) on the information society and to recommend policy. Nora and Minc's report is simply one manifestation of a very comprehensive information strategy mounted by the government of France in the last decade. Its *dirigisme* has been attended with some successes – notably the revitalization of telecommunications and telecommunication manufacturing in France but in other, largely software oriented sectors, success has been less evident. In European Data Base services – the computerized delivery of information to subscribers usually through a Videotex system – Britain leads with an annual market of $235 million, France, third to the UK and West Germany, has a market size of $150 million and the leading suppliers are loss makers (Frost and Sullivan, 1983, quoted in the *Financial Times*, 13 April 1983, p. 16). The leading British supplier, Reuter, announced profits of £35 million in 1983 – a 100 per cent increase on the previous year. Comparative advantage resting here with British software producers in the European financial information market as it rests with US producers in the world entertainment market.

The strategy of the government of France has been largely formulated in the shadow of 'le défi américain' personified by Nora and Minc in the corporate personality of IBM:

> IBM is following a strategy that will enable it to set up a communications network and to control it. When it does it will encroach upon a traditional sphere of government power: communications. In the absence of a suitable policy alliances will develop that involve the administrator of the network and the American data banks to which it will facilitate access. (Nora and Minc, 1980, p. 6)

In Britain the seduction of government by the post-industrial society thesis has come relatively late, and is not distinguished by the virulent anti-Americanism of the French. For Nora and Minc the massed ranks of the European PTTs are the last line of defence possible against IBM; 'the only cartel capable of establishing a dialogue with IBM is one that could be formed from an alliance of telecommunications agencies' (Nora and Minc, 1980, p. 7), in consequence the British government's resolve to privatize its PTT – British Telecom – the choice of a US rather than a European standard for cellular radio (rewarded perhaps by Comsat's licensing of the British MAC satellite transmission system) and the reliance of the leading British manufacturers on US technology, for example, for large PABXs all products are ultimately of foreign, largely US origin (though Plessey claims its IDX is home-grown Rolm is currently suing Plessey in the US for breach of copyright) has provoked the French government to its familiar cry of 'perfide Albion', for example, in the 'great disappointment' of M. J.-P. Braunet, chairman of the state owned CIT – Alcatel at the harm to 'European collaboration' caused by the British cellular radio decision (*Financial Times*, 21 April 1983, p. 7).

Late and perfidious though British government's enthusiasm for the information society is, its commitment is as comprehensive as that of the French though the Conservative administration of Mrs Thatcher manoeuvres uneasily between the desire to take a leading role and its hostility to state *dirigisme*. Unfortunately though the Thatcher embrace of the information society has not been attended by the realization of one of Bell's more enticing predictions: British government discourse remains as untheorized as ever and one looks in vain to Mr Baker, the Minister charged with responsibility for information technology, for the cosmic utterances of Nora and Minc and their French epigones that better exemplify Bell's analysis:

> What is distinctive about the post industrial society is the change in the character of knowledge itself. What has become decisive for the organization of decisions and the direction of change is the centrality of theoretical knowledge – the primacy of theory over empiricism and the codification of knowledge into abstract systems used to illuminate many different and varied areas of experience. (Bell, 1976, p. 20)

Production/Distribution Balance – Film and Television

In this article I do not propose to consider the matters of telecommunications policy, but rather the consequences of the information society initiatives for broadcasting in the UK. Both because of the place of public service broadcasting in UK cultural life and because of the success of British television software sales to foreign markets. To some extent this is an arbitrary separation, although in the UK broadcasting and telcommunications have remained largely distinct technologies and institutions, the convergence that we are currently experiencing is replete with precedents. The telephone system that had developed in the UK principally as a 'contentless' system in which the numbers of transmitting and receiving stations existed in symmetrical relationships has 'broadcast' elements – the speaking clock, cricket scores and financial statistics services, 'Dial-a-Disc' and 'Bedtime Stories'. And in the early 1920s the Electrophone Company offered London subscribers the possibility of auditing one of a number of London theatres or on Sundays a chosen church service replayed from a range of places of worship. The Electrophone was killed by radio, though radio in turn provided a stimulus to the development of wired systems offering subscribers relays of broadcast radio services. And cable television in the UK is largely the child of the introduction of commercial television in 1955 when for a considerable time markets existed for the relay of a good broadcast television signal to areas shielded by the local topography (for example, Sheffield, and the area of south-east London served currently by Greenwich Cablevision) from the transmitter or which was at the edge of a number of stations transmission areas (for example Swindon).

In the UK, as in most European countries, the broadcasting order has developed constrained by shortage of spectrum capacity relative to that outside Europe, for example in the USA. The geographical proximity of European countries has permitted fewer channels for terrestrial broadcast services in a single country than elsewhere. It is customarily argued that this shortage of spectrum capacity has both necessitated and legitimized regulation by the state and that in a number of European countries a fortuitous 'fit' developed between the resources available for national program (software) *production* and the (limited by spectrum availability) capacity of the *distribution* system. This 'fit' resulted in a stable broadcasting system ecology in which national broadcasting systems distributing substantially indigenous product developed, offering a model instance of the planned evolution of a viable and popular national cultural industry. France, West Germany and the UK exemplified the 'fit' and the health of their broadcasting systems compared favourably with the crises of small countries such as Denmark, the Netherlands, or Belgium in which the revenues generated (whether from the sale of broadcasting receiving licences, levies on the sale of receiving apparatus or components, from advertising or directly from the state budget), were insufficient to fund the quantity and quality of programme material required for the capacity of the terrestrial broadcast distribution system.

The introduction of new distribution technologies, whether cable or direct broadcast satellites, separately or in conjunction, will upset this comfortable symbiosis by expanding distribution channels, creating a demand for software that cannot be met by the national production industry. The consequential importation of software from overseas will attract audiences away from existing services and reduce the revenues accruing to existing services (whether by having smaller audiences to sell to advertisers or by reducing the political acceptability of expenditure from the state budget or the levying of broadcast receiving licence fees), thus reducing the quality of indigenously produced software and initiating a spiral of decline. The history of the film industry in the UK is the classic example used to support this melancholy prognosis. The PEP report of 1952 defined the problem thus:

> The British film industry could not pay its way without a substantial export market. The home market could not compare with the home market of the American industry which was already several times as large. As soon as American production expanded and with its expansion introduced a new and more expensive type of film, there was no longer the same demand in the United States for British films which were of a cheaper and less polished kind. Without an overseas market British producers could not afford to increase the quality and consequently the expense of their films and without that extra quality they could not hope to compete with the Americans . . . Even in these days of sound the film trade is an international one and the American industry with its enormous home market has most of the advantages. Although in the history of film production many millions of pounds have been wasted, the fact remains that in all but exceptional circumstances the making of films which are both commercially and technically good costs a great deal of money; because of the extent of their home market the American producers are in the best position to meet financial necessities. (PEP, 1952, p. 29)

Though these remarks were made in respect of the period before the First World War the structural problem defined here was enduring and, I suggest, will endure:

> In 1926 the proportion of British films shown over the country as a whole appears to have been not more then 5%. The actual proportion of exhibitions of British films on the screen at that time was probably well below 5% owing to the larger percentage

of exhibition dates secured by American films through the system of blind and block booking. (Moyne Committee Report, para 5, quoted in PEP, 1952, p. 41)

In 1927 the first of the legal measures enacted by the British government to protect national film production was enacted following the Moyne Committee Report: the Cinematograph Films Act checking the practices of blind and block bookings imposed on exhibitors by the strength of the US major producers and introducing quotas of British films for exhibitors and distributors. The quotas began in 1928 at 7.5 per cent for distribution and 5 per cent for exhibitions and rose to 20 per cent in 1935. US interests remained dominant within the industry – particularly important was their commanding position in the distribution sector but government action – particularly quota requirements – had lifted British feature film production to 228 films in 1938 from 96 in 1930 (PEP, 1952, pp. 60, 68). The stimulus offered by quota applied only to the home market and to import substitution; it did not enable producers to successfully exploit world markets. But import substitution and the amortization of production costs by exhibition solely in the British market did not permit 'quality' film production and advantage remained with the US production industry:

> Quality films were expensive; the British market alone was not large enough to recover their costs of production; therefore quality films must have a world market. (PEP, 1952, p. 69)

But:

> British films could not capture a big enough share of the world market, more particularly of the American market, and the confidence which led to the expansion of the industry and the concomitant loans was unjustified. (PEP, 1952, p. 70)

And:

> An assessment of the comparative markets available to British and American producers in 1936 showed that in terms of seating capacity the American home market was two and a half times

as large as the British domestic market and that the annual net box-office receipts were four times as large; that 'owing . . . to the common language, nearly every American film is available for and is sent to, all other English speaking countries, giving a much larger market still to the American product and a correspondingly reduced one to British films'. (PEP, 1952, p. 74)

The Cinematograph Films Act of 1938 revised quota requirements to extend protection to short films (pressure had come from John Grierson and documentary film-makers) by establishing a separate short film quota and (to raise the quality of British productions), establishing a minimum cost of £7500 labour costs per film and of £1 per foot of film for quota eligibility. Films with higher labour costs of £3 per foot counted for double quota and £5 per foot treble quota.

In 1944 a further Committee of Enquiry into the film industry, the Palache Committee, was appointed and whilst not all of the committee's recommendations were implemented some of its arguments are worth recording for their recognition of the cultural significance of the cinematograph film commodity:

A cinematograph film represents something more than a mere commodity to be bartered against others. Already the screen has great influence both politically and culturally over the minds of the people. Its potentialities are vast, as a vehicle for expression of national life, ideals and tradition, as a dramatic and artistic medium and as an instrument for propaganda . . . The British public are vitally concerned that the British cinematograph industry should not be allowed to become either a mere reflection of a foreign atmosphere or a channel for disseminating the ideas and aspirations, no matter how worthy in themselves, of one or two dominating personalities in the country. (PEP, 1952, p. 90)

In 1947 Customs Duty of 75 per cent was imposed on all imported films – this 'Dalton Duty' was imposed 'because the country cannot afford to allocate the dollars necessary to pay for the exhibition of American films in this country at the present time' (*Hansard*, 3 November 1947, quoted in PEP 1952, p. 99) and constituted the most effective protection enjoyed to date by the British film production industry. The 'ad valorem' duty was removed in 1948 after pressure from British exhibitors and American producers in exchange for agreement from the US producers for a phased remission to the US of revenues earned in the UK and measures to promote circulation of British films in the US and US investment in the British industry. In 1948 the recommendations of the Moyne (1927) and Palache (1944) Committees that financial support for British film production should be available was implemented with the establishment of the National Film Finance Corporation. However, the 1948 Cinematograph Films Act removed quota for distributors (retaining it at 45 per cent for first feature exhibition and 25 per cent for supporting programs) and reduced the labour cost per foot requirement for quota elibility by 50 per cent.

In 1949 the reports of the Plant and Gater Committees (on distribution and exhibition of cinematographic films and on film production costs, respectively were published: their consensual view was that receipts from the share of the domestic market remaining to British producers were still insufficient to sustain film production in Britain, and that the structure of the distribution (dominated by US companies) and exhibition sectors (dominated by two companies with agreements with the US majors resulting in a predominance of US product exhibited) militated against a successful British production sector. *Plus ça change plus c'est la même chose*.

'It is abundantly clear', said Lord Lucas (the government spokesman in the House of Lords), 'that a reorganization is necessary upon the distributive side of this industry and in the arrangements for marketing' (PEP, 1952, p. 124).

The problems of distribution and exhibition were never satisfactorily tackled but in 1950 the British Film Production Fund (usually known as the Eady Levy after the civil servant Sir William Eady) was set up. The fund levies a percentage of exhibitors revenues on admission tickets, and channels the revenues to British producers of British films. Producers benefit (as do a number of other bodies such as the British Film Institute and the Children's Film Foundation), in proportion to the distributors' gross revenues earned by his or her film. Thus Eady taxes the exhibitor's revenue for all (including non-British) films shown and distributes the revenue to the producers of British films. Eady was given the force of statute in 1957 and has reduced the gap between the capacity of the distribution/exhibition sector and the production sector by directing revenues from distribution/exhibition to support production.

The regime established by the early 1950s of quota, the National Film Finance Corporation and the Eady Levy has persisted for thirty years. During those thirty years the fortunes of the British film industry ebbed and flowed; a pool of skills for film production was maintained (though as the Interim Action Committee on the Film Industry observed in 1979 these skills 'can be used in other sectors of industry, for example in the building trade'), revenues circulated between sectors of the industry and between government and industry (Coulson-Thomas argues persuasively that the financial effect of government intervention in the film industry has been to transfer funds from industry to government; revenues gained from, for example, entertainments tax and corporation tax outweigh revenues lost through the NFFC or the 100 per cent first-year capital allowances against tax given to British film productions), Ealing comedies came and went, the British social realist films of the late 1950s and early 1960s came and went, *Star Wars*, *Alien* and *Superman* (all British films for the purposes of the Eady Levy and the British government), came and went. In the late 1970s success was such that 'earnings by British film producers from performances overseas have been greater than the money paid out by British exhibitors for screening Hollywood films' (Porter, 1979, p. 221). But the forces identified by Porter in 1979 as central forces behind the British production industry's success – the 'vertically integrated multinational corporations' of ACC and EMI have rapidly faded from the scene. The recent success of British cinema – *Chariots of Fire* and *Gandhi* are independent productions. British success in the international marketplace, history shows is short-lived and insecure. The long-term movement of the industry has been one of decline – by the early 1980s the British film production industry was making too few films for exhibitions to fulfil quota requirements and in 1982 the quota requirements were reduced to 0 per cent.

Some contra-indications to this melancholy prognosis are clearly visible. *Chariots of Fire's* success has been followed this year by the perhaps even more emphatic success of *Gandhi*, an Anglo-Indian production with, as in the old days of the Raj, British predominance (60 per cent of the £11 million came from Goldcrest

Films a backer of *Chariots of Fire*, and part of the Pearson
Longman conglomerate which includes among its extensive media
holdings *The Financial Times*, Longmans Publishing and Penguin Books). However although Goldcrest have clearly picked
two winners the success of their films is neither unprecedented
nor does it compensate for the inactivity of the traditional big
indigenous fish in the British pool – Thorn–EMI, Rank and
Associated Communication. *The Financial Times* itself headlined
its report (13 April 1983) of *Gandhi*'s scoop: '8 Oscars do not
a thriving film industry make'. In three years of the late 1940s
a similar euphoria about the British industry was talked up on
the basis of Oscar successes. In 1946 *The Seventh Veil* got an
Oscar for its script and Laurence Olivier an honorary award for
Henry V. In 1947 *Great Expectations* and *Black Narcissus* divided
the Cinematography and Art Direction Academy Awards. In
1948 *Hamlet* and *The Red Shoes* divided a music award and
Hamlet received the best picture and Laurence Olivier the best
actor awards. Also in 1948 the Rank group produced more than
50 per cent of British features and lost £3,350,000 even after
massaging the annual accounts with £1,296,466 of non-recurring
credits (PEP, 1952, p. 109) on film production. The PEP Report
comments:

> The statement of the Rank production losses was the epitaph
> of another era in British film history. But by the time the
> announcement was made, in September 1949, the continuance
> of film-making in this country had already become dependent
> on loans from public funds. (PEP, 1952, p. 109)

Though state intervention kept an industry in place and permitted
sporadic successes, from *The Red Shoes* to *Chariots of Fire*, and
Gandhi, the structural problems of US predominance in the
distribution sector, the exhibition duopoly with its agreements
with the US majors 'crowding out' British productions and the
small size of the British market compared with that of the US
market have in the long-run supervened.

Broadcast television has developed in Britain as a vertically
integrated production/distribution/exhibition entity in which state
policy has denied entry in all three sectors to competitors of
the BBC and the ITCA companies (the companies exclusively

franchised by the IBA to sell broadcast advertising in a particular geographical area and which produce the bulk of television programming for the first commercial television channel and a growing proportion of the programming for Channel 4) until the establishment in 1982 of Channel 4 which has little in-house production capacity. Competing producers are further restricted by an 86 per cent quota for British productions prescribed by the IBA and 'informally' practised by the BBC, though Chapman reckons non-British material at nearer 20 per cent of broadcasts (Chapman, 1981). TV production in the UK has thus been protected by import quotas and control of distribution capacity in a way that the UK film industry never was.

The secure home base of the British television contractors and the potential it offers for secure profits is tempered by the financial regime contrived by the Treasury and the IBA in which an excess profits tax is levied on the profits generated in the UK. That is on the surplus of advertising revenue that remains after costs of programming, the IBA transmitter rentals etc. have been paid for. Profits accruing from sales of programming overseas do not attract excess profits levy. In the year to 31 March 1983, 60 per cent of Thames Television's (the major programme company franchised by the IBA) profits came from overseas programme sales. The licensing and fiscal régime is therefore one that encourages high expenditure on programming (with possible disadvantages to the British public of transfer pricing shifting profit to associated companies, costs of programming inflated by high wage and salary costs and programming oriented to foreign sales not domestic tastes) and foreign sales. On balance though the system serves the public well and has harnessed the revenues generated in the British exhibition and distribution sector to support an internationally competitive production sector consistently producing for domestic and foreign consumption, quality product.

Competition in the sections of distribution and exhibition has been restricted by the limitations of terrestrial broadcast technology. (The propagation characteristics of Herzian waves at the frequencies available for television broadcasts have meant that no offshore television stations serving UK audiences could be established, there is not and has not been a television equivalent to offshore radio stations such as Radio Luxembourg and Radio Caroline or to the spill-over of US transmissions into Canada that debilitated Canadian TV production, and by the government declining to allocate all of the spectrum capacity at its disposal for terrestrial TV broadcasting. It is often assumed that there has been a shortage of spectrum capacity for European countries, an objective block to the creation of a plurality of television broadcasters, but whilst spectrum capacity is finite the limits of capacity have, in Britain (and in most other countries including the USA), not yet been reached. The Home Office report on Direct Broadcasting by Satellite (1981) observed that capacity exists for a further terrestrial broadcast television channel. (This would be achieved by re-engineering the VHF 405 line services. These are to be closed in 1984 and the frequencies allocated not to broadcasting but to land mobile radio services. If transmission quality comparable to that of United States television were accepted other TV channels would be available for terrestrial broadcasting.) The report also observed that introduction of the four operating terrestrial broadcast television channels has been phased in order, *inter alia*, to ensure that the productive capacity of the domestic hardware and software industry, the capabilities of the human skills and talent pool etc. are not exhausted, thus opening the door to import penetration. BBC Television was re-introduced after World War II in 1946, a commercial television channel was first introduced in 1955, the second BBC channel began in 1964 and Channel 4 in 1982 (the introduction of which was preceded by strenuous attempts, some successful, to foster new British programme producers and was attended by considerable scepticism from the ITCA companies as to Channel 4's abilities to fill its schedules).

There is evidence to suggest that expansion of distribution capacity to four channels has overstretched resources. Thames Television's chairman Hugh Dundas regards Thames' contribution of £20 million to Channel 4 as 'intolerable'. Subscriptions to Channel 4 of £100 million from the ITCA companies, 14 per cent of their revenue, for which they are enabled to sell Channel 4 advertising is matched by derisory advertising revenues. Circumstances are still very exceptional and no firm judgement can be reached for revenues from advertising on Channel 4 are depressed because of an enduring dispute between Equity (the performers union) and the Institute of Practitioners in Advertising. However, audiences for Channel 4 peak at about 10 per cent of the peak audiences for ITV and generally remain low. Indeed at Christmas 1982 the Channel 4 audience was only 3.5 per cent of TV viewers.

S4C (Sianel Pedwar Cymru) the largely Welsh language fourth channel for Wales has been extremely successful in attracting audiences and is clearly much valued in Wales, but its costs of £48 million per year (Wordley, 1983) can never hope to be matched by advertising revenues.

Breakfast TV, another recent initiative, has the commercial station TV-am achieving audiences of 200,000 (15 per cent of the audiences for the BBC's competing breakfast programme) and losing between £500,000 and £1 million per month. Perhaps the point has been reached where capacity of the British television distribution system has outgrown the capacity of the production sector and its revenue base.

The history of the broadcasting industry in the United States offers interesting material for consideration. The US experience is customarily invoked by advocates of additional services and a market-based broadcasting order. The US system offers consumers in major markets more signals than does UK TV, but here too the system has reached limits, set not by the state but by the market. In most US markets UHF frequencies are available for additional terrestrial broadcast television. The limit to system expansion is reached at the point where the cost per 1000 viewers incurred by the broadcaster in reaching an audience exceeds the revenue that accrues to the broadcaster from the sale of that increment of the audience to advertisers, and at the point where the costs to a cable operator of extending a cable relay system that distributes the signals of distant stations to subscribers exceed the revenues generated from the subscribers. These are limits established in *consumption*. However, there are limits to the US system imposed by *production* factors by the need to concentrate revenues generated in the distribution sector for production. Though US broadcasting is performed by a great plurality of independent stations (nearly 1300 TV stations is the figure given by Head [1976, p. 169] the broadcasting order is dominated by three entities: the networks. Head glosses his history of television – embedded in his general account *Broadcasting in America* in which the same tendencies towards concentration of production and networking are recounted in US radio's history – thus:

The economies of the medium drove it inexorably toward syndication. This was true at the local as well as at the network level. Local live production eventually dwindled to news, sports and children's programming, plus a sprinkling of religious, public affairs, homemaking and agricultural features. And even these few so-called live programs draw much of their content from syndicated material: news agency stories, kiddie cartoons, Department of Agriculture films and canned religious features. A good deal of the newsfilm seen on the local programs of network affiliates consists either of news stories syndicated by the networks to their affiliates 'down the line', at times when the relay facilities lie idle, or of taped repeats of network news stories. (Head, 1976)

The concentration of resources necessary to produce programming of acceptable quality produced in US radio four networks (though it could be argued that market conditions permitted only three, the compulsory divestiture in 1943 – prompted by the FCC – by NBC of one of its networks created an unstable situation with the fourth network, Mutual, always financially vulnerable) the greater resources necessary for television production permitted in the US – the largest and richest of world TV markets – only three major production entities.

The tendency for concentration within a national market observed by Head is now taking place on an international scale. Broadcasting, then, has not been constrained by a shortage of spectrum capacity in the UK for the limit of spectrum capacity has not yet been reached but rather by a consistent and remarkably enduring series of political and cultural judgements that the national interest is best served by restricting supply of programming to that amount that can be financed and produced indigenously. There has been a tendency towards the same regime in the USA as a consequence of market pressures.

Unlike the experience of the film production industry in Britain, the television production industry has been able to benefit from a secure home base from which to colonize foreign software markets. The limitation of distribution capacity (and the imposition of an 85 per cent British quota) enabled production to amortize its costs at home and compete on the world market on the same basis as US producers. The film industry never enjoyed this situation, the distribution and exhibition sector of the film trade in the UK had capacity to fill beyond that capable of being filled by the British production industry. The expansion of television's distribution capacity by DBS and cable currently advocated by Mrs Thatcher's government is likely to reduce the British TV production industry, even protected by quota (and the Cable White Paper, 1983, prefers rather to take into account the proportion of British material intended by franchisees for transmission in judging competing applications for franchises than to continue with an explicit quota. There are, I think, good grounds for scepticism as to whether such 'intentions' are likely to prove enduring), to the condition of the film production industry. But to a government orientated to the market as a better guarantee of the public interest than regulation 'intentions' are likely to prove more than sufficient.

The Market and the Role of the State

British government policy for the information society has been governed by two contradictory principles, that of promoting the role of the market and that of foregrounding the role of the state in an attempt to create the concentration of resources necessary for innovation and development. But though the role of government remains an active one (for example, in funding the Alvey program of computer development with £200 million), it is the ideology of the market that reigns supreme – the ideology of public service manifested through public sector institutions such as the BBC and British Telecom, with their commitment to universal service and constant pricing through cross-subsidy and through the regulation of commercial broadcasting has been rejected (see Garnham, 1983). The assumption is overwhelmingly that the public interest is, *necessarily*, best served by the market: 'Government policy is one of introducing and promoting competition so that both industry and the consumer can benefit' (HMSO, 1983, p. 69). British Telecom's network monopoly has been ended with the licensing of the Mercury telecommunications system, competition in supply of terminals, radiotelephony, value added services has been introduced and the government currently has a bill for the privatization of British Telecom before Parliament. But of the range of measures and projects that are currently being promoted it is cable to which the government is most firmly committed and which has caught the imagination of the public. The entire stock, 2000 copies, of the Stationery Office's holding of the cable White Paper, *The Development of Cable Systems and Services*, was sold out by 10:00 a.m. on the day following the announcement of the publication to Parliament. Whilst the White Paper (HMSO, 1983) on cable development was jointly produced by the Home Office (generally thought to favour paternalism, control and public service) and the Department of Industry (the market, deregulation and competition), and contains ritual obeisances to the sanctified principles of protecting the public interest through administrative measures the dominant motif is that of the market:

> In the Government's view cable has the potential for increasing the range of good quality services available to the public, and this will best be encouraged by giving the consumer the opportunity to determine what he is willing to buy. (HMSO, 1983, p. 56)

The week of the cable White Paper also saw the publication in *The Times* (26 April 1983, p. 12) of an article by Howard Davies, a recently retired Treasury civil servant, advocating 'dismemberment or even abolition of the BBC', the allocation of radio frequencies by auction and predicting that, should the Thatcher government be returned to power following the 1983 election, a 'radical reappraisal of public service broadcasting' will ensue. It is clear that the dominant (though by no means the only) thread in government thinking is the assumption that market-determined allocations are necessarily superior to other forms of allocation in directing resources and in achieving an equitable distribution of benefits. Other commentators do not share this optimism. Melody (1980) points out that 'transaction and enforcement costs as well as loss of spectrum use would far exceed any claimed allocation efficiency benefits flowing from the introduction of market principles into spectrum allocation' and whilst there is undoubtedly an attractive note struck in Davies' contention, of British broadcasting, that 'the principal beneficiaries . . . are as with any monopoly its employees', he does not consider the introduction into the BBC of an elected control structure accountable to the public as an alternative to the beneficent hand of the market in checking the luxuries enjoyed at viewers' and listeners' expense (whether the BBC staffs' realization of pet artistic projects or in more material sources of gratification). Nor, perhaps it is needless to say, are the benefits enjoyed by the holders of power in non-monopoly private enterprises considered by Mr Davies. And the 'creaking expensive and out of touch with its taxpayer-viewers' system deplored by Davies succeeds in delivering product to consumers at a cost of 1.5 to 2 pence per viewing hour per viewer (Ehrenberg and Barwise, 1982). Admittedly this calculation is performed on the basis that spectrum resources are costed at zero, but even at the level of costs of £6.50 to £9.95 per month charged by the Pay TV operators operating *existing* cable systems, ten to fifteen viewer hours per day are required for each cable subscription to deliver comparable cost-benefits to those of broadcast television. Many more viewer hours per day will be required for cable systems requiring new infrastructure and entailing consequentially higher subscription fees from consumers to deliver the cost/benefit relationship of existing broadcast TV.

Winners and Losers: Hardware and Software

The Cable White Paper (HMSO, 1983) though makes clear, as have previous government statements and reports, that the unquantifiable benefits of taming the BBC and introducing the market principle aside, the major role of pay television delivered by broadband cable is to act as a locomotive for the information society. The proposed Cable Authority is, for example, charged with 'responsibility to promote interactive services' (p. 24), 'wideband cable systems', it is argued, 'offer the opportunity for non-entertainment services to be made available to subscribers at marginal price levels since the basic system and infrastructure costs will have been absorbed by the entertainment services' (p. 15). There is, I believe, considerable reason to be sceptical of this scenario, there is no firm evidence that a market for cable television exists that is sufficiently large to amortize the capital costs of the infrastructure. Costs of cabling could be reduced under a number of scenarios that range from using British Telecom ducts and ceding it a *de facto* monopoly in hardware provision to exploiting (as Rothschild's bank did with its acquisition of the assets, holes in the ground, of the London Hydraulic Company) the sewers, disused tramway ducts or any of the underused or discarded existing holes in the ground. Given a cable system in place then the problem becomes one of securing subscriptions. The experience of the thirteen areas experimentally licensed for pay TV has been very varied but not overall encouraging. Of 300,000 homes passed by cable only 19,000 subscribed to the pay services. The successful penetration of cable in Belgium (64.1 per cent), Canada (57 per cent), and the Netherlands (55 per cent) (Shaw, 1981), has been due to the low quality of broadcast television in those countries *relative* to that available in neighbouring countries broadcasting in a comprehensible language. Thus cable has enabled Dutch subscribers to consume West German television funded by a domestic market more than four times as large as the Netherlands, as has Canadian cable enabled Canadians to consume US television funded by the US domestic market larger by a factor of ten than the Canadian market. (Why one wonders given an extensive cable infrastructure in these countries all at least as technically advanced as the UK and all more prosperous has not the cornucopia of interactive services and the transition to the post-industrial society eventuated there?) The pay cable experience in the USA is most pertinent to the situation in the UK. And here there is disagreement about the benefits in TV programming quality brought by cable. Davies asserts that:

> cable has already revolutionized television in large areas of the US. And as the IEA authors (C. G. Veljanovski and W. D. Bishop in 'Choice by Cable', Institute of Economic Affairs, London RC) point out, the choice available to viewers in Manhattan in quality and variety makes a nonsense of the traditional 'quality' argument for the BBC. (Davies, *ibid*)

Winston argues the reverse – his argument is not such as to be represented in a single quotation though the title of his article 'Unusual rubbish' encapsulates his view of Manhattan cable programming. Quality is a problematic – though vital – criterion, but Winston establishes a case to answer; a challenge yet to be taken up by cable advocates. He states:

There are for all intents and purposes only four broadcast television networks in the United States. . . . Within any one of them, I regarded it as an achievement to be able to distinguish commercials from programmes, so dense and complex in the presentational style. Final programme credits are regularly augmented by voice over promotions for coming shows . . . so fast and furious is the pace of this electronic juggernaut that programme junctions simply get overridden and lost in the rush. This accepted and amazing cacophony is a base element in creating the false notion of the possibility of a television of abundance. (Winston, 1982, p. 156)

and

In any given month those services (i.e. Manhattan movie channel pay-cable RC) offer around fifty-one per cent identical product – over six months they played 'Rocky II' 44 times. 'The Muppet Movie' 37 times . . . 'And Justice for All' 30 times, 'Close Encounters' 41 times and 'Superman' 53 times. (Winston, 1982, p. 157)

Melvin Goldberg (a vice-president of the broadcaster ABC and therefore perhaps a partisan witness) states that 12.6 million households in the US (i.e. approx. 17 per cent) subscribe to pay cable, and that of homes receiving 20 or more channels only 8.1 channels were viewed (a view is registered if a channel is viewed for a minimum of 10 minutes per month) (Goldberg, 1982). Cable in the USA has experienced at least one false dawn in which Teleprompter (one of the two franchises for Manhattan) suffered severe financial setbacks in the early 1970s and to survive surrendered expensive franchises granted elsewhere than Manhattan.

The *Financial Times* of 6 July 1982 reports losses of between $10 million and $15 million for Getty Oil's sports network (ESPN), the news service of Ted Turner is in financial trouble losing in 1981 $13.4 million on sales of $95 million. CBS has closed its arts/cultural channel. The sole major success in the programmers serving US pay cable is that of Home Box Office which reaching 8 million subscribers (i.e. about 12 per cent of US households) generated $75 million profit on a $315 million turnover (*Financial*

Times, 6 July 1982, p. 20). But HBO was charging a premium of $9 per month for its service in addition to a basic cable charge of say $10 per month (Cohen, 1981). The UK equivalent would be perhaps £12 per month – higher by perhaps 20 to 40 per cent than the fee charged in the experimental British pay TV operations which have themselves had an indifferent success. Given the differences in the broadcasting orders of the UK, the USA and the extensively cabled countries there seems room for substantial doubt as to the likely success of cable TV in the UK.

The uptake in the USA for interactive services delivered by broadband cable is put by Winston (Winston, 1982) at 0.001 per cent of cable homes. All the services currently canvassed by cable advocates can, with the exception of high speed bulk data transfer, be performed over the narrowband telephone system, on which there is (at the level of the local loop which is the level at which cable is being promoted) growing (with digitalization, improvements in switching, etc.) surplus capacity. Even in the wildest fantasies of Daniel Bell and Kenneth Baker there can surely be limited demand by domestic consumers for high speed bulk data transfer and one needs look no further than the experience of AT&T with Picturephone to develop some scepticism about demand for picture telephony. The evidence is that the 64 kilobit/second infrastructure of the British Telecommunication system is adequate for all foreseeable 'need pulled' services – where demand develops for increased transmission capacity it is at the level of trunk routes where concentration may be performed, *ad hoc* increases in capacity delivered whether by cable, terrestrial microwave or satellite. In any case with the establishment of the Mercury networks a massive increase in trunk capacity in Britain is about to be implemented. It seems likely that cabling of Britain, if undertaken, and there are signs that few investors will be found (see *The Sunday Times*, 1 May 1983, p. 63, and the *Financial Times*, 28 April 1983, p. 20), will be an investment in an unnecessary duplicated, unplanned communication infrastructure replete with diseconomies of scale as was the excess railway capacity constructed in the railway mania of the nineteenth century. There seems no reason to dissent from the conclusions of the West German Commission for the Development of the Telecommunications System (KtK, 1976, p. 194) that:

There was no urgent and acute additional demand for an increased number of television programmes. The demand for picture telephony is also low; the costs to meet this demand would be high. On the other hand, the (narrowband) telecommunications network, that is the telephone network in particular, provides an infrastructure whose qualitative possibilities are by far not as yet exploited to the maximum.

There is growing evidence that cable in the UK is an unattractive investment. DeLoitte, Haskins and Sells (one of the consultants and analysts most favourably inclined towards cable) predict fairly modest returns for cable operations and stress that financial success hangs on two factors: the availability of existing ducts and the reduction of rental fees for feature films by the MPEA (Motion Picture Exporters Association of America). For Luton and Dunstable (a prosperous concentrated settlement north of London with excellent road, rail and air communications) a post-tax rate return of 6 to 7 per cent for the first franchise period is predicted with a pre-tax rate of return (i.e. for corporations with losses to set against cable earnings) of 12 to 14 per cent (*The Financial Times*, 28 February 1983, p. 4). Pre-tax redemption yields on British government stocks in excess of 11 per cent can currently be achieved; with that return available on very low risk readily marketable investments cable, offering a 3 per cent maximum additional return, looks very speculative.

Even assuming that the half of the UK that generous estimates calculate might be cabled is cabled benefits to the national economy look very marginal. The Greater London Council Economic Policy Group (GLC, 1982) calculate (in an extensive report covering other impacts than employment) an employment gain in the UK by 1990 of 23,000 jobs but a loss of 25,000 jobs in other sectors notably in software production. The consultants CSP, in a report for British Telecom (CSP, 1982), predict an employment gain of 13,750 jobs by 1990 assuming no job loss in software production and an employment growth of 9,000 jobs in the telecommunications/information technology industry by 1990 given a 'high growth investment scenario: accompanied by a growing negative UK balance of trade in this sector of £318 million in 1990'.

Pessimism about technological change and cultural decline are, of course, enduring British tropes. Lord Reith's, in retrospect, hysterical jeremiad against the introduction of commercial television, only continued the long and mistaken tradition of inveighing against 'illth' and innovations in cultural forms tracked, *inter alia*, by Ruskin, Arnold, Eliot and Leavis. But the banality of the prose of Reith's epigone Lord Thompson (Chairman of the IBA), and the retrospective knowledge that Matthew Arnold disparaged the novel and exalted poetry as the Crown of Literature, when Dickens, George Eliot and Mrs Gaskell were writing and that commercial television in spite of Reith's predictions has given us *Strangers, The Sweeney, Out, Harry's Game, Bill Brand* does not necessarily mean that cultural pessimism is misplaced in the current instance. Or that concern for the nature of programming is the prerogative only of the middle class, who, pace Davies (1983), consume at the expense of the poor 'the unconstrained artistic endeavours of BBC drama producers which largely benefit the middle classes'.

The experience of Canada (see Collins, 1982) has demonstrated the problems for cultural sovereignty, for the quality of mass culture, and for the domestic software production industry of expansion of distribution capacity to a level beyond that which a flow of programming from domestic producers can fill. More does not necessarily mean worse – the fortuitously contrived regime for ITV in the UK shows that – but it may. When one considers that cable has been successful only in those markets where superior television is available in a comprehensible language from a neighbouring country, or where the quality (of transmission, interruption by advertisements and of programming) of television is such as to dispose audiences to subscribe to cable to get a decent signal, ad-free programmes and a greater variety of rubbish, than one has to see a certain Machiavellian logic to the scenario hinted at by Davies. If cable needs bad broadcast television to be successful then broadcast television in Britain will have to be worsened.

Whether Mrs Thatcher and Mr Baker have *The Prince* for bedside reading is not known but they, as ruling princes in the UK, have amply demonstrated their ability to rule by fear. The possibility of a cable demarche, however risky a new enterprise for the prince and princess to introduce, should not be ignored, particularly since the CDU government in West Germany is following the same line of march. The government's commitment to cable and satellite television and its communication policies generally drawn on two of its most potent ideological reflexes to technology and to the market. When technology offers the possibility of the introduction of a market rather than an administered public service regime than its seductions are too powerful to resist. But given the costs of entry to the new information technologies, the problematic risk/reward relationships and increasing resistance to an economic and political rationale that seeks to eliminate the category public good from policy discourse paradoxically government will have to dangle larger and larger carrots in front of the donkeys in order to get them to market. The downside risks of impact on the software industries, overinvestment in infrastructure capacity, and high level of public satisfaction with existing services may yet mean that there are too few donkeys drawn by the carrots to make a market. The whip has been applied to British Telecom; it may be that other public sector institutions animated in however traduced and ossified a fashion by public service goals will next feel it across their backs.

Davies is probably right; the BBC and IBA are next. But application of whip or carrot will not resolve the central contradiction in the government's position – its commitment to a market regime, and competition within the boundaries of the UK for industries to which economies of scale apply and which operate in an environment of fierce international competition. Deregulation may have been good for the United States; it is too soon to judge the life expectancy of the Baby Bells (each of which is about the size of British Telecom, itself enormous in the UK industrial landscape), but what was good in the United States for the United States may turn out in Britain to be similarly good for the Unites States.

There will be 'winners' as well as 'losers' in the UK, but government's legitimacy rests on its ability to represent general and collective interest not sectional and particular interests. The government of Mrs Thatcher judges that the general interest (or public interest though that term is anathema to it) is best served by a rapid move to a market system of allocations with government action directed towards the removal of regulation and selective state support for elite companies that may be trained and hardened for international competition. In the long-term the market system may be a superior system for allocating and generating resources and many spots on the British industrial landscape evidence the debilitating effects of protection from competition. (The telecommunications equipment manufacturing industry is perhaps the prime example.)

But competitors do not enter the marketplace equally well fitted for competition nor are the benefits of market allocations distributed either equally or equitably. It is one thing for a government elected by and disposing of its power within a nation-state to engineer a reconstruction of market forces. Winners and losers remain within those national boundaries. In international competition, even granting the proposition of market theorists that the market is the least worst system of allocation, the winners may be outside the boundaries of the nation-state and the losers within it.

Nor is it necessarily the case that the 'winners' in the international marketplace are those made lean and fit by exposure to competition at home. L. M. Ericsson has used the base of its cosy relationship with the Swedish PTT to become a major force in the world telecommunications equipment market; Plessey favoured similarly in British Telecom's procurement, is being sued by Rolm for theft of intellectual property. Competition among manufacturers of Prestel terminals has had the effect of raising the unit cost of a terminal above that that would have obtained with a monopoly supplier and has slowed the penetration of interactive videotex in the UK and reduced potential revenues for the information providers and British Telecom.

UK Government policy then is directed towards hastening the birth of the information society in the UK, but its analysis that pay television delivered through the establishment of a broad band cable network (though even the most optimistic advocates of cable concede that 50 per cent of the UK will remain uncabled), will act as a locomotive drawing prosperity and a raft of information services in its wake seems extremely unlikely. However, expansion of UK television distribution capacity, a policy aimed at stimulating hardware industries important sections of which are of questionable international competitiveness (the head of British Telecom's research laboratories at Martlesham – the modest but capable UK equivalent of Bell Labs – Mr May, recently observed that after a working life attempting successful collaboration with the British Telecommunication equipment manufacturing industry he welcomed the aspect of Conservative government telecoms policy that would permit British Telecom to buy reliable foreign manufactured equipment in the future), is likely to adversely impact on the British software industry. Is there any reason to doubt that the consistent success of the British television programme production industry has been conditional on its protection by quota and restriction of distribution capacity from the dumping of US programming? The British film production industry has been reduced to a marginal viability in circumstances similar to those that current government policy will reproduce for the television production industry.

In 1958 Ealing Film Studios closed for film production and has since been used for production by the BBC. The commemorative plaque marking the demise of Ealing Films reads: 'Here during a quarter of a century were made many films projecting Britain and the British character.' Current government policy will leave the BBC few options but to erect a similar memorial.

The fruits of the UK government's policies, questions of quality, cultural sovereignty and public good aside, are likely to be those of import penetration, job losses, weakening of the software industries in spite of the large sums of public money devoted to inducing the birth of the information society in the UK. The British competitor in the international lemming race towards the information society may yet best serve the public interest by falling at the first fence.

This chapter was first published in 1983 in *Media Culture and Society* vol. 5, no. 3/4, and reprinted in *Media Culture and Society. A Critical Reader*. (London: Sage, 1986).

References

Bell, D. (1976), *The Coming of the Post Industrial Society* (Harmondsworth: Peregrine).

Chapman, G. (1981), *International Television Flow in West Europe*, International Institute of Communication Conference Report.

Cohen, F. (1981), 'The US cable explosion. Home Box Office and Others', *InterMedia*, November.

Collins, R. (1982), *Lessons for the Old Countries. Broadcasting and National Culture in Canada*, Canada House Lecture, London, Canadian High Commission.

CSP (1982), *Telecommunications and the Economy*, London.

Coulson-Thomas, C. (1981), *The British Film Production Industry and Government Support*. MA thesis, Polytechnic of Central London.

Ehrenberg, A. and Barwise, T. (1982), *How much does U.K. Television Cost?*, London Business School.

Garnham, N. (1983), 'Public service versus the Market', *Screen* vol. 24, no. 1, January–February.

GLC (1982). *Cabling in London*. Report of Economic Policy Group, London.

Goldberg, M. (1982), 'Will the US networks survive the 1980s?', *InterMedia*. November.

Government of Canada (1983), *Towards a New National Broadcasting Policy*. Department of Communications, Government of Canada.

Head, S. (1976), *Broadcasting in America* (Boston: Houghton Mifflin).

HMSO (1983), *The Development of Cable Systems and Services*, Cmnd 8866 (London: HMSO).

Hoskins, C., and McFadyen, S. (1982), 'Market Structure and Television Programming Performance in Canada and the UK. A Comparative Study', *Canadian Public Policy*, Summer.

ITAP (1982), *Cable Systems*. A report by the Information Technology Advisory Panel (London: HMSO).

KtK (1976), Commission for the Development of the Telecommunications System, *Telecommunications Report* (Bonn: Federal Ministry of Posts and Telecommunications).

Kumar, K. (1978), *Prophecy and Progress* (Harmondsworth: Penguin).

Melody, W. (1979), 'Are satellites the pyramids of the 20th Century?', *Search*, vol. 6, no. 2.

Melody, W. (1980), 'Radio spectrum allocation: role of the market', *American Economic Review*, vol. 70, no. 2, March.

Melody, W. (1982), *Direct Broadcast Satellites. The Canadian Experience*. Paper at symposium 'Satellite Communication: National Media Systems and International Communications Policies', Hans Bredow Institute, University of Hamburg, December.

Nora, S. and Minc, A. (1980), *The Computerization of Society* (Cambridge: MIT Press).

PEP (1952), *The British Film Industry*. Political and Economic Planning, London.

Porter, V. (1979), 'Film policy for the 80s', *Sight and Sound*, Autumn.

Shaw, J. (1981), 'ITV must respond to satellite opportunities', *InterMedia*, July.

Wall, S. (1977), The U.K.: an information economy?, British Telecom mimeo.

Winston, B. (1982), 'Unusual rubbish', *Sight and Sound*, Summer.

Wordley, R. (1983), Letter to *The Times*, 22 March 1983.

Chapter 7

Wall-to-Wall *Dallas*? The US–UK Trade in Television

Media analysis is in danger of repeating the behaviour of the Bourbons: learning nothing and forgetting nothing. Slowly and laboriously, simple behaviourist stimulus and response models of effects and audience research are being driven from the field by more nuanced and mediated models of the consumption and effects of the mass media. A variety of studies, including Hall's *Encoding and Decoding* (Hall, 1980) and Morley's *The Nationwide Audience* (Morley, 1980) have asserted the differentiality of audience understandings and actions. Yet this understanding of the specificity of micro-cosmic responses to television programmes is rarely replicated when the macro-cosmic impact of programming is considered. Studies of world information flows assert confidently that imperialistic relationships exist, that cultural imperialism is rampant and that everywhere the media are American (see Schiller, 1969, Smith, 1980, Tunstall, 1977, Varis, 1974). However, much evidence suggests that the same differential found at the micro-levels of consumption is found at the macro-level, though there has been little reconsideration of the media imperialism thesis other than Lee (1980) and Ravault (1980). In Europe the alarm at the impact of American television programming (for which *Dallas* has become a codeword) has continued, becoming sufficiently fashionable to have assumed the dimensions of moral panic. 'Wall to Wall Dallas' is by now the accepted shorthand of critics anticipating the effects of the general introduction of pay cable television to the UK (Chris Dunkley even used that as the title for his recent book [Dunkley, 1985]) and a French government minister attacked Luxembourg's broadcast satellite (a delivery system for American

151

programming) as a 'Coca-Cola' satellite 'attacking our artistic and cultural integrity' (in *Financial Times*, 31 May 1984, p. 3). Indeed, the dreaded *Dallas* was chosen by the Commission of the European Communities to exemplify the perils of non-European television:

> There is already a certain uniformity in the range of films screened on television in the Community. Programmes such as *'Dallas'* are carried by almost every television channel in the member states. The creation of a common market for television production is thus one essential step if the dominance of the big American media corporations is to be counterbalanced. (Commission of the European Communities, 1984, p. 47)

National broadcasting authorities have recently attempted to regain audiences lost to *Dallas* by reworking it in a national idiom – for example, France's *Chateauvallon*, Canada's *Vanderberg* and the Netherlands' *Herrenstraat 10*. These initiatives are in turn perceived as imitative amplifications of US imperialism and distinctive symptoms of the decline of authentic national cultural production. But the impact of *Dallas*, and of US television in general, is far from unambiguous.

The trade in television programming between the USA and the UK is not one of unequal exchange from which only the USA benefits. The factors that have sustained US dominance of the world trade in audio-visual media, whether films for theatrical exhibition or programming for television, may be changing and new opportunities arising for foreign producers to exploit in the US domestic market the comparative advantages that have hitherto been the prerogative of American producers. Twenty years ago the American automobile industry's command of its domestic market was considered unassailable. It was unimaginable that Americans would drive anything other than six-seated V8s. Now Chrysler has gone to the wall and come back again and the bottom end of the US automobile market is dominated by Toyota, Nissan and Subaru, the top by BMW and Mercedes Benz. There are grounds for believing that US television programming may experience similar import penetration to that experienced by the United States automobile market.

Information is a tradeable product like vehicles, fish, coal and chemicals. Just as nation-states see the terms of trade and import/export ratios in coal and fish as legitimate national interests, so do they in information products. Given that comparative advantage in the production of tradeable products resides at different times with different producers, there is no particular economic reason why a nation-state should seek autarchy in the production of information goods any more than Switzerland should seek to be self-sufficient in seafish, Britain in bananas or Egypt in forest products. In respect of the production of other commodities an international division of labour takes place, why not with information goods?

The evidence of history is that for the kind of information product represented by *Dallas* (high-budget soap opera/family melodrama narrative fiction) the United States has long been the overwhelmingly dominant producer.

> By 1925 a third of all foreign revenue came from the United Kingdom alone, where American films captured 95% of the market. In the same period, 77% of the features shown in France came from the United States, as did about 66% in Italy. (Guback, 1976)

In 1925, Guback states, 235 million feet of motion pictures were exported and 7 million feet imported by the United States. That country's dominance in the world market for audio-visual information goods has been consolidated by successive innovations in technology and product and by raising the costs of production and therefore barriers to the entry of competitors to the market (the star system, sound, colour, wide screen, 3D, epic scale, special effects and so on). In most European countries, a national film production industry survives only through state subsidy and import quotas. The US industry has very successfully exploited its major comparative advantage, the large size of its (rather chauvinistic) domestic market. Gordon (1976) shows the relative size of the US and EEC film markets in 1972 in Table 7.1.

The large size of the US domestic market, its resistance to penetration by foreign product and the evolution of large firms able to produce on a scale appropriate to a business in which demand for its products in general has co-existed with considerable market capriciousness *vis-à-vis* particular products (of ten films one may make very high profits, seven may lose greater or less

Table 7.1 Box office grosses in $ millions, 1972

US	1300
Italy	364
France	202
W Germany	186
Britain	154
Belgium	33
Netherlands	29
Denmark	23
EEC	991

amounts, three may break even, thus long-term success will only be available to large-scale producers) has given the US film and production industry very substantial advantages in the international audio-visual information goods markets. Many of these characteristics have been replicated in the television programming market. Varis (1974) has shown the United States' importation of foreign television programming to be exceptionally low (between 1 per cent and 2 per cent imports). The US market for television programming in 1980 was 2.8 billion dollars (Grieve, Horner and Associates, 1981, pp. 108–9). This sum is enormous in comparison with the size of the UK programming market: £937 million in 1982 (derived from Broadcasting Research Unit, 1983). The US market was divided into these proportions between the networks 63 per cent, syndication and barter (i.e., the independents) 23 per cent, PBS 4 per cent, pay TV 9 per cent, the UK market between ITV 69 per cent, and BBC 31 per cent.

However, the dominance of US producers in European markets is considerably less marked when the television distribution and exhibition medium is considered than it was, and is, with film. Film distribution in Europe was, and is, dominated by US companies – in television (with some recent exceptions – notably Italy) distribution and exhibition is the monopoly of a state agency or is closely regulated by the state. The film exhibition sector in Europe expanded beyond the capacity of domestic producers and a conflict of interests developed between the domestic exhibition sector, enjoying a kind of comprador relationship with US producers and distributors, and the domestic production sector. Exhibitors in Britain had to be compelled by quota legislation to exhibit British films – their economic interests were in general better served by exhibiting imported material made with higher budgets and featuring international stars, and sold to exhibitors at low cost. In 1982 in a belated recognition that the British film production industry was producing too few films for the exhibition sector to fulfil its 15 per cent British quota, the quota was reduced to zero per cent by the national government.

In contrast to the long dominance of the United States in the film business British television has been more resistant to US penetration. In 1981 television transmission of non British/non EEC programming was, for commercial television, limited to 14 per cent. In October 1984 this quota was raised by 1.5 per cent to permit more programming from the Commonwealth. No formal restrictions exist for the BBC which has in general limited itself to the 14 per cent prescribed by the statute for commercial television. However, there are signs that the BBC's financial difficulties are leading to its transmission of increasing quantities of foreign programming. In 1982 (Broadcasting Research Unit, 1983) 31 per cent of the Corporation's prime-time television came from overseas, 26 per cent from the USA. Seventeen per cent of BBC1 programming that year was of non-BBC origin, 22 per cent of BBC2 programming was of non-BBC origin (although these percentages may, of course, have included British or EEC material originated 'out of house'). The balance of trade in television programmes between the UK and North America (statistics that disaggregate Canada and the USA are unavailable), over the last five years for which information is available, has turned against the UK. However, a longer term indexical analysis modifies this conclusion by demonstrating that there is considerable variation in the trading relationships between the UK and North America:

Table 7.2 Balance of trade in television programmes between UK and North America, £m

1977	1978	1979	1980	1981	1982	1983	1984
+ 11	+ 5	+ 3	+ 12	+ 2	− 1	0	− 13

Source: British Business, September 16, 1983; October 5, 1984; August 30, 1985; September 9, 1985.

During the period 1977–84 UK exporters maintained the largest proportion of their sales to North America. (The North American component of overall TV programme sales was 56 per cent both in 1977 and 1984 and varied between 43 and 61 per cent overall.) But UK importers increased the proportion of overall purchases from Norrth America (the North American component of overall TV programme imports varied between 43 per cent in 1977 and 71 per cent in 1984).

Essentially British television distribution/exhibition capacity has been rationed by the national government. The protected and rationed domestic distribution/exhibition sector has permitted the production of high budget, high production values, quality programming in the UK. Revenues from the sale of audiences to advertisers or from the sale of broadcast receiving licenses are deployed to supply programmes to a market that is both guaranteed 84.5 per cent of broadcast hours for UK/EEC programmes) and limited (four channels). Control of the distribution/exhibition sector is tight and has permitted the growth of a production sector in Britain where the quality and quantity of domestically produced programmes strengthens the bargaining position of British broadcasters in their negotiations for the purchase of foreign programming and whose own products can successfully be sold in international markets.

At a level of economic analysis it is at least an open question whether the public interest in the UK has been best served by the film industry regime; supplying the British entertainment information goods market with cheaply purchased high budget quality products imported largely from the USA; or the television industry regime of denying entry to 86 per cent of the British entertainment information goods market to foreign productions. However, it is clear that with information goods other criteria than purely economic ones obtain. One of my purposes has been to show that some form of economic analysis and policy has to be formulated if questions of communication sovereignty and cultural imperialism are to be addressed sensibly, but the arguments about a New World Information Order, free flows versus balanced flows etc., show that many interests see more than economics at stake in the production and consumption of information goods.

Concern about the effects of mass communications has been persistent since the beginning of the mass media era whether that is dated from Gutenberg's or Marconi's time. However, in the decades since World War II the focus of concern has shifted from that for individuals, under-represented or vulnerable groups within a particular nation-state to concern with and for the nation itself. The threat to communications sovereignty latent since the beginning of the twentieth century and slowly actualized in North America (Canadian subordination to US broadcasting remains the classic, even though earliest, instance) has with the triple impact of new distribution technologies, new ideologies of deregulation, and the accelerating demand for quantities of high-budget but low-cost software, become a matter of general concern. In Western Europe, national governments have lost confidence in their ability to maintain communications sovereignty buttressed by national newspaper and publishing industries and state control of broadcasting. Italy's experience, following the Tele-Biella judgement, of the national broadcasting monopoly's vanishing access to the Italian people in favour of unregulated private broadcasters distributing largely US programming is exemplary. Moreover, the critique of the loss of communications sovereignty customarily runs in harness with a qualitative judgement that the new order and its product is inferior to the old. The concept of cultural imperialism is dependent on qualitative and quantitative judgements. The conditions of quantitative subordination are economic and organizational, the conditions of qualitative subordination are cultural and aesthetic.

It is an enduring European trope to hold up a mirror to US chauvinism. In the UK critical concern focuses on the proliferation of US-style hamburger outlets, not on the proliferation of Turkish, Greek and Lebanese kebab houses, or French, Italian, Indian and Chinese restaurants. The productivity of US cultural influences are very quickly forgotten – for example, the appropriation of its practices by modernist artists (as Brecht and Grosz), the impact of Hollywood cinema on the Nouvelle Vague, the New German Cinema, or on Italian film-makers like Sergio Leone or, as has recently been claimed, Gianni Amelio.

The shift in film and television production (though as indicated above, a shift that is far from total), from an artisanal mode of production where products are strongly marked by an authorial signature, whether that of director or scriptwriter, to series production in which it hardly makes sense to ask who is the author of *Dallas* or *Coronation Street*, is customarily deplored as a particularly insidious form of cultural imperialism. Yet this seems to me no more cultural imperialism than the adoption in Britain of the electrical engineering manufacturing techniques of Halske and Siemens, Pascalian mathematics or the astronomical theories of Copernicus and Galileo. US television series production techniques have dominated television in Britain since the 60s, co-existing with (some would claim making possible) British television's substantial dominance of the UK audience ratings. It is this format that broadcast media have uniquely made possible and conjured into existence.

Radio and television's creation of an audience consuming upwards of four hours of broadcasting per day and a 'flow' of programming makes possible and demands temporally extensive continuous fictions in a way that neither the newspapers nor the cinema did. Cultural forms like *Coronation Street* and *Dr Who* have endured in the UK for more than twenty years. What literary or dramatic precedents are there for narratives that exist without closure for such duration? It is this shift in programme form, the demand from audiences for choice *and* high budget productions, that has created an international market-place for products like *Dallas*, although US producers, though paramount in this international market-place, are not the only players. A condition of consistent success in the international market is the production of product appealing to international tastes and with a national content confined to the internationally current stereotypes of individual national histories and formations. Thus British television presents to the world a costumed image of Britain as a rigidly but harmoniously hierarchized class society: *Brideshead Revisited, The Six Wives of Henry VIII, Upstairs, Downstairs;* Japan the shogun and samurai pasts; Italy *The Borgias. Dallas, Dynasty, Hotel* and *Flamingo Road* represent the United States to international television viewers in contemporary melodrama in which the values of capitalist business and the family are presented both positively and negatively. But so popular are serial melodramas generally on British TV, that in May 1983, *Dallas* came only eleventh in the 50 highest audiences of the month, beaten by sundry episodes of the ITV serials *Coronation Street* and *Crossroads*. (Of the 50, 24 were watching domestic melodramas, of which 22 were of British and 2 of US origin.)

None the less, screening American programming is an attractive option for British broadcasters. By doing so, programmes with high production budgets acquired at low cost will tend to attract and retain audiences at a lower cost per 1000 viewers than will domestically produced material. To establish relative production and acquisition costs of the programming is extremely difficult. The industry is a remarkably secretive one and both sellers and buyers are reluctant to reveal the costs of transactions. To these difficulties should be added those of fluctuating sterling/dollar rates and significant and rapid changes in production costs. (Grieve, Horner cite a 60 per cent rise in cost per episode of *Lou Grant* between 1977 and 1981 [1984, p. 94].) Both factors mean that the figures that follow should be treated with some caution. However, they are figures around which there is significant convergence from a variety of sources, industry journals, consultants' reports, or my interviews (mostly off the record) with industry sources.

In 1983 *Variety* (14 September 1983, p. 40) estimated the UK costs per hour of TV programming as follows: ITV £40,000; BBC £30,000; Channel 4 £25,000; bought-in programmes £2,000. In the next month the same paper (*Variety*, 5 October 1983, pp. 56, 57, 70, 71) estimated the production fee per episode of US TV series as follows: *Dynasty* $850,000; *Hotel* $700,000; *Dallas* $850,000; *Falcon Crest* $750,000; *Knots Landing* $650,000; *St Elsewhere* $750,000 (i.e., for an hour of product). A year earlier *TV World* (July 1982, p. 46) estimated the following world prices for US sales of half hour TV series: Belgium $1000–1500; France $8500–10,000; Italy $4000–4200; Netherlands $1900–2000; Spain $1400–1900; UK $9000–10,000; West Germany $8500–18,000.

However, *Broadcasting* points out that half hours are:

considerably cheaper . . .less than 50% of what it costs . . . to license a full hour episode . . . the reasons half hours are considerably less expensive . . . than full hours are numerous but heading the list is that video tape is used . . . Another factor that contributes to the less expensive half hour show is that they are usually produced on permanent sets in studios and do not require the elaborate location shooting and special effects often required by full hour dramas. (*Broadcasting*, 22 October 1984, p. 70).

The *TV World* figures for exhibition prices are likely to be less reliable than *Variety's* for production prices, but even as ballpark estimates it can be seen that for, say, an episode of *Dynasty* costing $850,000 a TV channel in the UK paid about $20,000, and the Netherlands $4000.

In 1985 *Variety* reported that the BBC had been acquiring *Dallas* for $43,000 per episode and that unprecedented competition between the BBC and the British commercial company Thames led the BBC to bid $47,500 per episode for the rival – and successful – bidder to secure the series for $60,000 per episode. *Variety* noted that 'this may be a record for a series import in the British market' (*Variety*, 23 January 1985, p. 1). Programming costs per 1000 viewers for the BBC showing *Dallas* in a May 1983 screening attracting 12.7 million viewers at a cost per episode estimated at $43,000 would then have been $3.39. If we calculate the cost per 1000 of the highest-rated British programme transmitted by the BBC in May 1983, *That's Life* , screened to 12.6 million viewers at *Variety's* figure of £30,000 or $47,000 per hour it will have a cost per 1000 viewers that is higher than the cost of *Dallas*, i.e., $3.70 per 1000. The economic benefits of showing *Dallas* hardly need underlining.

With a more successful US programme than *Dallas* benefits are even higher. In 1984, the *Financial Times* estimated the cost to the BBC of the eight-hour US mini-series *The Thorn Birds* as £600,000. The last episode's screening attracted an audience of 15.75 million viewers (then the BBC's biggest audience for more than two years, though still well below peak audiences for *Coronation Street*, a serial that has run on ITV for 25 years). The *Financial Times* hypothesized the costs of the BBC originating *The Thorn Birds* at a minimum of £2 million (*Financial Times*, 1 February 1984, p. 19). However, if we believe those commentators who suggest that the BBC's screening of *The Thorn Birds* was the provocation that led the government to establish the Peacock Committee to review BBC funding, the costs of *The Thorn Birds* may have been very high indeed.

British TV is required to exhibit 84.5 per cent British/EEC productions and has developed a successful production strategy for British and international markets. Thames Television produces 950 hours of programming annually at a cost of £30,000,000 (*Variety*, 27 April 1983), i.e., at an average cost per hour of approximately £31,600, of which an unspecified number of hours produced revenues from foreign sales of £18,000,000 (of which £9 million were US sales and £2.5 million Australian). *The Sunday Times* (5 February, 1984, p. 51) estimates revenues from US sales of $20,000 per hour for British producers, i.e., there are grounds for belief that British producers are able to sell an hour of television into the US market at about the same price that US producers sell an hour of television into the British market. I have been unable to confirm this supposition since US commercial stations and distributors have been unwilling to reveal the acquisition costs to US television stations of British programming (for example, of *The Benny Hill Show*, cited as yielding 'the biggest grosses of any overseas production in the USA' (*TV World*, October 1985, p. 52). Nor are audience ratings in the public domain in the United States. However, interviews with a senior executive in Mobil Oil (the sponsor of *Masterpiece Theatre* on PBS) and senior figures in PBS and the Corporation for Public Broadcasting have enabled me to establish acquisition costs of programming for *Masterpiece Theatre* and ratings for representative screenings.

Masterpiece Theatre acquires its programmes principally from the UK and to a lesser extent from other anglophone producers such as Ireland and Australia. A June 1983 screening (chosen as close as possible to the May 1983 screening of *Dallas* already discussed) of an episode of the BBC drama *Sons and Lovers* achieved a share of 4.2 per cent of the US national audience (reached by 273 PBS stations offering *Masterpiece Theatre*) or 3.5 million households, each of which is estimated to have a prime-time viewing population of 1.7 people. Therefore 5,950,000 Americans watched an episode of *Sons and Lovers* (after at least three previous episodes had been transmitted and an audience for the series built). If we assume an acquisition cost of $100,000 per hour for *Sons and Lovers* (at the low end of the $100,000/200,000 per hour range of acquisition costs cited for *Masterpiece Theatre*) we find a cost per 1000 viewers of $16.8. Compared to the BBC's cost per 1000 viewers of $3.39 for *Dallas*, *Masterpiece Theatre*'s British programming looks expensive. Though the cost of acquisition by Mobil is, of course, less than the cost of production of a comparable production *ab initio*.

Other evidence suggests that a price of $100,000 per hour for quality drama for the US market is plausible. The Canadian

Broadcasting Corporation sold its most successful drama series *Empire Inc.* to Metromedia for US commercial syndication for $500,000 plus a percentage of revenue for three two-hour programmes (re-edited from the original six one-hour episodes sold to the BBC for $25,000 per hour). However, it is clear that although British producers are more successful than any others at securing US sales (and are second only to the US in sales to third countries), they are still hampered by the small size of the British home market compared to that of the US domestic market. Their success is conditional, I suggest, on the restriction of non-EEC entrants to the UK market to 14 per cent of programme hours transmitted. British producers are also disadvantaged in that while British and European audiences are very receptive to US programming, US audiences are less receptive to European product. Much of Thames TV's revenue from foreign sales comes from format sales rather than directly from programme sales. The US *Three's Company* was developed from Thames' *Man about the House*. In 1984 *Variety* (25 January 1984, p. 43) estimated that US syndication sales on the project had realized $150,000,000, of which Thames took 12.5 per cent ($19,000,000). In contrast the *Benny Hill* shows sold directly to the US in the same version as shown in the UK annually realise $15,000,000 in US markets.

A very strong incentive has existed for British commercial contractors to maximize revenues from foreign programme sales. Until 1986 the excess profits tax levied on profits originating from UK revenues did not apply to profits originating from overseas. As the National Economic Research Associates stated to the Peacock Committee: '*The optimal tax strategy would be to shift revenues to overseas sales while costs are allocated to national programming*' (National Economic Research Associates (NERA), 1985, p. 31). In 1982/3 the commercial contractor with the highest advertising revenue (Thames Television) was able to escape levy completely following the strategy described by NERA. Now the government is to modify the levy arrangements by reducing levy on UK profits to 45 per cent of profits exceeding £800,000 and applying a 22.5 per cent levy on overseas profits. But it remains to be seen whether the Inland Revenue and the IBA will be able to exact levy either from UK-based companies such as Zenith Films (wholly owned by Central Television but not licenced by the IBA and conducted as an 'at arm's length' business with no evident connection to Central's franchise to transmit programmes and sell television advertising time in the English Midlands); to extraterritorial companies such as Thames' joint venture in California, Grand Central Productions; or to sales of intellectual property, such as format rights, that have no direct connection to the franchised activities of an ITV company.

The strength of the US market and its resistance to colonization by foreign information goods is the foundation of the success of US producers in world markets. But there are interesting signs that the comparative advantage long enjoyed by US audio-visual media producers may be ending. The major strength of the US producers has been their ability to recoup their production costs – even costs of $850,000 per hour – from US sales. This ability is in turn dependent on customers' – US television stations' – ability to pay such sums for programming. This ability is in turn conditional on the existence of a small number of exhibition channels – the networks – and their ability to command the lion's share of TV advertising revenues and recycle them (after taking profits and network costs) to producers. But now it seems that the dominance of the networks is waning. Independent broadcasters are increasingly challenging the networks and are – within the limits of FCC regulation – constituting themselves through common ownership and syndication of programming as challengers to the networks. Grieve, Horner project a trend in which the US network share continues to decline:

Table 7.3 Percentage share of viewing

	1975	1981	1986	1991
Network stations	84	75	67	56
Independent & public	16	22	22	23
Pay services	—	2	7	13
Non-pay cable services	—	1	3	7

Source: Grieve, Horner and Associates, 1981, p. 4.

If the attrition of the networks' share of audiences and revenues continues to be faster than growth in aggregate revenues then the revenue pool will be shared more evenly among a greater number of broadcasters with each commanding less resources than do the biggest current ones. The ability to pay for the production costs of an episode of, say, *Dallas* at an acquisition cost of

$750,000–800,000 for an initial screening and $65,000–70,000 for a second screening (*Broadcasting*, 22 October 1984, p. 70) will decline. But the ability of a greater number to pay intermediate prices for programming will rise. In this new regime, where very high cost programming may no longer be afforded and in which demand and ability to pay for low to mid-cost programming increases, there may well be increased opportunities for sales to the USA by foreign producers. Increase in US distribution capacity (through licensing of new terrestrial broadcasters and satellite and cable delivered pay television) and redistribution of advertising revenue among broadcasters are likely to diminish the comparative advantage of a strong home market resistant to foreign products long enjoyed by US film and TV producers. But there are also counter-indications to this scenario: the merger of one network, ABC, with one of the principal independent groups, Capital Cities Communications (*Philadelphia Inquirer*, 19 March 1985, p. 1) to form the US' largest broadcasting group suggests that other resolutions of this contradiction are possible.

Studying the trade in TV programming between the US and the UK shows that the media imperialism thesis is by no means clearly demonstrated. UK producers are able to sell to the US markets on considerably better terms than US producers are able to sell to the UK. The volume of trade between the US and UK in TV programming now favours the US but there are grounds for supposing that that balance may in the future become less unfavourable to the UK. This does not disprove the general thesis that media imperialism is practised by the United States, but it does suggest that the thesis demands more thorough demonstration than it customarily receives. The tasks for advocates of the thesis are not only to demonstrate (as I suspect could be done) that the US/UK trade is an exceptional one and may best be regarded – as does Tunstall (1977) – as the UK acting as a kind of cadet to the USA in the imperialism game. Other tasks include showing that an adverse balance of trade in one sector, cultural goods, correlates with a general economic, political or cultural subordination. As Ravault (1980) points out, this is not easy to do. Countries such as West Germany and Japan or the Nordic countries have all combined economic prosperity and political and cultural independence with high levels of importation of cultural goods from the anglophone block, notably the USA, UK and Australia. It would further require demonstration that consumption of US cultural goods produces the feared threat to cultural integrity and independence of consumers and a disadvantageous homogenization and 'Americanization' of audiences. Katz and Liebes's work (1986), among others, suggests that different audiences produce highly differentiated readings of *Dallas*. These appropriations of *Dallas* may, of course, though different, be equally 'bad' for audiences but here, too, there are some grounds for scepticism. Since the 1950s work of film theorists has established a convincing aesthetic and cultural case for Hollywood cinema of the 1940s, 50s and early 60s. Contemporary feminist film theory positively re-appropriates the despised melodramas and women's weepies of the American cinema. If it can be done for Universal films, why not for Lorimar television?

A number of Québécois writers have testifed to the positive influence of the US mass media in breaking the grip of 'La Grande Noirceur' in Quebec and the development of a modern secular society in francophone North America. Gilles Carle's recollection of his childhood may stand as emblematic of this testimony that not all transborder data flows are baleful indices of the rest of the world's subordination as periphery to the dominant central metropole of the United States:

> Our radio picked up Buffalo and Montreal, always together, never separate, so that the religious broadcasts always had a pleasant background of country and western music . . . We seven children would thus recite our rosaries at a gallop, learning that in Quebec the most contradictory dreams are possible. (Leach, 1984, p. 162)

I wish to acknowledge my debt to Philip Hayward for his assistance in preparing some of the statistical information which I have presented here and on which I have drawn for my analysis.

This chapter was first published in *Screen*, vol. 27, no. 3/4 (1986), and subsequently in C. Schneider and B. Wallis (eds.) *Global Television* (Cambridge: MIT Press, 1988).

References

Balio, T. (1976), *The American Film Industry* (Madison: University of Wisconsin Press).

Broadcasting Research Unit (1983), A Report from the Working Party on the New Technologies (London: Broadcasting Research Unit).

Commission of the European Communities (1984), *Television Without Frontiers*, Com (84) 300 final. Office for Official Publications of the European Communities. Luxembourg.

Dunkley, C. (1985), *TV Today and Tomorrow. Wall to Wall Dallas* (Harmondsworth: Penguin).

Gordon, D. (1976), 'Why the Movie Majors are Major', in Balio op. cit.

Grieve, Horner and Associates (Undated, probably 1981), *A Study of the United States Market for Television Programs*, Consultants' report (Toronto).

Guback, T. (1976), 'Hollywood's International Market', in Balio op. cit.

Hall, S. (1980), 'Encoding/Decoding', in S. Hall et al. (eds.) *Culture Media Language* (London: Hutchinson).

Katz, E., and Liebes, T. (1986), 'Mutual Aid in the Decoding of Dallas' in P. Drummond and R. Paterson (eds.) *Television in Transition* (London: British Film Institute).

Leach, J. (1984), 'The Sins of Gilles Carle', in S. Feldman (ed.) *Take Two* (Toronto: Irwin).

Lee, C. C. (1980), *Media Imperialism Reconsidered* (Beverly Hills: Sage).

Morley, D. (1980), *The Nationwide Audience*, (London: British Film Institute).

NERA (National Economic Research Associates) (1985), *Report to the Committee on Financing the BBC* The Peacock Committee (London: HMSO).

Ravault, R–J. (1980), 'De l'exploitation des despotes culturels' par les téléspectateurs', A. Mear (ed.) in *Recherches québécoises sur la télévision* (Montreal: Editions Albert Saint Martin).

Schiller, H. (1969), *Mass Communications and American Empire* (New York: A. M. Kelley).

Smith, A. (1980), *The Geopolitics of Information* (New York: Oxford University Press).

Tunstall, J. (1977), *The Media are American* (London: Constable).

Varis, T. (1974), 'The global traffic in television', in *Journal of Communication*, vol. 24, no. 1, Winter.

Chapter 8

Broadcasting and National Culture in Canada

Radio and TV piping American programmes into Canadian homes, have created mass taste on a continental basis. The Canadian response has been to force the burden of nationalism on to the new media. The CBC is hailed by the Committee on Broadcasting as the most important single instrument available for the development and maintenance of the unity of Canada; it is hardly surprising that the committee then finds CBC wanting. (Watkins, 1966, p. 297)

The contradictory and antagonistic relationship between Canada's political institutions (the Canadian state) and the internationalizing tendencies of the capitalist market is an enduring theme in Canadian history and Canadian studies. Nowhere more than in broadcasting has this perennial conflict been identified as both baleful and pervasive. In studies of international media relationships (and in the literature of media imperialism in particular) the Canadian case is frequently also taken as representative. Schiller's pathbreaking *Mass Communications and American Empire* cites Canada as a paradigm of media imperialism:

Canada's radio and television air waves are dominated by American programs. Many Canadians feel consequently, that much of the broadcasting they see and hear is not serving Canadian needs. (Schiller, 1969, p. 79)

Moreover Canada has also been taken to foreshadow anticipated developments in European broadcasting (see *inter alia* Collins, 1989; Juneau, 1984; Gerlach, 1988).

The Free Trade agreement between Canada and the United States (negotiated in 1987/8) exempted the 'cultural industries', including broadcasting, from its provisions. This exclusion testifies to both Canada's deep commitment to what it has termed 'cultural and communication sovereignty' and a very significant concession by the United States. For the USA is in (chronic) deficit in international trade; one of the few fields in which it enjoys a positive balance of trade is in cultural/information goods and services (the US surplus on films runs to approximately $1 billion annually). Canada–US relations in the field of the cultural industries are particularly important for both countries. Canada believes its national identity, sovereignty and continued existence are at stake, the United States has in question one of the few economic sectors in which its producers are internationally competitive. Conflicts of interest are apparent in most areas of international trade, but information trades, though becoming economically more important as the 'post-industrial' or information society develops, are peculiarly vexed. For not only do information markets exhibit in intensified form a general characteristic of capitalist markets, to expand as a division of labour takes place on the basis of comparative advantage, but information trades also put in question the continuing existence of the values, beliefs and identities of the trading partners.

Information has peculiar economic characteristics: it is not exhausted in consumption – a television programme once viewed remains available for consumption in another place and at another time. It has low marginal costs of reproduction (the first copy cost of a film includes the capital cost of studio premises and plant, labour costs as well as the film stock used in producing the first copy, but second and subsequent copy costs are little more than the costs of striking an extra print from a negative) and tends to return more than proportional increases in profit to producers as consumption rises and markets are extended. Information often has no physical mass – as for example when transmitted using radio waves – and even when in physical form such as a book or film is easily and cheaply transportable. Such characteristics mean information markets have a pronounced tendency to extend in time and space. Of course there are many factors that inhibit such market tendencies: distribution costs rise as markets expand, consumer resistance to products may become more significant as producer and consumer are further and further apart, and so on. A most significant obstacle to the extension of information markets has been the difference in language (and culture) of trading partners. *Le Monde*'s market hardly extends beyond the boundaries of francophone Europe for example. But the 49th Parallel has been surprisingly permeable and the French language has only slowed, but not blocked, the creation of 'continental' North American information markets. The 'threat' to Canada has come from the attractiveness of American products to Canadian consumers. Canadian state intervention in markets (whether to promote Canadian substitutes to foreign goods or through quotas to restrict consumer access to desired foreign products) has been justified on the grounds of maximizing the benefit to Canada as a whole at the expense of admitted loss of benefits by individuals or groups of consumers. For though aggregate welfare benefits may, in theory, be maximized by the operations of the invisible hand in the market, resulting welfare gains may be inequitably and unequally allocated. The beneficiary of a more efficient integrated continental market (and there is never unanimity that such a market will be optimally efficient) may be the United States rather than Canada. Thus market allocations (which in aggregate may indeed maximize wealth) may be resisted by individuals and communities in order to better serve their own and their community's interests even if aggregate welfare is thereby diminished. History is replete with examples of 'unequal' trading relationships, and the operations of unregulated international capitalist markets are often understood in Canada as promoting Canada's dependency on other more powerful actors in the world economy rather than serving Canada's authentic interests. Watkins for example argues that: 'the greatest potential for Canada as a national society may lie in a substantial rejection of the market economy' (Watkins, 1966, p. 299). Canada's nineteenth-century National Policy represented just such a rejection of the guidance afforded by the invisible hand and Canadian broadcasting policy has long been marked by similar considerations.

The incandescent controversies over the contemporary Free Trade agreement with the United States have turned in part on whether Canada is likely to be economically advantaged by Free Trade but also on non-economic questions of power and control. Krasner (1985) persuasively argues that there are many instances of states refusing economic development and auugmented wealth and economic efficiency in order to retain political power that would otherwise be lost. Canadian political intervention in markets, whether by federal or provincial governments, has been animated by concerns over retention of power even at the expense of diminished economic efficiency, as well as by concern over the economic disadvantaging of Canadian interests in free markets. In policy fields such as these there is a particular sensitivity when information is the product in question. Different criteria from those pertaining to trade in steel or shoes are applied to information trades. Information, it is believed, is so important to the formation of ideas and identity and to the political process that either no restrictions on its movement are justified (the free market of ideas, no prior restraint, First Amendment rights, free flow of information) or more restrictions on its circulation than on the movement of steel and shoes are justified (censorship, tendency to deprave and corrupt, national security, balanced flows, national identity and culture). Canada lies, and is not alone in doing so, in a contradictory position on such questions.

The Canadian state actively intervenes in information markets to promote production and consumption of certain information goods and services and to inhibit that of others. It inhibits information flows through measures such as content quotas for Canadian broadcasters, requiring commercial television to transmit Canadian programmes for half of their prime time schedule, and through censorship: there is no lawful access to pornography in Canada (Jarvie, 1987). It promotes the circulation of information by providing (through public sector bodies such as TV Ontario or the National Film Board or through subsidy to private sector producers via agencies such as Telefilm Canada) information goods and services which would not otherwise exist. But Canada is not Romania, its inhibitory reflexes are seldom exercised with oppressive diligence. For example, the 1968 Canadian Broadcasting Act (the legislation which currently governs broadcasting in Canada) defines in its third part a 'right to freedom of expression and the right of persons to receive programs'. Moreover the state's presence in information markets is small compared to that of the private sector. In spite of Hardin's description of Canada as a 'public enterprise economy' (Hardin, 1974) in information, as in most other areas of economic activity, Canada is overwhelmingly a capitalist economy.

In Canadian broadcasting the contradictions between the internationalizing tendencies of markets and the imperatives of national policy and institutions are particularly sharply defined. For radio waves do not respect frontiers; as the director of Canada's Radio Services stated in 1925, 'the aether disregards all boundaries' (cited in Peers, 1969, p. 13). This is a particularly troubling condition for on broadcasting, many Canadians (and others) assume, hangs Canada's continued existence as a sovereign state. Broadcasting is seen both to exemplify a distinctive and vital difference between Canada and the United States and to be the bearer of Canada's national culture, on which the continued survival of the Canadian state is assumed to depend. One of the central elements, Hardin argued, of Canadian national identity was its public broadcasting culture (Hardin, 1974). And indeed the 1968 Broadcasting Act (part 3a) defines broadcasting to be based on public property and as a 'single system':

> Broadcasting undertakings in Canada make use of radio frequencies that are public property and such undertakings constitute a single system, herein referred to as the Canadian broadcasting system, comprising public and private elements.

In which the public interest and the 'national broadcasting service' (that is CBC/Radio Canada) are paramount (part 3h).

> Where any conflict arises between the objectives of the national broadcasting service and the interests of the private element of the Canadian broadcasting system, it shall be resolved in the public interest but paramount consideration shall be given to objectives of the national broadcasting service.

The state and the public sector were invested with the leading role in Canadian broadcasting because of the 49th Parallel's permeability to radio and television broadcasting from the United States and in the belief that Canada's national existence and sovereignty were thereby threatened.

A central tenet of nationalist theory is that states are weak if there is an absence of fit between political institutions and national communities. States and nations are only secure when they are integrated and isomorphic. Nations are in turn conceived of as

groups defined by a shared ethnicity, belief system and language –
by, in short, a shared culture. Broadcasting now accounts for a large
proportion of individuals' cultural consumption; Canadians in 1984
watched 23.6 hours of television (Caplan and Sauvageau, 1986, p.
85) and listened to 19.9 hours of radio each week. If viewing and
listening includes (as it does in Canada) a high proportion of foreign
programmes then, it is assumed, national political sovereignty
is at risk. Canadians have long consumed a remarkably high
proportion of American broadcasts. Peers in his magnificent
history of broadcasting in Canada from 1920 to 1968 testifies to
the early establishment of this pattern of consumption:

> Nine tenths of the radio fans in this Dominion hear three or
> four times as many United States stations as Canadian. Few
> fans, no matter in what part of Canada they live, can regularly
> pick up more than three or four different Canadian stations;
> any fan with a good set can log a score of American stations.
> (Peers, 1969, p. 20)

A pattern which continues in the 1980s. English Canadian television viewers watch Canadian programmes only 29 per cent of
the time, though French Canadians view Canadian programmes
68 per cent of the time (Caplan and Sauvageau, 1986, p. 95).
Such long established consumption habits provide the principal
rationale for public regulation of commercial broadcasting and
for the continued maintenance of public sector broadcasters in
Canada. For it is assumed that without such provisions by the
Canadian state (to inhibit the flow of US programmes into Canada
and to provide a countervailing Canadian alternative) Canada
would be unable to maintain its sovereignty and would become
assimilated into a 'continental' political, cultural and economic
system in which it would become indistinguishable from the USA.
As Graham Spry, founder of the Canadian Radio League – later
the Broadcasting League – which successfully lobbied in the 1930s
for the establishment of the CBC, said: 'The choice is the state or
the United States.' Spry's views, though alas no longer vigorously
advanced by him in person, remain alive. The CBC's evidence
to the Federal Task Force on Broadcasting Policy in 1985 stated:
'At the very heart of our sovereignty is our culture. There can be
no political sovereignty without cultural sovereignty' (Canadian

Broadcasting Corporation, 1985, p. 9). Spry, the CBC and the Canadian state strategy for broadcasting have all assumed that deviations from a normative symmetry between the cultural and the political are aberrant, unstable and unsustainable. These are classically *nationalistic* assumptions. Nationalism is an ideology that is pervasively recognized as important. Underhill refers to it as the 'dominant twentieth century form of religion' (Underhill, 1986, p. xvi) and Minogue as 'the foremost ideology of the modern world' (Minogue, 1967, p. 8) but about which there is small consensus of judgement. Minogue contemptuously describes it as 'a political movement depending on a feeling of collective grievance against foreigners' (Minogue, 1967, p. 25) but it is more productively conceived, following Gellner, as 'the striving to make culture and polity congruent, to endow a culture with its own political roof' (Gellner, 1983, p. 43). That is, to make a nation politically sovereign. As Breuilly states, 'Nationalism is above and beyond all else about politics' (Breuilly, 1985, p. 1). But the political project of nationalism depends on the prior existence of a nation. That is on a community which shares common characteristics of ethnicity, religion, economic interest, physical location, history, culture and language which engender the 'natural and spontaneous solidarity that exists among members of a human group sharing a historical and cultural tradition' (Brunet, 1966, p. 47).

Canada fits few of the stipulative precepts of nationalism. Canadians are bound together by few of the characteristics customarily seen as proper to a nation. In nationalist terms a bilingual and multicultural 'nation' is a contradiction in terms. The French Canadian nationalist Tardivel pointed out that from the perspective of nationalism Canada is a 'beautiful theory but it is nothing but a theory' (cited in Cook, 1969, p. 151). And English Canada, though customarily conceived as one of Canada's 'two nations' although more or less sharing a language, has few of the other shared, integrating characteristics of a nation (whereas Quebec satisfies the nationalist prescriptions). Porter emphasizes the diverse nature of English Canada:

It is unlikely that any other society has resembled a huge demographic railway station as much as has the non-French part of Canada. (Porter, 1965, p. 33)

Yet Canada is a stable political unit even though it only weakly conforms to the nationalist model. It is not an old style, classic nation state but none the less survives successfully. This absence of fit between culture and polity, Canada's non-conformity to nationalist precepts, has deeply troubled Canadian intellectual and political elites, and 'nation-building' (for states create nations as well as nations states), not least in broadcasting, in order to rectify the anomalous absence of congruence between culture and polity in Canada has become established as a major political goal.

In television the troubling absence of congruence between polity and culture is very striking. Francophone viewers seldom watch English Canadian programmes and anglophone viewers even less watch French Canadian programmes. But both Canadian language communities consume much American broadcasting. The spectacular success in Quebec of the television drama series *Lance et Compte* (Radio Canada, 1986) was attended by derisory anglophone audiences for the series. Whether this is because the anglophone version was censored and the nudity evident in the original French version eliminated is not clear. In any event the difference in the two versions testifies to important cultural differences between the two communities: divided not only by language but also by degrees of tolerance of representation of sexual activity and sexual difference. The earlier drama series *Duplessis* (Radio Canada, 1977) attracted audiences of two million in Quebec (that is a quarter of the population and a considerably higher share of the TV audience) but when shown to English Canadians it achieved a derisory audience share of 4.5 per cent. Hétu and Renaud observe that CBC's *The Nature of Things*, a series produced for twenty-seven years and sold to thirty countries, has never been shown in Canada in French. They further point out in their analysis of magazine programmes that:

> L'information collective, celle qui crée une reconnaissance commune d'une realité commune, celle qui est à la base d'un sentiment d'appartenance et d'identification à une nation n'éxisterait donc qu'à travers onze émissions dont trois francophones ne rendent compte que du Québec et huit anglophones ne citant que le Canada anglais.

[Shared information, which creates a shared awareness of a common reality and which is the foundation of a sense of belonging and of national identity, existed only in eleven programmes. Of which three in French took account only of Quebec and eight in English represented only English Canada.] (Hétu and Renaud, 1987, p. 48)

In television at least the classic Canadian 'two solitudes' continue to prevail. Table 8.1 shows that in both Canadian language communities American television is widely consumed (given that 'foreign' and 'American' are virtually synonymous terms in this respect) amounting in English Canada to a majority of viewing time. Although the statistics shown in Table 8.1 refer to 1984, the condition they exemplify is long standing and stems from two factors: first the permeability of the 49th Parallel to radio waves and reception in Canada of trans-border spillover of American signals, now largely redistributed through Canadian owned and controlled satellite and cable systems; secondly the low cost and high attractiveness of American television programmes. Since the inception of radio broadcasting Canadians have received broadcasts from the United States. Most Canadians now have access, via cable or satellite, to five American broadcast channels (NBC, CBS, ABC, PBS and an independent broadcaster). Cable television in

Table 8.1 Percentages of anglophone and francophone broadcast and viewing time for types of Canadian and foreign programming, 1984

Broadcasting time					Viewing time			
Anglophone		Francophone			Anglophone		Francophone	
Can.	For.	Can.	For.		Can.	For.	Can.	For.
28	72	57	43	all programmes	29	71	68	23
46	54	99	1	news	89	11	100	0
52	48	78	22	public affairs	62	38	99	1
68	32	92	8	sports	71	29	96	4
2	98	10	90	drama	2	98	20	80
25	75	66	34	variety/ music/quiz	18	82	87	13

Source: Caplan and Sauvageau, 1986, p. 95.

Canada began in 1952 in London, Ontario (before CBC established Canada's first television services), as a relay system for US signals. In 1985 sixty four per cent of Canadian homes subscribed to cable TV which offers subscribers an average twenty seven signals (Hind Smith, 1985, p. 11).

Provision of American television via cable benefits the Canadian agents directly involved. The subscriber receives signals which are not available off-air for an average $64 per annum (though in some markets this average is substantially exceeded. In Toronto, for example, enhanced service, including pay channels, costs $43 per month.) The cable operator receives a product gratis which is then profitably sold: McFadyen, Hoskins and Gillen estimate an annual average rate of return to cable operators of 24 per cent (McFadyen, Hoskins and Gillen, 1980, p. 242). It is widely accepted that the success of Canadian cable operators depends on their ability to deliver American television to subscribers. See *inter alia* Caplan and Sauvageau's judgement: 'What cable television offered Canadians was essentially the three American commercial networks plus PBS. Known as "three plus one" this combination proved attractive' (Caplan and Sauvageau, 1986, p. 545). But there is less certainty as to whether the US broadcaster benefits. On one hand the US broadcaster does gain by acquiring a larger audience which may be profitably sold to advertisers (and the United States' public broadcaster, PBS, partly funded by viewer subscriptions, gains additional subscribers. For example PBS received via cable in Alberta has drawn over 40 per cent of its subscriptions from Canadian donors.) On the other hand, Americans have complained that Canadian redistribution of US signals for profit is a form of copyright theft or piracy. The Federal Communications Commission and the US Department of Commerce complained in 1985 to the Canadian Radio-Television and Telecommunications Commission (CRTC) about redistribution of US signals via a Canadian satellite. The FCC and DoC stated that re-transmission of US broadcasts had 'long been of serious US concern' and pointed out that the 1985 'Shamrock Summit' between the Canadian Prime Minister Brian Mulroney and then United States' President Ronald Reagan had resolved on 'cooperation to protect intellectual property rights' which were being infringed by Canadian cable and satellite enterprises (Caplan and Sauvageau, 1986, p. 654–5).

Canadian viewers' access to American programmes is not wholly dependent on access to American signals. The programme schedules of Canadian broadcasters are replete with US programmes. For Canadian broadcasters can best maximize audiences at lowest cost by scheduling American programmes. A single episode of a representative US teleseries, *Dallas*, costs $850,000 to produce (*Variety*, 5 October 1983). A US television network acquiring *Dallas* for first screening pays in the region of $750,000 for a broadcast licence. The producers of *Dallas* are able to secure another $65,000 in the US second run (syndication) television market (*Broadcast*, 22 October 1984). Producers of programmes such as *Dallas* are able therefore to amortize nearly all (and often all) their high production costs in the US domestic market. However *Dallas* is not destroyed in consumption in the US market and remains available for export sale, its producers requiring only to recoup the marginal cost of an extra film print or videotape and the costs of marketing and distribution for profit to accrue from such sales. Products such as *Dallas* have proven very popular with television audiences outside the USA and sales are readily secured. Broadcasters thereby acquire a programme likely to be attractive to audiences at considerably less than the cost of producing a domestic substitute. For example, at $43,000 per episode (*Variety*, 23 January 1985) the BBC pays more for *Dallas* than for any other US teleseries (and more than ITV for its US acquisitions): the normal cost of acquisition of half-hour US programmes for UK exhibition ranges between $1,200 and $14,000. At prices ranging per half-hour from $15,000 to $20,000 US (*Variety*, 17 April 1985), Canadian broadcasters pay more than UK broadcasters for US product, in part because they compete against each other for 'hot' products, whereas the BBC and ITV/Channel 4 in the UK have an understanding not to bid against each other. But even at $43,000 per episode *Dallas* is very cheap in relation both to its production costs and to the cost of substitute UK or Canadian production. The nearest Canadian equivalent to *Dallas*, CBC's six part series *Empire Inc* cost $5.8 million Canadian (Auditor General, 1984, p. 34). That is $483,000 per half hour. The financial incentives to scheduling imported rather than home-produced programming are obvious. As McFadyen, Hoskins and Gillen state:

An extra hour a day of prime-time Canadian programming adds $4.4m to $6.8m to a television station's expenses. As

their expenses, on average, are \$5.6m a year this represents
about a doubling of their expenses. It is scarcely surprising
that Canadian television broadcasters are reluctant to invest in
Canadian programming. (McFadyen, Hoskins and Gillen, 1980,
p. 159)

However it is important to stress that although there are formidable
economic benefits to broadcasters, whether private or public, of
scheduling imported – usually US – programming, these benefits
cannot be realized unless the foreign programming acquired is
attractive to audiences.

The Canadian state has intervened in the broadcasting market
in three ways: one, public sector supply of goods undersupplied (or
inefficiently supplied) by the market; two, regulation of the private
sector to compel commercial organizations to provide services they
otherwise would not, the stick; and three, subsidy to encourage or
make possible private sector production of goods that otherwise
would be undersupplied, the carrot. The rationale for such policies
has been the assumption that programme offer is imperfectly
matched to demand and that an unsatisfied demand for Canadian
programming exists which is, and will remain, unsatisfied by the
broadcasting market. The federal agencies principally responsible
for each of these strategies of intervention are the CBC/Radio
Canada, the CRTC and Téléfilm Canada. These bodies are echoed
at the provincial level by, for example, Access Alberta, Quebec's
Radio Québec, Régie de la Cinéma et du Vidéo and the Régie
des services publics and by Ontario's subsidy and favourable tax
treatment of film and television programme production and TV
Ontario. Table 8.2 shows that three federal agencies of public
broadcasting, regulation and subsidy (Téléfilm Canada, the CBC,
the CRTC) account for the lion's share of federal government
expenditure on culture, for 69.2 per cent.

Such has been the character of Canadian broadcasting: the
market delivering American programming (whether by American
broadcasters in trans-border spillover and relayed by cable or
by Canadian broadcasters because of its relative cheapness and
attractiveness to Canadian audiences) and the Canadian state
devoting considerable resources to the Canadianization of its
broadcasting environment. Although Canada has existed as a
stable political unit throughout seventy years of broadcasting, the

Table 8.2 Canadian Federal budget estimates for expenditure on culture ($m), 1984/5

Arts & Culture	90.4
Canada Council	69.6
Canadian Arts Center	14.8
CBC	895.7
CFDC (Telefilm Canada)	54.8
CRTC	25.5
National Film Board	62.5
National Library	29.8
National Museums	69.5
Public Archives	39.4
Social Sciences and Humanities Research Council (SSHRC)	56.9
Total	1409.4

Source: Cinema Canada, no. 126, January 1986, p. 9 (figures as source).

absence of correspondence between polity and culture, inherent in Canadian audiences' consumption of United States' broadcasting, has consistently been seen as unsustainable and dangerous. A symptom of the attention given to this matter is the number of government committees and commissions charged with recommending initiatives in broadcasting policy. Between 1928 and 1978 there were thirteen policy commissions and five revisions of the Broadcasting Act. Initiatives since 1978 have included the Applebaum-Hébert report (1982), the policy reviews (DoC 1983a, 1983b, 1984) of the Liberal government (which commissioned Applebaum and Hébert's *Report of the Federal Cultural Policy Review Committee*) and the Auditor General's (1984) report on the CBC. The Progressive Conservatives have continued in like vein, with the Mulroney government establishing a 'Task Force on Broadcasting Policy' in 1985. The Caplan-Sauvageau Report (as the Task Force's report is usually known) appeared a year and a half later in 1986.

The Task Force's analysis and recommendations are consistent with the long established primacy in official rhetoric ceded to the CBC and to regulation in order to compensate for the market's failure to 'safeguard enrich and strengthen' Canadian identity and culture. The Caplan-Sauvageau Report stated that its 'first priority is to make the broadcasting system serve Canadian culture' (Caplan and Sauvageau, 1986, p. 41). Its recommendations were to strengthen the CBC, to regulate broadcasting more stringently and to establish 'a new network or two of an overwhelmingly Canadian kind' (a satellite to cable TV Canada channel and probably a CBC all-news channel) in order to compensate for the perceived continuing failure of the broadcasting market. (Caplan and Sauvageau's proposals are succinctly presented in an article/interview in *Broadcast* with Dr Gerald Caplan (*Broadcast*, 16 October 1987, p. 26–78).) The TV Canada channel, the Task Force's major proposal, was to be funded by a compulsory levy on cable subscribers and programmed, in the main, by public sector producers, the National Film Board, the CBC, the provincial public broadcasters such as TV Ontario, and French language programming from Canadian public sources and from TV5 (the international francophone channel principally programmed by the European francophone states). The Task Force declined to follow the path blazed in the early 1980s by the Applebaum-Hébert Committee (1982) which broke with tradition and followed fashionable world trends by flirting with market mechanisms. However, though more recent in its appearance than Applebaum-Hébert, it seems likely that Caplan-Sauvageau will remain as a monument to a long tradition in Canadian broadcasting policy rather than as a guide to government actions. Rather the new path blazed by Applebaum-Hébert (which recommended a move towards market allocations and made a powerful critique of the state's agencies) and consolidated by the Liberal government of the early eighties is likely to be followed rather than the return to 'the good old things' advocated by Caplan-Sauvageau. The Task Force's recommendations have been ignored and Flora MacDonald, when Minister of Communications, stated that Caplan-Sauvageau, though 731 pages long, is 'not the last word' in broadcasting policy. Certainly the government's cuts in the CBC's budget, its refusal to authorize TV Canada and to initiate a stricter regulatory regime suggest that the fate of the Caplan-Sauvageau Report will be to gather dust rather than to animate policy.

Broadcasting policy in Canada in the 1980s has oscillated between adherence to the nationalist policy of compensation for perceived market failure (regulation, state enterprises) and an embrace of the market because of a perceived failure of the state agencies and initiatives. Overall it has been characterized by a shift away from the use of public sector bodies and regulation towards subsidy and market mechanisms. The Canadian loss of faith in the state as an agency superior to the market is of course not a wholly Canadian phenomenon. There are powerful winds in the sails of the argosies of deregulation and the market across the world. Examples include France's sale of its first television channel to the private sector, West Germany's introduction of commercial TV, the FCC's 'deregulation' of communications in the USA (memorialized in the remark of the FCC chairman Mark Fowler that television is simply a 'toaster with pictures'), and the proposals of the UK government to sell television franchises and radio frequencies. But this global change in the direction of the wind is particularly controversial in Canada because of the long held nationalist belief in the importance of a shared culture (and a culture differentiated from that of other states and nations) as a condition of political stability and sovereignty. Conservative governments in Canada have formerly been as well disposed to public broadcasting as have Liberals (indeed Canada's Radio Broadcasting Act, first establishing a public sector broadcaster and regulator in Canada, was passed by a Conservative government in 1932 one week after tabling of the report it had commissioned from the Special Committee on Radio Broadcasting).

In 1980 the Liberals, the party of government in Canada for all but nine months of the twenty one years preceding 1984, established a Federal Cultural Policy Review Committee: the so-called Applebert Committee – named after its co-chairmen Louis Applebaum and Jacques Hébert – which reported in 1982. The government produced three major audio-visual policy documents: *Towards a New National Broadcasting Policy* (1983), *Building for the Future, Towards a Distinctive CBC* (1983) and *The National Film and Video Policy* (1984). These developments articulated three major new themes: the substitution of the carrot for the stick (financial inducements to achieve desired ends rather than regulation to prevent undesired outcomes and the substitution of a market for an administered regime), a critique of the public sector (including proposals such that Canada's goals would in future be sought through a fostering of private sector initiatives rather than public sector institutions), and subordination of cultural to industrial/economic priorities.

The Applebaum-Hébert report concedes the force of the dominant Canadian view that the market imperfectly allocates

resources· to the cultural sector. But argues that although a
condition of market failure *does* obtain where culture is concerned
the market may still be a less worse system of resource allocation
than others. It should therefore not be rejected as an instrument
of cultural policy. For, the Committee argued, market failure is
neither a phenomenon peculiar to Canada (and therefore requiring
uniquely Canadian solutions) nor is market failure confined to the
cultural sector. Cultural markets fail pervasively, the Committee
argued, because:

> The market cannot reflect . . . lasting benefits. To the writer,
> the composer, the painter or the scholar, the market presents
> a demand that reflects only the benefit to his or her own
> generation. Yet each generation must not only preserve and
> pass on all that is significant in its own cultural inheritance, but
> most also add to that stock new elements of its own creation,
> for which the demand of its own time may be small but from
> which large future benefits may flow. In a sense then it is the
> crucial function of the patron of culture – whether a Medici or
> a Canada Council – to serve as agent on behalf of the future.
> (Applebaum and Hébert, 1982, p. 65)

Although this is a powerful argument it does not account for the
production of culture in the past on the basis of its present rather
than future value. The work of many cultural producers was sold
as a commodity, both church and state were (and remain) patrons
of cultural producers, and are able to realize the benefits from art
works over a period longer than an individual lifetime. But, as
the report goes on to argue, recognition of market failure and
a compensatory role for the state does not resolve the problem
of resource allocation. Market failure is a condition in which the
market is unable to allocate resources satisfactorily. It is not a
condition in which another agency will, of necessity, do better.
Patrons, whether Medici, the Roman Catholic Church or the
Canada Council, have to decide which among several activities (for
which contemporary demand is small but which may realize future
benefits) is to be supported. Culture is but one possible claimant
to resources on grounds of market failure: scientific research,
education, pollution control or infrastructure construction are also
contenders for resources and, like culture, may not yield sufficient

benefits in quick time to secure funding from the market. And, as Applebert observes, two further problems remain:

> How much is needed to remedy these failures? And where should the additional resources be directed? The market is in fact the only mechanism available for measuring demand in terms that can be translated into quantity of resources and when the market fails we can only guess at the scale of the remedies required. (Applebaum and Hébert, 1982, p. 66)

Applebert was highly critical of the state's record in the cultural sector. For Applebert, the CBC and National Film Board, free of the disciplines of the market, were wasteful and sclerotic, and had become the fief of insiders who were unresponsive to changed circumstances and protective of their privileged position. Because of the deficiencies of the state's custody and the difficulties of establishing satisfactory administered systems, Applebert judged that, in spite of market failure, the market is likely to be superior to the state as a resource allocator in the cultural field. The Applebert Committee opened the shooting season on the CBC thus:

> The Committee fully endorses the criticism heard during our public hearing that CBC television is not sufficiently open to Canadian creative talent and, more importantly, that it does not foster the growth of talent sufficiently . . . the result is a hardening of creative arteries and protection of the institutional status quo. The CBC is that type of over-protected operation. It is not a monopolist, but the fact that it receives so much of its gross income from Parliament effectively shields it and its employees from having to respond to changed circumstances. (Applebaum and Hébert, 1982, pp. 276–7)

More of the same was dished out to the other sacred cow of the public sector, the National Film Board:

> The Board's output of new work no longer represents a significant film experience for the Canadian public. Its short films are seldom shown in Canadian theatres because owners do not believe these films have audience appeal. Nor are current NFB productions a staple of either television programming or even the curricula of educational institutions in Canada. The NFB's displacement

from centre stage has occurred for a number of reasons, of which institutional inertia is not the least important . . . The NFB's share of the federal government's resources for film cannot be justified if judged by the cultural benefits Canadians now receive from the NFB. (Applebaum and Hébert, 1982, pp. 263–4)

The Committee's negative judgement on the CBC was echoed by a report on the CBC by the Auditor General of Canada which stated:

> The Corporation had not developed systems and procedures to enable the radio and TV plant managers to calculate the annual production capacity of plants and match available resources with demand. Excess or under-capacity was not identified for individual plants or for the Corporation as a whole. Operational programming and capital decisions were made without such information. CBC plants did not have systems for measuring the unproductive time of technicians. Incremental budgeting practices, staffing for peak work loads, the failure to use load levelling and the lack of information on standby and idle time all suggested that there would be a surplus of available technician time. Information on utilization of studios, rehearsal rooms and videotape recorders was also not used or not produced. Weaknesses were noted in material management practices and policies and procedures to ensure economy and efficiency were required in connection with storage in television plants and for maintenance of equipment. (Auditor General, 1984, para. 3.9)

Neither the general difficulty of separating overhead and incremental costs nor the peculiar problems of working in an industry whose prime resource, according to Al Johnson the past president of CBC, is 'genius' (interview with the author March 1985) explain or justify the conditions identified by the Applebaum Hébert Committee and by the Auditor General. The report continues in like vein:

> The Head Office financial management function did not fully play its control and service role of developing corporate financial policies . . . Financial information and cost accounting systems do not yet provide useful reliable consistent and timely

information . . . Despite its importance to the Corporation the management of human resources has been weak. (Auditor General, 1984, paras 3.10 and 3.11)

Because market failure has customarily been assumed (thus necessitating and legitimizing regulation and public sector agencies), the problems that attend non-market, administered allocations had, before the eighties, seldom been recognized in Canadian broadcasting policy. Applebaum and Hébert and the Auditor General point to the ossification that develops in such non-market systems and in the institutions they spawn.

Brimelow (1986) makes the case in more general (and vigorous) terms. He argues that a 'new class' has developed in Canada which uses its political power in order to capture state organizations and resources for its own rather than the public's interest. This manoeuvre, whereby an elite 'captures' public sector institutions and resources, is performed under cover of a nationalist rhetoric of market failure. Brimelow's is a controversial thesis but repays attention. Hardin (1985) makes similar arguments and contends that the state regulation of broadcasting in Canada institutionalized elite prerogatives under a rhetoric of Canadianization. Hardin's critique focuses on broadcasting regulation and on the CRTC (rather than on the public bodies which exercised the Auditor General and Applebaum-Hébert), and not, as did Brimelow's on a many-tentacled and pervasive Ottawa-centred new class. Voices such as these are new to the broadcasting policy discourse in Canada. The old voices (as we hear in Caplan-Sauvageau) are far from stilled. Indeed Applebaum and Hébert's critique was itself the occasion for vituperative criticism by *inter alios* Crean (1983) and Gathercole (1983).

The critique of public sector institutions and state allocations for ossification, clientism and elite capture have opened the way for a developing new understanding of Canadian broadcasting's dynamics and for attention to the role of elites in Canadian broadcasting. Elite capture is perhaps as important a cause of Canadian television audiences' consumption of American programming as is market failure and American market power. For broadcasting displays a highly imperfect signalling system between consumers and producers. Whether financed by advertising or subscription in a market or by state budgets or licence fees in a public service mode, final consumers of broadcasting have few means through which to signal the direction and intensity of their preferences. There are three important channels through which feedback, however attenuated, circulates: audience research; consumers' letters and telephone calls to broadcasters; and comment and criticism in the press. All three channels relay messages of uncertain reliability and representativeness. Audience research is the least unreliable of the available indicators. But its characteristic product, ratings, indicates at best, aggregate consumption and what, among available alternatives, audiences prefer. Ratings do not reveal either what characteristics audiences dislike in the programmes they avoid or what they like in the programmes they consume. Nor do ratings reveal whether alternative unoffered programme choices would be preferred by audiences rather than those which were actually available and watched. Such signals as broadcasters do receive on the important matter of programme construction and content principally come from other broadcasters (whether over a drink or in the prize-givings judged by their peers, the Genies, Emmys, Logies, or BAFTA awards) and from critics who tend to be members of the same cultural and metropolitan elites as are broadcasters themselves.

Given such problems it is surprising how little Canadian research exists on Canadian television audiences' attitudes. Moreover although audience behaviour is better documented there are still major lacunae in the material available in the public domain. The main quantitative research, that of the Bureau of Broadcast Measurement (BBM) is confidential to its clients. The Caplan-Sauvageau report is representative in that it devotes 47 out of its 731 pages to a chapter entitled 'Programs and Audiences' in which there is a wealth of information on programme offer but little on actual consumption beyond an account of temporal shifts in viewing behaviour and tabulations of viewing by programme category, national origin and type of transmitting station. The ratings (which describe audience behaviour) reflect a pervasive consumption of US television (whether delivered by US or Canadian broadcasters), however ratings reflect only a response to programme *offer* which may not correspond to audience *demand*.

A customary interpretation of ratings in Canada would be to identify audience consumption of American programming (particularly of drama, an area where it is overwhelming) as indicating a preference for such material. Indeed that is broadly how Canadian commercial broadcasters interpret the ratings. Consequently they schedule American drama to the extent permitted by the CRTC's Canadian content regulations. A quirk of another CRTC regulation (the simultaneous substitution rule, which requires Canadian cable operators to substitute a Canadian station's signal for a US signal when both stations are simultaneously transmitting the same programme) gives Canadian broadcasters an incentive to mimic the schedule of US television broadcasters. But nationalist policy makers and broadcasters do not so interpret the ratings. For them ratings signals are signs of market failure which require compensatory action by the state to remedy the market's undersupply of Canadian programming.

The paucity of information in the public domain prohibits us from confidently drawing conclusions, but a number of studies suggest that Canadian television audiences' consumption of non-Canadian programmes reflects not, as Caplan–Sauvageau and the nationalist orthodoxy state, undersupply of Canadian programming, but active preference for American programming. That is, audience studies show not that the market is failing but rather that it is responding to authentic audience preferences. Other sources include Hothi (1981), Goldfarb (1983), Canada/Québec (1985) and Harrison, Young, Pesonan and Newell (1986).

Hothi cites a 1977 study commissioned by the CRTC which states that 'American programs are considered to be better than Canadian programs in a ratio of three to one' (Hothi, 1981, p. 22). Canada/Québec – an interesting study which both exemplifies the flirtation between the newly elected Mulroney federal administration and the then soon to be defeated Parti Québécois government, and stands as one of a few Canadian audience studies based on interviews, and which thus researches audience attitudes rather than simply monitoring consumption – suggests a similar positive evaluation of American *vis-à-vis* Canadian programming:

Pour la majorité des participants la télévision francophone est une télévision qui présente la pauvreté et râbache les oreilles avec la misère québecoise (*Bonheur d'Occasion, Maria Chapdelaine, Entre Chien et Loup*). C'est une télévision axée sur le passé (*Le Parc des Braves, Le Temps d'Une Paix*). C'est une télévision centrée sur le noyau familial, témoignant d'une dynamique sociale restreinte et non d'horizons ouverts sur le monde. Enfin, c'est une télévision viellissante. Au début de la télévision, c'était des jeunes artistes et créateurs; ceux-ci sont devenus vieux et se répètent. Il faudrait renouveler le bassin de vedettes, d'animateurs et de créateurs.

[French television, for most respondents, is a television which irritates the eyes and ears with its insistent presentation of deprivation and Quebecois wretchedness. (As in *Bonheur d'Occasion*, *Maria Chapdelaine*, *Entre Chien et Loup*.) It's a television concerned with the past (*Le Parc des Braves*, *Le Temps d'Une Paix*). It's an introverted television testifying to a straightjacketed social dynamic and is not open to the rest of the world. In the end it's an obsolete television. At the inception of television there were young artists and producers, these have now aged and become stuck in their ways. It's necessary to renew the talent pool of stars, producers and artists.]

A l'opposé, la télévision américaine apparaît comme une télévision véhiculant la richesse (*Dallas*, *Hotel*, *Dynasty*) le rêve et l'éspoir (*The Price is Right*). On la dit axée sur le futur: 'Les horizons sont ouverts' et on lui donne la charactéristique de pensée positive.

[On the other hand American television was perceived as the bearer of abundance (*Dallas*, *Hotel*, *Dynasty*), of dreams and of hope (*The Price is Right*). Respondents said it was future orientated 'The horizons are open' and attributed an optimism to American television.] (Canada/Québec, 1985, p. 47)

The most recent relevant study, that authored by Harrison, Young, Pesonan and Newell (1986), cited as HYPN, was commissioned by the Caplan Sauvageau Task Force but was mentioned only once in the 731 pages of the Task Force's report. HYPN's findings directly contradict those of the Task Force and challenge an axiom of Canadian broadcasting policy: that underconsumption of Canadian programming is due to underprovision of Canadian programming. Rather than supporting the policy recommended by the Task Force (increasing the supply of Canadian programmes) the analyses of HYPN and of Canada/Québec suggest rather that the content of Canadian programmes is less pleasing to audiences than is that of American programmes. Similarly HYPN found that availability of a greater variety of timing options – delivering a greater variety of Canadian programming – led to a reduction in consumption of Canadian programming. That is audiences discriminated *against* Canadian programming.

> The ongoing decision by Women 18+ to view or not to view Canadian programming is not a function of Canadian programming availability . . . The more TV system options available to women the less time women spend with Canadian programming and this dynamic takes place in the face of the fact that a greater variety of Canadian programs are available to women with greater TV system viewing options. (HYPN, 1986, p. 38)

HYPN considered three categories of viewer of which women over the age of eighteen were the biggest users of television. This class of viewer was a good proxy for other classes. Although men over the age of eighteen consumed less television than women in the same age group, men exhibited similar consumption patterns (although they did consume more Canadian programming than did women because of their greater viewing of live sport, much of which is Canadian). HYPN's finding that increased availability of Canadian programming does not produce greater consumption of Canadian programming is important. For it suggests that there is no unsatisfied demand for Canadian programming among the Canadian television audience and thus that Canadian broadcasting policy is based on a misrecognition of reality.

The HYPN findings which I have highlighted should be treated with caution. HYPN's study is but one interpretation of a snapshot of audience behaviour, but it suggests that more research should be done to explore the hypothesis that Canadian audiences are not dissatisfied with the television programming offer (albeit overwhelmingly non-Canadian) available to them in Canada. There are other findings in HYPN's study which challenge central assumptions in nationalist broadcasting policy. Notably that 'there are significant numbers of women who avoid Canadian programming', (HYPN, 1986, p. 41). They also find that in Ontario (HYPN, 1986, pp. 35–6) the most watched television system is the US commercial system (in all other provinces it is the Canadian commercial networks CTV or TVA that have the largest viewing share). Given Ontario's 'overconsumption' of US television one would expect to find (were the suppositions of nationalists about the influence of television viewing on national identity and consciousness well founded) that Ontario would be the most 'continental' in its attitudes of the Canadian provinces. Whereas, to take but one recent and highly significant indicator, opposition to free trade has been stronger in Ontario than in any other province.

There are reasons for scepticism about how far patterns of television consumption indicate popular preferences and values. There is little explicit public dissatisfaction with Canadian public sector broadcasting. Canadians still watch substantial quantities of Canadian television even though most of their viewing is of American television (Starowicz [1984] estimates that 66 per cent of programmes offered to Canadian audiences are American and that 75 per cent of Canadian viewing hours are of American programmes) and they continue to give public assent to a high-profile Canadian nationalism. However, there are grounds for doubt as to whether the main rationale for state intervention in the broadcasting market in Canada is soundly based. HYPN suggests thaat Canadian programmes are not undersupplied, and the conclusion could plausibly be drawn from the Harrison, Young, Pesonan and Newell study that it is the *kind* of Canadian programming – not the quantity – that is the problem. That different rather than more Canadian television is required to win Canadian audiences for Canadian programming.

The continued existence of Canada as a sovereign state, despite it having little television programming shared by the two national communities and much viewing time devoted to foreign programmes, suggests that the nationalist axiom that political sovereignty and stability depend on cultural and communication sovereignty is misconceived. Undesirable consequences flow from these twin misconceptions.

> Radio and television have been used or misused in a largely futile attempt to foster nationalism, with a consequent failure to exploit adequately the potential of public ownership of the media to offset commercialism and provide free education. (Watkins, 1966, p. 295)

For Watkins the privileging of a nationalist vocation for Canadian broadcasting has been at the expense of its public service vocation. Public service broadcasting is conceived to address and serve a variety of 'publics'. Its pluralistic and minoritarian aims are hard to reconcile with a nationalist and majoritarian project for broadcasting. For a national service must achieve a mass audience in order to knit the nation together into its 'imagined community' (Anderson, 1983). Canadian audiences obdurately consume less Canadian programming than they are offered. The comparative economic advantage of US producers enjoying the world's largest market is undoubtedly an important factor in Americans' success in the production of television programming which is consistently attractive to Canadian (and international) audiences. But so too may be the textual, cultural characteristics of US programmes. There is, according to Hoskins and Mirus, a low cultural discount attaching to American television programmes. By cultural discount they mean that

> a particular program rooted in one culture, and thus attractive in that environment will have a diminished appeal elsewhere as viewers find it difficult to identify with the style, values and behavioral patterns of the material in question. (Hoskins and Mirus, 1987, p. 23)

A major factor in cultural discount is language (the lowest international discount factor attaches to the English language). But language is far from the only factor which contributes to cultural discount. For example, Quebec viewers watch more English language programming than they watch French language programming from metropolitan France, in spite of the factor of linguistic discount. It is possible (though 'proof' would require a comprehensive and inventive research programme) that the Canadian cultural imperatives which stress the 'miserabilist' elements in Canada's cultural traditions (see *inter alia* Atwood, 1972; Feldman, 1984; Frye, 1971 and 1972; Houle, 1980; McGregor, 1985), and which nationalist cultural policies and national cultural elites demand be foregrounded in Canadian television programming, produce a 'diminished appeal'. This diminished appeal may discount the value of Canadian content to Canadian (and other) audiences. Certainly this is what the responses of those polled in Canada/Québec (1985) suggest.

The assumption that national identity and cultural identity are recto and verso of an integral whole leads to the demand, the insistence that a Canadian cultural identity be manifested to complement an established Canadian citizenship. Because most Canadians most of the time watch American rather than Canadian television, nationhood is at risk and a countervailing Canadian force has to be mobilized across the 'aether'. Because this Canadian content must be different from the threatening international/continental/American culture, it can have few of the characteristics of American content. One finds Canadian commentators, who constitute an important source of legitimacy for and feedback to broadcasters, such as Morris Wolfe (*Saturday Night's* TV critic for a decade) asserting an intrinsic qualitative difference between Canadian and American television.

> Much of the American television (and film) is about the American dream – the world as we wish it could be, a place in which goodness and reason prevail and things work out for the best. Much of Canadian television (and film) on the other hand, is about reality – the grey world as we actually find it. American television tells lies. (Wolfe, 1985, p. 78)

Wolfe's characterization corresponds closely to that identified by Quebecois TV viewers (who contrasted American television 'véhiculant la richesse, le rêve et l'éspoir' to Canadian television 'témoignant d'une dynamique sociale restreinte et non d'horizons ouverts sur le monde. Enfin c'est une télévision vieillissante' ([Canada/Québec, 1985, p. 47]), but whereas viewers' preference was for American television, Wolfe's is for Canadian. Here Wolfe is representative of Canada's cultural elite and articulates norms shared by many Canadian broadcasters but, it seems, by few viewers. The effect of reproduction of a Canadian culture different from American (because 'grey' and not a 'dream', negative not positive) is to amplify class stratification in the cultural consumption, the cultural universe, of Canadians. It *divides* rather than *unifies* the national community. The gap between the Canadian nationalist elites and the Canadian television audience seems to be such that a cultural discount applies to Canadian performance programming when consumed by Canadian audiences and that an effect of nationalist cultural policy has been to raise this discount factor.

The Caplan–Sauvageau Report runs counter both to the critique of the public sector, and to the market-based proposals of Applebaum-Hébert and the policies promulgated by government, both the former Liberal government in its last years and the current Conservative government. Its proposals express a long established conception of broadcasting in Canada as an exemplary instance of market failure, and the consequential necessity for the state and public sector to compensate for the failure of the market through regulation, public sector provision or subsidy to induce commercial interests to provide services that otherwise would not be available to Canadian viewers and listeners. But there are indications that Canadian television audiences discriminate against the Canadian programming which regulation and the public sector provides, and that the Canadian content and culture demanded by audiences is not undersupplied by the market. Or if there is an undersupply then the present compensatory Canadian offer does not satisfy audience requirements.

The assumption of market failure has led television producers in Canada to mistrust the signals sent by audiences via ratings and to read them not as an indicator of audience desire for popular entertainment, which could and should be met with Canadian programming of a more plebeian kind than is customarily offered by Canadian public broadcasters, but rather as an index of American market power which requires the compensatory assertion of an insistent Canadian difference. This reflex confirms a laager mentality – or garrison mentality as Frye put it (Frye, 1971 and 1972) – and blocks adaptation of programme offer to audience demand. However, the Canadian polity seems to have been little harmed either by its citizens' predilictions for United States broadcasting or the imperfect accommodation to popular taste of its own cultural elites. Canada seems better to exemplify the proposition that there is a weak rather than a strong linkage between citizenship (political identity), and television viewing (cultural identity). As Desaulniers argues in a provocative and persuasive article:

Il y a autant d'écart entre identité nationale et identité culturelle qu'entre système digital et système analogique, on est ou non Canadien, mais on peut être plus ou moins culturellement Canadien.

[There is no more equivalence between national identity and cultural identity than there is between a digital and an analogue system. One either is or is not a Canadian citizen, but one can be culturally Canadian in varying degrees.] (Desaulniers, 1987, p. 37)

In spite of the two solitudes of Canada's language communities, the pervasive consumption of American television by English Canadians (and to a significant and growing extent by francophones) and the amplification of class stratification by nationalist cultural principles and policies, the Canadian state has held together since the birth of broadcasting. It better exemplifies Trudeau's forward-looking vision of Canada as an anticipation of a new form of human society where citizenship and ethnic and cultural identity are decoupled than the classic nineteenth-century European nation-state struggling to come into being on which cultural nationalists insist. The nationalist precept that 'There can be no political sovereignty without cultural sovereignty' (CBC, 1985, p. 9), though insistently iterated in discussion of Canadian broadcasting, seems falsified rather than verified by the case of Canadian television.

Canada best exemplifies not an old style nation but an early instance of a new form of human society. Trudeau recognizes the existence of national communities but argues against the nationalist programme of political sovereignty for nations in a distinct nation-state: 'It is not the concept of nation that is retrograde: it is the idea that the nation must necessarily be sovereign' (Trudeau, 1968, p. 179). He proposes for Canada – and here he draws on a long continuity in Canadian political theory dating at least to Doutre's notion of 'universal nationality' (Doutre, 1864, p. 113) – a decoupling of nationality and political institutions. A programme opposed to the classic nationalist project of 'striving to make culture and polity congruent, to endow a culture with its own political roof and not more than one roof at that' (Gellner, 1983, p. 43). For Trudeau, Canada's future is the collaboration of Canadian national communities in order to establish not a nation-state but 'a truly pluralistic state, Canada could become the envied seat of a form of federalism that belongs to tomorrow's world. Better than the American melting pot' (Trudeau, 1968, pp. 178–9).

But the absent fit between Canadian polity and culture identified by Trudeau as an opportunity is more often seen as a problem. Canada is not a nation-state, it is as Ramsay Cook (1977) stated, 'a nationalist state'. There have been few Canadians who have followed Trudeau's lucid theory, a theory which recognizes the potency of nationalist sentiment in Canada but also advances a model for political organization to turn to advantage the elements in the Canadian condition which so trouble nationalists and which have been so important in the development of Canada's broadcasting policy. The absence of a unitary national culture in Canada has permitted remarkable political achievements such as the successful integration of a separate state (Newfoundland), and the 'third force' the 27 per cent of Canadians in 1981 not of 'charter race' origin, into the Canadian polity (*Canadian Encyclopaedia*, 1985, p. 595).

The immediate future for Canadian broadcasting is unclear. Caplan–Sauvageau was delivered to the Minister of Communications in September 1986. Of its recommendations only one, that the CBC operate an all-news channel, has been realized (Newsworld began on 31 July 1989). Otherwise little has happened. *De facto* therefore the policy is the status quo – a status quo defined in the long run by the nationalist project of Canadian broadcasting policy, in the middle run by the market orientated recommendations of Applebaum-Hébert and the Liberals' policies of the mid-1980s and in the short run by a disinclination of government to pursue the recommendations of its Task Force on Broadcasting Policy. The status quo is centred on an acceptance of Canadian viewers' consumption of American television whilst providing a Canadian alternative through the public sector (more disciplined by market organization and financial stringency than broadcasting would like) for those Canadians who wish to consume its products.

Canada is a state without a shared symbolic culture. It has rather a distinctive and shared 'anthropological' culture different from that of the rest of the North American continent, to draw on a distinction made by Raymond Williams in his

discussions of the category 'culture' which he names as 'one of
the two or three most complicated words in the English language'
(Williams, 1976, p.76). Canada has a welfare state, a more communitarian, less violent and less individualistic ethos compared to
that of the USA. Its cities (including the fourth and fifth biggest in
North America) are clearly more successful human communities
than are their equivalents in the USA. It is in this 'anthropological
culture' put and kept in place by systems of law and politics that
Canada's national culture and its distinctive differences from the
USA inhere, not in its symbolic culture. Canadians' use of their
leisure time to watch American television seems to have no
stronger link to their political actions, their assumptions of citizenship and national self-definitions than does their choice to eat
in Indian, Chinese, French rather than Canadian restaurants.

This chapter was first published in 1989 in the *British Journal
of Canadian Studies*, vol. 4, no. 1.

References

Anderson, B. (1983), *Imagined Communities: Reflections on the Origins
and Spread of Nationalism* (London: Verso).
Applebaum, L. and Hébert, J. (chairmen) (1982), *Report of the Federal
Cultural Policy Review Committee* (Ottawa: Ministry of Supply and
Services).
Atwood, M. (1972), *Survival* (Toronto: Anansi).
Auditor General (1984), *Comprehensive Audit of the CBC. Auditor
General's Report to the Board of Directors* (Ottawa: Canadian
Broadcasting Corporation).
Breuilly, J. (1985), *Nationalism and the State* (Manchester: Manchester
University Press).
Brimelow, P. (1986), *The Patriot Game* (Toronto: Key Porter Books).
Brunet, M. (1966), *The French Canadians' Search for a Fatherland*,
in P. Russell (ed.) *Nationalism in Canada* (Toronto: McGraw-
Hill).
Canada/Québec (1985), *L'Avenir de la Télévision Francophone* (Ottawa
and Quebec: Ministries of Communication Canada and Quebec).
——. (1985) *The Canadian Encyclopaedia* (Edmonton: Hurtig).
Canadian Broadcasting Corporation (CBC) (1985), *Let's Do It!* (Ottawa:
CBC).
Caplan, G. and Sauvageau, F. (chairmen) (1986), *Report of the Task
Force on Broadcasting Policy*, (Ottawa: Ministry of Supply and
Services).

Collins, R. (1989), 'Broadcasting – The United Kingdom and Europe in the 1990s', in *Rundfunk und Fernsehen* 1989, no. 2/3, Hamburg.

Cook, R. (1977) *The Maple Leaf for Ever* (Toronto: Copp Clark & Pitman).

Crean, S. (1983), 'Understanding Applebert' *in Canadian Forum*, vol. 18, no. 727, April.

Department of Communications (DOC) (1983a), *Building for the Future: Towards a Distinctive CBC* (Ottawa: DOC).

Department of Communications (DOC) (1983b), *Culture and Communication* (Ottawa: Ministry of Supply and Services).

Department of Communications (DOC) (1984), *The National Film and Video Policy* (Ottawa: DOC).

Desaulniers, J–P (1987), 'L'Histoire sans Leçon. What does Canada want?', in *TSF Magazine*, no. 4, Université du Québec à Montréal.

Doutre, G. (1864), 'The principle of nationalities' in R. Cook (ed.) *French Canadian Nationalism*, (1969) (Toronto: Macmillan).

Feldman, S. (1984), 'The silent subject in English Canadian film', in S. Feldman (ed.) *Take Two* (1984) (Toronto: Irwin).

Frye, N. (1971), *The Bush Garden* (Toronto: Anansi).

Frye, N. (1972) *Divisions on a Ground* (Toronto: Anansi).

Gathercole, S. (1983), 'Refusing the challenge', in *Canadian Forum*, vol. 17, no. 725, February.

Gellner, E. (1983), *Nations and Nationalism* (Oxford: Blackwell).

Gerlach, D. (1988), 'Broadcasting in Canada – A Yardstick for Europe?', in *European Broadcasting Union Review* (Programmes Administration Law) vol. 39, no. 1, January.

Goldfarb Consultants (1983), *The Culture of Canada* Research Report for the Department of Communications (Toronto).

Hardin, H. (1974), *A Nation Unaware* (Vancouver: J. Douglas).

Hardin, H. (1985), *Closed Circuits* (Vancouver: Douglas & McIntyre).

Harrison, Young, Pesonan and Newell Inc. (1986), *Canadian TV Viewing Habits. A Study of how Canadians use the Television Medium which concentrates on how Canadians view Canadian programming*. Mimeo (Ottawa: Department of Communications).

Hétu, A. M. and Renaud, C. (1987), *Le Magazine Télévise au Canada* (Montréal: Hétu Renaud Recherche).

Hind Smith, M. (1985), cited in *New Media Markets* vol. 3, no. 20, 5 October 1985.

Hoskins, C. and Mirus, R. (1987), *A Study of the Economic, Social and Cultural Reasons for the significant international popularity of television fiction produced in the United States*, Mimeo (Edmonton: University of Alberta).

Hothi, H. (1981), *Light and Heavy Viewers*, Mimeo (Ottawa: CRTC Research Directorate).

Houle, M. (1980), 'Some ideological and thematic aspects of the Quebecois cinema', in P. Verroneau and P. Handling (eds.) *Self Portrait. Essays on the Canadian and Quebec Cinema* (Ottawa: Canadian Film Institute).

Jarvie, I. (1987) 'The sociology of the pornography debate', in *Philosophy of the Social Sciences*, vol. 17, no. 2.

Juneau, P. (1984), 'Audience fragmentation and cultural erosion', in *European Broadcasting Union Review* (Programmes Administration Law), vol. 35, no. 2.

Krasner, S. (1985), *Structural Conflict* (Berkeley: University of California Press).

McFadyen, S., Hoskins, C. and Gillen, D. (1980), *Canadian Broadcasting, Market Structure and Economic Performance* (Montreal: Institute for Public Policy).

McGregor, G. (1985), *The Wacousta Syndrome* (Toronto: University of Toronto Press).

Minogue, K. (1967), *Nationalism* (London: Methuen).

Peers, F. (1969), *The Politics of Canadian Broadcasting 1920–51* (Toronto: University of Toronto Press).

Porter, J. (1965), *The Vertical Mosaic: An analysis of Social Class and Power in Canada* (Toronto: University of Toronto Press).

Schiller, H. (1969), *Mass Communications and American Empire* (New York: A. M. Kelley).

Starowicz, M. (1984), *Slow Dissolve*, address at University of Calgary. abbreviated version in *This Magazine*, vol. 19, no. 1, April 1985.

Tardivel, J-P. (1904), *Concerning the Geography of a Great, Unified Canada*, extract cited in R. Cook (ed.) *French Canadian Nationalism* (1969) (Toronto: Macmillan), p. 151.

Trudeau, P. (1968), *Federalism and the French Canadians* (New York: St Martins Press).

Underhill, F. (1966), 'Foreword', in P. Russell (ed.) *Nationalism in Canada* (Toronto: McGraw-Hill).

Watkins, M. (1966), 'Technology and Nationalism', in P. Russell (ed.) *Nationalism in Canada* (Toronto: McGraw-Hill).

Williams, R. (1976), *Keywords* (London: Fontana).

Wolfe, M. (1985), *Jolts. The TV Wasteland and the Canadian Oasis* (Toronto: Lorimer).

Chapter 9

National Culture: A Contradiction in Terms?

Introduction

More and more, television is becoming transnationalized under the influence of, sometimes complementary, sometimes contradictory, economic and political forces. Audiences' expectations are ratcheted up as they are exposed to high-budget productions, and accordingly higher and higher programme costs need to be amortized in larger and larger markets which increasingly cross national boundaries. Cost-spreading is achieved through programme sales, co-productions and all manner of inventive twinning, presale and co-venture agreements (see Collins, Garnham and Locksley, 1988; Porter, 1985; and Renaud and Litman, 1985). Economic pressures leading to transnationalization are matched by political pressures, including the efforts of European institutions, such as the European Commission, which seek greater economic and/or political integration between hitherto separate and sovereign states. The single European market in goods and services, including television (by 1992), is but one, albeit the most ambitious and comprehensive, integrative project (see *inter alia* Commission of the European Communities, 1984 and 1986; and Schwartz, 1985). The transnationalization of culture is both a cause and a consequence of the political and economic processes through which television is becoming transnationalized.

The notion 'national culture' is both a central organizing category constituting a point of reference and a centre of value in shaping economic and cultural production, and a mystifying category error. The term 'national culture' fits the reality of

television less and less though it has been an important goal in
the past and in a programmatic and 'scaled up' version promises
to do so in the future. For the creation of a single European
market (in at least some eyes) is conditional on the creation
of a 'European nation'; a political and economic unit which will
need its own shared culture to unify the new community *and*
separate it from others. Implicit already are the problems. In
the old Europe of nation-states there was (and is) no symmetry
between political institutions and nations. The submerged nations
of the Welsh, Basques, Corsicans, Wends and so on do not have
the states which nationalist ideology demands should be theirs.
Nor is the German nation organized in one state, or the Irish,
or the Jews, and so on. Just as Italy was for Metternich only a
geographical expression so, it seems, is Europe. But just as Italy
created its unity ('Italia felo de se'), so, it is believed, must Europe
on the lines of congruence between nation and state, between
'culture' and political institutions. Both advocates of a European
nation, such as Jacques Delors, and those who resist it, notably
Margaret Thatcher (who argues instead for a pragmatic association of sovereign nation states – see her notorious Bruges speech
[Thatcher, 1988]) ground their arguments in similar nationalist
precepts and demand that culture and political institutions should
be isomorphic. This ideology of nationalism centres on the belief
that there are 'natural' communities sharing ethnicity, location,
history, belief, language and economic interest that 'naturally'
should enjoy political sovereignty in a 'nation-state'. And that
nation-states are the building blocks only from which a stable
and productive political order can be made.

Nationalism is self-evidently a powerful force and a concept
with real analytical power. But it is not the only form in which
human sociality is expressed and realized, and is neither the sole
basis on which stable and legitimate political institutions can be
built nor necessarily the best conceptual basis for understanding the forces in play in the contemporary politics, culture
and economics of television. Although nationalist assumptions
underpin much discussion of the restratification of television
markets and the transnationalization of culture, I believe it
makes more sense to decouple polity from culture. To recognize
the undoubted existence of national communities and the power
of patriotic sentiment but not to accept that such communities

and sentiments are either necessary or optimal bases for political institutions, for states. I attempt to show in this paper that there is no necessary congruence between the frontiers of states and those of cultural communities, that the transnationalization of television is driven by both economic and political imperatives, that positive consequences can follow (and in the case of UK television have followed) from transnationalization and that the integrity and survival of states is less strongly linked to cultural sovereignty and the maintenance of national culture than is often supposed.

Co-Productions

Co-productions are becoming an increasingly important form of internationlization of the content of television programmes. Television Business International (TBI) (October 1989, pp. 127–34) lists 442 co-productions in progress, or recently completed, at October 1989. Co-productions reflect both economic and political pressures for collaboration in production between partners of different nationalities. Drama is the highest cost television programme form and therefore the point at which economic pressures (making for internationalization) are likely to be most acutely experienced. Yet although economic and political imperatives may occasion increasing numbers of international co-productions, a successful co-production must satisfy essentially cultural criteria; it must please different audiences which often have few assumptions and cultural reflexes in common. A successful co-production, a term used here to signify a variety of collaborative arrangements between production partners, whether or not a true co-production, with equivalent financial and creative contributions from partners, must be 'amphibious', that is, acceptable to audiences in different markets. Most co-productions are therefore between partners in a single international language community. Of the 82 UK co-productions listed by Television Business International, only 18 included non-anglophone partners and of these only 10 were with exclusively non-English-speaking partners. It is in such products that a successful 'internationalization' of content has become most evident. However, particularly in contemporary

Western Europe, there are increasingly strong countervailing political forces which promote co-productions between production partners drawn from distinct language communities and for audiences lacking competence in the language of the co-produced programme, who are also often resistant to subtitled and/or dubbed programmes. Successful co-productions are conditional on the programme subject being of interest to audiences in all the markets which the co-production partners serve. Opportunities to co-produce are limited when the aspirant partners come from, and are making products for, markets where target viewers have little historical experience and few cultural reference points in common. Anglophone audiences seem particularly resistant to consumption of programming made in languages other than English. United States viewers are notorious for their intolerance of exogenous programming, hence the extraordinarily low percentage of foreign programmes on US screens detected by Varis (1974 and 1984). Colin Leventhal, Programme Acquisitions Officer for Channel 4 (and now a member of the Channel 4 board) commented on UK audiences' resistance to dubbed and subtitled programmes, noting that women are particularly disinclined to watch subtitled programmes (interview by author, May 1986). Hence the long history of co-production between anglophone partners, and between the United Kingdom and the United States in particular. Such productions have characteristically had a mid-Atlantic character (for which they have often been anathematised). But co-productions with anglophone (and particularly American) partners are not the only manifestations of a pervasive internationalization of UK television production. The political imperative of Europeanization bears fruit in television co-productions and joint ventures. UK producers are vigorously breeding families of twins, triplets and sextuplets with European partners. The most striking example is Channel 4's participation in the European Co-production Association.

The European Co-production Association was established in 1985 as a vehicle for collaboration in production between European public broadcasters (see Ungureit, 1988). Channel 4 shared parentage of an interesting progeny; the *Eurocops* sextuplets which were made to increase the exposure of European television audiences to programming from other European producers.

Eurocops was the first of a series of planned drama initiatives (and was screened in 1988), in which Channel 4 (UK), RAI (Italy), ORF (Austria), ZDF (West Germany), Antenne 2 (France), SRG (Switzerland) and latterly RTVE (Spain) have collaborated. The first fruits of this transnational co-operation (in which the Austrian and Swiss partners commit half the resources committed by the larger countries and in consequence take half any revenues resulting from sales) are a series on the European Science research programme led by ZDF, a motor racing series led by RAI and the *Eurocops* sextuplets. Future projects on the French Revolution, Mozart's travels and Alexander the Great may more closely fit the 'European culture and tradition' desired by the parents for their offspring. The aims of the Production Association are:

> the long term making and exploiting of joint productions by the contracting partners, and especially long running drama series, in the television field. The programmes made by the production association are to deal with European subjects, to make known the European culture of the past, present and future and, last but not least, to contribute to the presentation and reinforcement of the artistic and production related infrastructure in European countries. (Ungureit, 1988, p. 17)

The Association committed £22.7 million to approximately 50 hours of programmes (*Financial Times* 17 March 1988, p. 2), an average budget of £450,000 per hour – high for drama production in Europe. (Ungureit states [p. 17] that a budget of ECU 70m was established for 100 hours of programming. His figures indicate a programme budget of £466,000 per hour, closely comparable to that indicated in the *Financial Times*). Even though Channel 4 contributed only one-fifth of this budget, its costs were high in relation to the channel's average cost of programming (in 1986 circa £24,000, rising in 1988 to £26,500, and declining in 1989 to £25,700 per hour) and to the cost of programming it acquires off the shelf. However though collaboration on *Eurocops* has successfully augmented the budget per hour of drama programming enjoyed by the co-production partners, assessment of the project's success must comprehend the response of viewers to the *Eurocops* (and other joint venture) programmes.

It is hard to make a sensible comparison between the reception of *Eurocops* programmes in different West European television markets. Programmes were shown on different days and at different times and against different alternative viewing possibilities in each of the six partners' markets. (And Swiss television did not screen the French episode of *Eurocops*.) Moreover, viewing figures in some markets are expressed in terms of ratings (the average percentage of all individuals with a television receiver who watched) and in terms of share (the proportion of viewers who watched) in others. However it is clear that fewer television viewers in the UK than in France or Italy watched *Eurocops*. The UK-produced episode 'Hunting the Squirrel' achieved a UK rating of 4 per cent, a French rating of 12.1 per cent, and an Italian share of 19.75 per cent. The French episode 'Rapt à Paris' ('Kidnapping in Paris') scored a UK rating of 4 per cent, a French rating of 11.1 per cent and an Italian share of 25.68 per cent. Figures for Switzerland, Germany and Austria are incomplete. The viewing figures (albeit incomplete and imperfectly comparable) may suggest that UK viewers are less disposed than are other European television viewers to watch television from other European producers, although the UK episode of *Eurocops* scored a lower UK rating than did the Austrian episode 'Die Bestie vom Bisamberg' ('The Beast of Bisamberg'). Perhaps UK viewing of *Eurocops* was shaped by audience response to Channel 4, perceived as a minority channel, so that even a UK cop drama achieved a low rating. However Ungureit (Deputy Director of Programmes for ZDF, the West German participant in the Production Association) states that the dramas made by the Association exemplify a generally contradictory relationship between the aspirations of the producers, to make 'European' programming, and those of the audience, to be entertained. He states:

> Common to all is the intention to stress European values; this primarily concerns the traditions of non-standardized, non-levelled narrative form. It is quite obvious that this contains material for conflict if popular programmes are to be made. (Ungureit, 1988, p. 20)

European Culture

In Western Europe (which of course includes the UK), there are strong political forces which are shaping the internationalization of television, of which *Eurocops* is but one manifestation. In the European Commission and the Council of Europe a transnational 'European Culture' is being promoted as a defensive response to the transnational culture which the television market-place is creating. The alarm voiced in the Community and Council can cynically be regarded as the result of manoeuvering by European producer-interests and cultural elites as their assured markets and hegemony are threatened by migration of European television audiences to competing television programming originating from exogenous suppliers. Such alarm is directly proportional to the attractiveness of the foreign offerings to audiences which formerly, during the long heyday of national broadcasting sovereignty, could be taken for granted. But whether or not one finally wishes to make such cynical judgements it is important to recognize that there is an alternative (non-exclusive) explanation for such nationalist concerns. Described by Minogue (1967, p. 8) as 'the foremost ideology of the modern world' nationalism is a belief that human societies should be organized in politically sovereign states populated by a nation, and not more than one nation. The nation in turn being defined as a spontaneous association of humans bound together by shared language, culture, ethnicity and beliefs. Nationalism is a theory that stipulates a normative congruence of political institutions, economic activity and cultural identity and experience. Without such congruence, nationalists tend to believe, communities are unstable and their members are denied their patrimony of feeling 'at home'. It is a belief which, as Gellner states, strives 'to make culture and polity congruent, to endow a culture with its own political roof and not more than one roof at that' (Gellner, 1983, p. 43). Clearly such notions are, and have long been, very powerful. But equally clearly many human societies have not been of this kind. But nationalism is an ideology under pressure as the world economy becomes more integrated and interdependent, and the economic self-sufficiency of nation-states (even the largest, most developed and powerful such as the USA) less easy to sustain. The decoupling of politics and economics, of political institutions (states) exerting authority more and more precariously over economic activity which increasingly escapes its grasp (transnational corporations, mobile factors of production, a world economy into which more and more communities are integrated and over which fewer and fewer can successfully exercise control) are familiar motifs of our daily news. As of course is the decoupling of politics and culture, of cultural production and consumption from the citizenship of its authors and audiences in international high culture. But the international circulation of Mozart, Poussin, Borges and Tolstoy troubles few. What is troubling is the internationalization of mass culture, the consequential imputed threat to national identity and the stability of the political institutions and systems which are assumed to rest on it. One sees therefore attempts to keep 'polity and culture' congruent. Political units are scaled up but require a scaled up culture to sustain them. The European Economic Community is a case in point. The more it flexes its political and economic muscles, the more it requires a cultural dimension to match its increasingly prevalent description of itself as the European Community: not a loose collaboration of sovereign states in a pragmatic economic association but more and more an approximation to a sovereign state (in which are numbered citizens of Réunion, French Guiana, Guadeloupe and Martinique as the French Presidential elections reminded us). Cultural unities are required to fit the new political unities.

What then is the European culture required to sustain European political institutions? And what place does UK television have within it? To take the last question first. The UK and Ireland are almost unique in Europe (with the exception of Portugal) in being junior partners in an international language community. France is the centre for 'La Francophonie', Italian speakers are concentrated in Italy and contiguous areas, German speakers in the adjacent two Germanies, Austria and Switzerland (with West Germany by far the largest polity of German speakers). Spain it is true is outnumbered in 'La Hispanidad' by Latin American Hispanics but, Mexico excepted, is the largest single community of Spanish speakers and the centre of Spanish culture. The culture of the anglophone European societies is unrepresentatively decentred from Europe and part of an international (principally North Atlantic) anglophone unity rather than a European one.

The imperial past also of course orientates the UK outside Europe not only in reactionary sentiment but also because a legacy of Empire was the establishment of legal and political systems akin to those of Britain. Firms were, and are, organized across the Empire and the ties of blood and friendship, though weakening as each generation passes, are still potent. Ireland has something of the same consanguinity binding it to the Eastern seaboard of the USA. This is an experience unlike that of the other European states and is reflected in Britain's television and its TV programme trades. The main trading partner for UK television is not Europe but North America (Department of Trade returns do not disaggregate Canada and the USA). Is this pattern of trade evidence that the UK is not a 'good European' or that the UK's way of being European is different from that of other European states? Is European culture unitary or pluralistic and contradictory? If the latter, then from the point of view of nationalist theory, the super nation, Europe, is in trouble, for its polity and culture are not congruent. Although the European Commission's audio-visual policy is based on the nationalist assumptions that policy and culture should be congruent and that without such congruence the Community cannot thrive. Such assumptions underpin the Commission's MEDIA (Mésures pour Encourager le Développement de l'Industrie de production audiovisuelle) programme.

The economic and cultural dimensions of communication cannot be separated. The gap between the proliferation of equipment and media and the stagnation of creative content production capacities is a major problem for the societies of Europe; it lays them open to domination by other powers

Table 9.1 UK receipts from and expenditure on TV programmes (£m) 1987

	EEC	Other W Europe	USA & Canada	Other developed countries	Rest of world	US & Can share (%)
Receipt	28	7	54	21	8	46
Expenditure	19	11	66	6	8	60

Source: British Business 23 September 1988.

with a better performance in the programming content industry. (Commission óf the European Communities, 1986, p. 4)

The best known of the Commission's policies for television, its 'Television Without Frontiers' proposal (Commission of the European Communities, 1984) was for an abolition of frontiers *within* Europe but a creation and strengthening of frontiers between Europe and the rest of the world. In response to Europe's fortification of its frontiers Carla Hills, the US Trade representative, visited Europe in September 1989 promising to 'take a crowbar' to Fortress Europe. Her particular concern was the reactivated EC initiative to establish television programme quotas on a Community wide basis which resulted in an agreement, 3 October 1989, to establish quotas only 'where practicable'. The subtle manoeuvring for and against this initiative is well described in the *Financial Times* (11 September 1989, pp. 2 and 4).

Europe's proactive production and quota initiatives exemplify the nationalist aspiration to make culture and polity congruent within a Greater Europe. Although there are intimidating difficulties in the path of such a project, for European culture is as often a culture which distinguishes European communities from each other as it is shared between them, and even elements common to European states are often also shared with non-European states. Moreover if language is (as nationalist theorists customarily suggest) at the core of culture then the European Community (let alone Europe as a whole) is unlikely, if Kedourie is right, to achieve a common culture.

> Language is not only a vehicle for rational propositions, it is the outer expression of an inner experience, the outcome of a particular history, the legacy of a distinctive tradition. (Kedourie, 1966, p. 62).

There are nine official community languages (not counting the languages of the submerged nations, such as Basque, Welsh, Corsican and Gaelic). The forces of history and tradition that bind nations together have, in the recent past, separated Europe through war. And though there is a loosely shared system of beliefs that binds Western Europe (the inheritance of Christianity, democratic political systems, scientific rationalism and capitalist economics) these are not the exclusive prerogative of Western Europe. And what will become of European culture should Turkey, an Islamic (albeit modernized and secularized) state, join the Community? In January 1988 the Government of France sponsored an international symposium on European Cultural Identity. One hundred European intellectuals (broadly defined and including representatives from the evidently European states of Congo and Canada) addressed the question via a book *Lettres d'Europe* authored by

> onze écrivains français partent, chacun dans un pays de l'Europe des douze, à la rencontre d'hommes de culture, écrivains, cinéastes, universitaires . . . pour leur demander leur perception de notre culture. [eleven French writers, one to each of the European Community member states, met cultural leaders, writers, film-makers, scholars . . . to enquire about their view of our shared culture].
> (Symposium Internationale sur l'Identité Culturelle Europeénne [SIICE], 1988, p. 4).

The sponsors of such initiatives must shift their historical perspectives back very far indeed to find shared European projects and identities unspoiled by the inconvenient outbreaks of mass slaughter that have been so important a part of European history since the Middle Ages. Indeed it is to the Middle Ages that the sponsors of European cultural identity turn as a positive force to set against the negative of America which they customarily invoke ('devons nous craindre la déferlante américaine?' [must we fear the American flood?] SIICE, 1988, p. 3). The MEDIA programme supports a television series on mediaeval pilgrimages. For the Middle Ages were the last moment in European history when horizontal stratifications were more important than vertical ones. When religious, political, military and cultural elites circulated freely across the continent sharing language, religion, ethnicity, in short the attributes of a nation. After the Middle Ages the European nation-states formed themselves on a vertical basis, through exacerbating differences with neighbours (war) and accentuating similarities within the national community by expulsion and suppression of minorities. A less brutal congruence between polity and culture is now enjoined for Europe and, it seems, rejected only by the UK.

Il éxiste en Europe un large concensus sur la necessité de soutenir la production audio visuelle . . . La multiplication des coproductions entre partenaires européens est certainement l'une des voies du développement de la création audiovisuelle en Europe . . . A ce stade, les Douze (a l'éxception de la Grande-Bretagne) ainsi que la Suisse et la Suède, sont prêts s'associer à ce mecanisme, qui ferait l'objet d'un accord signé dans le cadre du Conseil de l'Europe.

[A substantial consensus exists in Europe about the necessity to support audio-visual production . . . The growth of European co-productions is certainly one route towards development of European audio-visual production . . . the European Community states (Great Britain excepted) and Sweden and Switzerland are ready to support such an initiative, which will be the aim of an agreement signed under the auspices of the Council of Europe]. (SIICE, 1988, pp. 5 and 6)

The producer interests are clear: the UK's producers prefer to maintain their existing place in the international market on a more or less free trade basis. Those of the other partners are better served by a protected European audio-visual space and subsidy measures. But it is not only producer interests that are at stake, though these are often constituted as equivalent to the national interest. Are producer interests in the UK or elsewhere in Europe the same as those of consumers? Here the evidence is less certain. European audiences have shown a long standing and pervasive readiness to consume 'American' culture (a readiness not confined to the masses, the positive appropriation of US culture by the Nouvelle Vague, New German Cinema, Brecht, Grosz and so on are too easily forgotten) but there is also clear evidence of preferences being exercised in favour of indigenous production when this addresses the needs and interests, the culture, of the audience.

Cultural Discount

The cost/revenue pressures that lead to collaboration between producers in co-production, pre-sale and twinning agreements also lead to extensive purchasing of programming in the international marketplace. The dynamics of this international trade are well known and are based on the low marginal cost of reproduction of film and television programmes and the ability of producers in large and prosperous markets (notably the USA) to recoup costs in home markets. Television programmes, one instance of internationally traded information products, are marked by intrinsic characteristics which limit their international circulation. Language and, to a lesser extent, culture are the most important of these characteristics. Information, though a product with potentially very low marginal costs of production and indestructible in consumption (and therefore a product which returns more than proportional rises in profits as consumption increases thus giving producers powerful incentives to extend their markets geographically) is not universally consumable. Linguistic and cultural barriers limit the extension of markets for information in ways that markets for textiles, grains, steel and many manufactured products are not. In the economics of information markets there is a particularly sharp contradiction between the potentiality to profit from low marginal costs of production through extension of markets in time and space, and consumer resistance to products which are incomprehensible (because in an unknown language) or are 'culturally' unfamiliar and unwelcome. Producers therefore experience very strong incentives to make products which are as widely acceptable as possible. In so doing not all producers are equally advantaged. Works in English enjoy enormous advantages, for not only are anglophones the largest and the richest world language community – excluding non-market economies of which the Chinese and Russian linguistic communities are the most important – but English is the dominant second language of the world. The size and wealth of the anglophone market provides producers of English language information with a considerable comparative advantage *vis-à-vis* producers in other languages. But it is important to recognize that this is a *potential* advantage which may or may not be realizable. Not all anglophone producers will succeed, and producers in other languages are not necessarily doomed to fail. Within the anglophone TV drama market a fairly stable division of labour has taken place with US producers making high cost melodramas, Australia moderately budgeted soaps and British producers high budget costume drama. Success is neither inevitable nor permanent but the anglophone market is sufficiently large for such specialization to take place. Such opportunities are denied to producers in smaller and poorer language communities who are faced with competing against the anglophone products – the costs of which have usually been fully recouped in the English language market – which are available for profitable sale into other language markets at little more than marginal cost (see Collins, 1986; and Hoskins, Mirus and Rozeboom, 1989). Moreover anglophone consumers tend to be less inclined to consume non-English-language products than are non-anglophones to consume English-language products. Anglophones have had fewer reasons than the speakers of other languages to consume information produced outside their language community; in consequence they have generally acquired neither the ability nor the tolerance to consume non-English-language information. The intolerance of UK television viewers for dubbed and subtitled programmes, and the paucity of foreign television on US screens (estimated by Varis [1984, p. 146] to account for only 3 per cent of prime time programming) exemplify this chauvinism.

Language is not the only factor which conditions market structure and promotes, or inhibits, the circulation of information. Hoskins and Mirus (1988) have coined the useful term 'cultural discount' to refer to loss of attractiveness or usefulness that obtains when information is marketed to consumers to whose cultural experience it is alien. Clearly cultural discount will vary depending on the proximity of producers and consumers and obtains *within* as well as between states. Thus a cultural discount obtains when *Tutti Frutti* is consumed by UK television viewers unfamiliar with the topography of Glasgow, the accents of Central Scotland and the music of the sixties. And when viewers and producers are separated by social class, Richards cites the *World Film News* survey published in 1937 to suggest that a higher cultural discount applied between British working-class cinema audiences and British films than between those audiences and American films. That is the notionally national culture of Britain was weaker than the transnational culture which bound working-class British audiences into a North Atlantic culture rather than into an exclusively British national culture. Exhibitors in working-class areas, Richards argues, were on the whole satisfied with the more vigorous American films . . . [but] practically unanimous in regarding the majority of British films as unsuitable for their audiences. British films, one Scottish exhibitor writes, should rather be called English films in a particularly parochial sense; they are more foreign to his audience than the products of Hollywood, over 6000 miles away. (Richards, 1984, p. 24)

The continued attractiveness of American audio-visual works to UK audiences was amply demonstrated by the BBC's dramatic loss of audience to commercial television in the late 1950s. Commercial television not only showed North Amercian programming and used North American formats and performers, but had the vitality and vigour that the 1930s cinema exhibitors identified as an attraction of American films for their audiences. Analogous patterns of audience 'leakage' away from the national programming diet provided by the state public broadcaster to competing American (or, when not produced in the USA, American-type) programming can be seen elsewhere in Europe. Sepstrup reveals the piquant information that Danish cable subscribers watch West German television not for a German alternative to what was then Danmark's Radio single TV channel but for West German television's American programming (Sepstrup, 1985)! One of the outstanding achievements of US cinema and television has been to develop programming which reduces 'cultural discount'. (Of course there is also a market for information products which exhibit a high cultural discount. Markets exist for French films that are emphatically French, for Japanese cinema because its rhetoric and locations are strange and for *Tutti Frutti* and *Minder* because of, not in spite of, their distinctive and different urban and plebian markings.) Clearly anglophone producers do enjoy a potential comparative advantage (and US producers in particular are advantaged) over competitors because of the characteristics of the English language market. But such advantages are potential advantages, their realization depends on a number of factors, not least their style and content. And European audiences' taste for American programming suggests that cultural communities are constituted as often *horizontally*, across national boundaries, as they are constituted *vertically*, within national boundaries.

Americanization

Various attempts have been made to account for the international attractiveness of American film and television. Bordwell, Staiger and Thompson (1985) argue rightly that 'a distinct and homogeneous style has dominated American studio filmmaking' (p. 3). How and why this 'distinct and homogeneous style' developed, its relation to the economic structure of the mass entertainment industry, and the reasons for its attractiveness to audiences has become an important focus for the attention of scholars. (See *inter alia* Bordwell, Staiger and Thompson, 1985; Gledhill, 1987; Pryluck, 1986; Thompson, 1986.) Among the factors that have contributed to the success of American producers in realizing their potential advantage are the profit-maximizing orientation of American producers, which has necessitated attention to the pleasure and gratification of audiences. The variety of populations immersed in the melting pot of the United States gave US producers a kind of microcosm of the developed world's population as a home market and the experience and values of the USA have long had a magnetic appeal outside its territories. The USA is, after all, the first post-revolutionary society with formally defined political and legal rights far in advance of those obtaining in most of the remainder of the world. Tracing the nature, origins and limits of the long enduring international appeal of US TV and cinema demands far more attention than I can give it here. My purposes for gesturing towards the problem, however briefly, are threefold. First, to establish that American audio-visual media offer an appeal that has long cut *horizontally* across the world audience, engaging the attention and mobilizing the enthusiasm of popular audiences (and often binding them into cultural unities that are transnational and horizontal rather than national or vertical). Second, such restratifications of national cultural communities separates elite from mass or popular taste and threatens the cultural hegemony enjoyed by national cultural elites (a hegemony that paradoxically is often based on a privileged familiarity with a high culture no more national than the 'coca-cola' culture of the masses). And third, the United States film and television industries owe their dominance of world audio-visual trades not only to market power, the machinations of Will Hays and Jack Valenti and to the comparative advantage of working in the biggest and richest of the world's language communities but also to their invention of a cultural form that is the closest to transnational acceptability of any yet contrived. For example *Eurocops* was beaten in the ratings on Channel 4 by *Kate and Allie, Hill Street Blues* and *St Elsewhere*. As de Sola Pool put it:

> The Americanization of world culture so often commented on and deplored might be better described as the discovery of what world cultural tastes actually are. (de Sola Pool, 1975, p. 48)

New cultural forms restratify communities. Insiders whose 'cultural capital' is invested in the old have an interest in resisting such changes. Insiders are unlikely to innovate, and where barriers to new market entrants exist latent consumer demand may be left unsatisfied. The history of broadcasting in the UK is replete with examples of such a situation. The demand for popular entertainment which the monopoly BBC left unsatisfied led in the 1930s to the establishment of English language services from Radio Luxembourg and Radio Normandie which attracted, at times, one in two UK listeners. British broadcasting has been more subject to competitive pressures than have been other West European systems. It is too easily forgotten that the UK had the first competitive television system in Europe and the first financed (in part) by advertising. Within this system there was, at times, an extraordinarily fruitful synthesis between the popular and the elite, a conjunction which was particularly evident in the BBC during the late fifties and early sixties when it adapted its programming to win back the audiences it had lost to commercial television. Americanization was a powerful element in this process, not only in the programmes (*77 Sunset Strip*, *Dragnet*) and formats *Take Your Pick, The $64,000 Question*) which UK broadcasters, including the BBC, imported from North America, but in an adoption of 'American' working practices. These were marked by a division of labour in production which led to what, hyperbolically, could be called the death of the author. The personnel and professional orientation of UK broadcasters during television's 'Golden Age' of TV drama (which followed the doubling of channel capacity and introduction of competition in the 1950s) was similarly 'Americanized'.

The BBC purchased thirty-five dramas from the CBC in Canada and hired the executive producer behind them, Sydney Newman. Newman, and the dramas he had developed in Canada, were attractive to the BBC because it was facing pressures from commercial broadcasting that had been faced earlier by the Canadian public broadcaster CBC. The competition from ITV which faced the BBC had been foreshadowed in the CBC's struggle with trans-border spillover from US television. In the CBC's response the BBC found a model. The qualities of the CBC programmes (and the usefulness of their 'author') inhered in their having been made in the face of competition from the US networks and Newman's consummate ability to reconcile the imperatives of quality and popularity. Newman's legacy was complex but central to it was his orientation to the popular. His assumption was that:

> The cost of art in our kind of society has to be in relation to the number of people whose imagination it will excite. (Newman, 1974)

Such priorities were very different from those which prevailed in the BBC before it was exposed to competition. Val Gielgud, the head of BBC TV drama from 1949 to 1952, and the effective head of BBC radio drama since 1929, found the BBC's radio soap *Mrs Dale's Diary:*

> socially corrupting by its monstrous flattery of the ego of the 'common man' and soul destroying to the actors, authors and producers concerned. (Briggs, 1979, p. 699)

Two points follow from this account. First, the media culture of the UK is one that has long been synthetic and appropriational. Second, it has been horizontally stratified with a powerful connection between subordinate classes and consumption of 'American' (whether or not 'made in the USA') information products not to mention a well-established pattern of adoption of American production arrangements and organization of the labour process in spite of the disdain of dominant groups for American culture. This suggests that national culture is, if not a category error, at least a misleading concept if the dynamics of these processes are to be captured‚ and understood. But there are important qualifications to be entered. The patterns of synthesis and appropriation performed in 'British' culture are strongly inflected by language. London is much closer to New York and New Zealand than it is to Paris. And consumption of television is strongly skewed towards consumption of British programmes. It is seldom that US material (let alone other foreign programmes) rises above eighth or tenth in the ratings. In part this is a function of scheduling. When the BBC responded to Downing Street's panic over TV and violence and shifted *Miami Vice* out of prime time its ratings declined. *Per contra* the BBC's rescheduling of the Australian soap *Neighbours* produced an extraordinary improvement in its ratings. In the week ending 23 August 1987, *Neighbours* was 91st in the UK ratings (and the previous week was 96th). When rescheduled in January 1988 it rose in the week ending 10 January to 8th position in the UK ratings. Dutch television has similar features (see *inter alia* Ang, 1985; Bekkers, 1987; for perceptive overviews). In spite of increasing access to transnational television whether delivered by satellite or terrestrial transmissions Dutch audiences prefer programmes and services of Dutch origin:

> Anything made in the Netherlands is always very popular. Dutch products always draw more viewers than similar products from abroad. (Bekkers, 1987, p. 34)

The Canadian Case

It is outside Europe that eyes turn when invoking a future for European television. Numerous commentators have argued that Canada has anticipated the future of European television (see *inter alia* Juneau, 1984; Collins, 1982; and Gerlach, 1988 for gloomy prognoses about the Canadianization of European television). Canada is invoked to exemplify the threat of the United States and the baleful consequences that attend loss of communication sovereignty and the absence of congruence between culture and polity which, it is assumed, inevitably obtains when more foreign than domestic television is viewed. Anglophone Canadians watch foreign programmes for 71 per cent of viewing time, francophones 32 per cent (Caplan and

Sauvageau, 1986, p. 95). The Canadian Broadcasting Corporation (CBC) stated in its evidence to the Government of Canada Task Force on Broadcasting Policy (the Caplan/Sauvageau Committee which reported in 1986): 'There can be no political sovereignty without cultural sovereignty' (CBC, 1985, p. 9). Palpably there can be, as the case of Canada demonstrates. Since the inception of broadcasting in North America in 1920 (XWA in Montreal and KDKA in Pittsburgh began regular broadcasts within a month of each other) Canadians have consumed large quantities of American radio and television. Far more than either Canadian language community consumes of the programming of the other Canadian language group. And as Hétu and Renaud (1987) point out there is little 'amphibious' programming scheduled to both communities (still less that is extensively watched by both) or that represents each to the other. Yet Canada holds together remarkably well. There is no evidence that it is becoming a 51st State. Canada better represents a weak rather than a strong connection between television consumption and political identity and citizenship. But overwhelmingly the Canadian broadcasting policy discourse proceeds from the same nationalistic assumption as the European, that of the normative congruence of polity and culture. However there are persuasive voices that argue that Canada anticipates a new form of human community in which polity and culture are decoupled rather than an imperfect realization of an old style nation-state to which condition Canada must struggle to aspire. Trudeau argues that

> It is not the concept of *nation* that is retrograde; it is the idea that the nation must necessarily be sovereign. (Trudeau, 1968, p. 151)

Trudeau points to the potentially infinite regress possible in constituting political unities. If a political unity is only legitimate insofar as it contains no minorities who do not recognize themselves and their experience and worldview in the unit then there are, for Trudeau, no possibilities of coherence or stable states. Nationalism realized in a nation-state is for Trudeau simply a barbaric archaism which belongs to 'a transitional period in world history' (Trudeau, 1968, p. 177). His conception of Canada is of a new kind of human society in which the maximal social unit –

the state – enjoys both the freely given allegiance of its citizens and embraces citizens unified by none of the forces that have traditionally integrated national communities: language, culture, religion, geography or economic interest. Trudeau's vision is quite simply that of an idea, a conception that seizes the opportunity presented by the historical accident of Canada to maximize the potential latent in so plural a human society by maintaining it as a unity out of which a new kind of human society may be conjured, rather than – as the nationalists of Canada's two founding groups tend to do – attempting to return to the point of origin, unravel the precarious unity of Canada and call into existence separate nation-states based on identities of language, culture and religion. Trudeau argues that a divorce between the paired concepts and practices of culture and politics that nationalism has wedded is necessary in order to create stable and decent contemporary societies. And that Canada represents both the potentiality and the necessity for such a decoupling. If the two Canadian nations will abandon their desires to make polity and culture fit, to make Canada a nation-state in which citizenship and cultural identity are congruent, only then will and can Canada be a 'peaceable kingdom'.

> If the two will collaborate at the hub of a truly pluralistic state, Canada could become the envied seat of a form of federalism that belongs to tomorrow's world. Better than the American melting pot. (Trudeau, 1968, pp. 178–9)

Trudeau's theory makes better sense of the Canadian case than does old style nationalism. His is a model that could and should be appropriated by contemporary Europe. A European orientation towards the bad new things rather than the good old ones (as Brecht urged), exemplified in Trudeau's conception which decouples culture and politics, promises to avoid the absurd spectacle of a retreat to the Middle Ages for a coherent vision of European identity, the involution of European cultural industries eschewing American products and models because they are un-European (and popular), and the slowing of adaptation to and synthesis with the 'American' style and content valued by audiences and which had so fruitful an impact on British TV drama of the 60s, on the Nouvelle Vague and New German Cinema.

More important still, Trudeau reminds us that there are alternatives to a modern reiteration of the doctrine of *'Cuius regio eius religio'*, which, freely translated, means 'the religion of the ruler is the religion of the ruled' or politics and religion must match. Trudeau's arguments substitute culture for religion which in the Europe of the past produced a plethora of illiberal brutalities in the name of political order. The United States, with its decoupling of religion from state, demonstrated in the eighteenth century that stable political units could be created without the doctrine of *cuius regio eius religio*; Canada in the twentieth century that culture and politics can be similarly decoupled without political institutions crumbling. As Desaulniers pertinently observes 'in terms of nationality a person is either Canadian or not, but culturally one may be Canadian in varying degrees' (Desaulniers, 1987, p. 151). In both instances North America represented more developed forms of human society than the European equivalents. We would be foolish to return to the Middle Ages (urged on by the interests of European audio-visual producers who decline to adapt to the tastes of their audiences) in a culturally autarchic version of Festung Europa.

Conclusion

Variety reports interestingly on, of all things, a film festival in Baghdad where the *absence* of products aimed at an international market amplified, it argues, incomprehension, misrecognition and hostility between peoples and states:

> If what was seen at this festival is representative there is little hope we in the West soon will find in the productions of the Islamic world programs that can make those complex cultures better understood. Second, the entire event demonstrates again the cultural as well as the political isolation of Israel from the Middle East – a culture which more than half of its Jewish settlers once shared in their countries of origin and which might yet serve their children as some basis for dialog with their Arab neighbour. (*Variety*, 13 April 1988, p. 64)

To be sure, to end the oppression of the Palestinian nation by the Israeli nation dialogue and understanding will not be sufficient. But *Variety* has located an important example of a structural condition. Production and consolidation of national culture necessarily means discrimination in favour of endogenous and against exogenous elements. Production for the international market-place requires rather a mediation between endogenous and exogenous elements. Admittedly the mediation of the market is performed on very unequal terms and the membrane that separates cultures is often only one-way permeable, from the West to the East, from the North to the South, from anglophones to non-English speakers and from the United States to the rest of the world. But in some sense an integrated market does demand dialogue, synthesis and adaptation, the *representation* of a culture to another rather than to itself. Not necessarily a bad thing. To that extent the erosion of national cultures and televisions under market pressures which engender co-production is positive.

Within any field of cultural production and consumption the terms national and international, chauvinistic or cosmopolitan are sites for conflict between different social, political and economic interests to appropriate the honorific categories and to assign the derogatory ones to others. Within Britain (or England if it makes the argument more palatable to those not *primus inter pares* in the Union) as within Europe there is competition for hegemony and resources between different cultural traditions and between pluralistic and prescriptive notions of culture and identity. Given the illiberal consequences within Britain of asserting a normative national culture and identity (a notion which of course requires the most Nelsonian view of history) I see no reason to support such a notion within a wider European context. Particularly when (and this is where the UK view does become different from that of other Europeans and the horrible notions of national interest and national culture do unfortunately fall back into congruency) the economic interests of UK producers and the cultural tastes of UK consumers are not likely to be served by a normative conception of European identity which designates the UK's experience of a culture orientated outward from Europe as being less European than are the European cultures which are either involuted or orientated east of the Elbe rather than west of Rockall. Clearly different interests are at stake and both cultural and financial capital is at risk in these struggles over identity. But underlying the problem is a theoretical conception of a normative and necessary congruence between political, cultural and economic forces, a congruence that as the world economy, foreign travel, movement of populations and international information markets become more pervasive will become less and less sustainable. Culture – tradeable information consumed for pleasure – has a curious status here. Other forms of discourse have successfully been decoupled from politics. We no longer attribute nationality to scientific or mathematical ideas, do not persist with Newtonian rather than Leibnitzian logarithms because one is English and the other German. Nor, happily, do we discriminate against Jewish science. Why should we animate similar concepts when we deal with the products consumed in our leisure time? The transnationalization of culture is a process (always partial) of organization of individuals into horizontal rather than vertical communities. It is a phenomenon that the dominant nationalist optic misrecognizes. The social productivity of the process is contradictory but at least some of the time benevolent and is one which (and here an English man writes as perhaps others interpellated by other discourses might not) by and large UK producers and consumers have benefited. The UK is in that sense different from other Western European states, not less European but differently European. Whether different in kind or only in degree is a question for another time. It is paradoxical but true that in respect of television the UK's national interest (and though an apostate in respect of my views on Canada in the 70s I have not, yet, reneged on my 70s distrust of that category) is best served by internationalism. Its economic advantage is owed in part to language but also to the competitive pressures exerted – to their long term benefit – on its cultural industries by US competition. The seductions of the USA to which British audiences have long been exposed uninsulated by so heavy a 'cultural discount' as those of other European states forced UK cultural industries to 'Americanize' in order to sustain their hold on audiences and produce efficiently. In the long term this has been a healthy process and has fitted UK producers well for the international market-place of the 80s and 90s. The nationalist paradigm of congruence of polity and culture has outworn its time. More and more this 'good old thing' is waning in its potency and the 'bad new thing', the Trudeauesque vision of a decoupled polity and culture, waxing. In time *cuius regio eius culturo* will be as quaint an archaism as *cuius regio eius religio*.

References

Ang, I. (1985), 'The Battle Between Television and its Audiences' in P. Drummond and R. Paterson (eds) *Television in Transition* (London: BFI).

Bekkers, W. (1987), 'The Dutch Public Broadcasting Services in a Multichannel Landscape', *European Broadcasting Union Review* (Programmes Administration Law) vol. 38, no. 6, November.

Bordwell, D., Staiger, J. and Thompson, K. (1985), *The Classical Hollywood Cinema: Film Style and Mode of Production to 1960* (New York: Columbia University Press).

Briggs, A. (1979), *Sound and Vision* Vol. IV, *The History of Broadcasting in the United Kingdom* (4 vols) (Oxford: Oxford University Press).

CBC (Canadian Broadcasting Corporation) (1985), *Let's Do It* (Ottawa: CBC).

Caplan, G. and Sauvageau, F. (chairman) (1986), *Report of the Task Force on Broadcasting Policy* (Ottawa: Ministry of Supply and Services).

Collins, R. (1982), *Lessons for the Old Countries: Broadcasting and National Culture in Canada*, Canada House Lecture 15 (London: Canadian High Commission).

Collins, R. (1986), 'Wall to Wall Dallas. The US–UK Trade in Television', *Screen* vol. 27, no. 3/4, May–August.

Collins, R., Garnham, N. and Locksley, G. (1988), *The Economics of Television. The UK Case* (London: Sage).

Commission of the European Communities (1984), *Television Without Frontiers*, COM(84) 300 final (Luxembourg: Office for Official Publications of the European Communities).

Commission of the European Communities (1986), *Action Programme for the European Audiovisual Media Products Industry* COM(86) 255 final (Brussels: Office for Official Publications of the European Communities).

de Sola Pool, I. (1975), 'Direct broadcast satellites and cultural integrity', in *Society* 12 (September–October).

Desaulniers, J-P. (1987), 'What does Canada want? or L'histoire sans leçon', *Media Culture and Society* vol. 9, no. 2.

Gellner, E. (1983), *Nations and Nationalism* (Oxford: Basil Blackwell).

Gerlach, P. (1988), 'Broadcasting in Canada – a yardstick for Europe?', *European Broadcasting Union Review* (Programmes Administration Law) vol. 39, no. 1, January.

Gledhill, C. (ed.) (1987), *Home Is Where the Heart Is* (London: BFI).

Hétu, A. M. and Renaud, C. (1987), *Le Magazine Télévisé au Canada* Hétu Renaud Recherche (Montréal: Conseil en Contenu Media).

Hoskins, C. and Mirus, R. (1988), 'Reasons for the US Dominance of the international trade in television programmes', in *Media Culture and Society*, vol. 10, no. 4.

Hoskins, C., Mirus, R. and Rozeboom, W. (1989), 'US television programs in the international market: unfair pricing?', in *Journal of Communication*, vol. 39, no. 2, Spring.

Juneau, P. (1984), 'Audience fragmentation and cultural erosion', *European Broadcasting Union Review* (Programmes Administration Law), vol. 35, no. 2, March.

Kedourie, E. (1966), *Nationalism* (London: Hutchinson).

Minogue, K. (1967), *Nationalism* (London: Methuen).

Newman, S. (1974), interviewed in *Cinema Canada*, no. 15.

OECD (Organisation for Economic Co-operation and Development) (1986), *OECD Observer*, 141, July.

Porter, V. (1985), 'European co-productions: aesthetic and cultural implications', *Journal of Area Studies*, no. 12, Autumn.

Pryluck, C. (1986), 'Industrialisation of entertainment in the United States', in B. Austin (ed.) *Current Research in Film* vol. 2 (Norwood, NJ: Ablex).

Renaud, J-L. and Litman, B. (1985), 'Changing dynamics of the overseas marketplace for TV programming: the rise of international co-production', *Telecommunications Policy*, vol. 9, no. 3, September.

Richards, J. (1984), *The Age of the Dream Palace: Cinema and Society in Britain 1930–39* (London: Routledge & Kegan Paul).

Schwartz, I. (1985), 'Broadcasting without frontiers in the European Community', *Media Law and Practice* (London: Frank Cass).

Sepstrup, P. (1985), *Commercial Transnational and Neighbour Country TV in Europe: Economic Consequences and Consumer Perspectives* (Arhus: Institut for Markedsokonomie Handelshojskolen i Arhus).

SIICE (Symposium International sur l'Identité Culturelle Européenne) (1988), mimeo, Paris.

Thatcher, M. (1988), 'On Europe'. Speech given on 20 September 1988 at Bruges.

Thompson, K. (1986), *Exporting Entertainment* (London: BFI).

Trudeau, P. (1968), *Federalism and the French Canadians* (New York: St Martin's Press).

Ungureit, H. (1988), 'The programmes of the European production Association', *European Broadcasting Union Review* (Programmes, Administration, Law) vol. 39, no. 3, May.

Varis, T. (1974), 'The global traffic in television', *Journal of Communication*, vol. 24, no. 1.

Varis, T. (1984), 'The international flow of television programs', *Journal of Communication* vol. 34, no. 1.

Chapter 10

Walling Germany with Brass: Theoretical Paradigms in British Studies of Television News

Sweet analytics, 'tis thou hast ravished me
(Marlowe: *Doctor Faustus* I, 33)

For the last decade news has been the principal television programme form studied by media sociologists in Britain. The first generation of studies (first for Britain, for the study of television news goes back at least as far as the Langs' study of the Chicago MacArthur day and its presentation on television [Lang and Lang, 1952]) exploded the broadcaster's claims to offer a neutral, impartial and unbiased version of reality to audiences. Whether analysing the professional practice of the newsmakers or news programmes themselves, this first generation of studies (Cohen and Young, 1973; Glasgow University Media Group, 1976 and 1980; Schlesinger 1978; Baggaley and Duck, 1976) were concerned with establishing that information in television news output was *produced*: selected, organized, structured and (necessarily) 'biased'. This critique has, as Anthony Smith says, become 'a firmly entrenched reverse view whereby objectivity is coming to be thought to be an impossible goal because all facts are taken from reality embedded in points of view. A framework of values is therefore implicit in all recordings of events' (Smith, 1977). A second generation of writers has begun to raise – and prompted by the South Atlantic war of 1982 we may anticipate growth in their volume of output – the *source* of the bias as the central question for study. How far is television news, and its producers, autonomous, and how much constrained by other centres of power? What is the nature of the 'determination' of television news and what are the relations between state, capital and television in the field?

Work by Connell (1978, 1979), Golding and Murdock (1979) and Sparks (1976, 1977) has, though not articulated at so great a length as the first generation studies, addressed the theoretical questions of autonomy and determination and relations of state, capital and television news. They offer a variety of theorizations of the degree to which the processes of ideological reproduction performed by TV news can be said to be determined by the economic and the political. Behind these works lies an extensive debate about the nature of the capitalist state marked by the work of Miliband (1969, 1972), Althusser (1971), Poulantzas (1972), and by West German theorization via translations edited by Holloway and Piccotto (1978). Harris (1983), and Hooper (1982), most recently address themselves concretely to the dance of the powerful negotiating the production of news' account of reality, particularly of the South Atlantic war.

The First Generation Paradigms

It is in the brief, but none the less important arguments of Sparks that the strongest 'integrationist' view – that is, the determination of TV news content by the economic – is articulated.

Sparks argues that television news is strongly determined by the mode of production of the society that generates it – capitalism in the case of the UK. He further argues that in the context of an intense phase of capitalist economic crisis we are witnessing a transition towards an increasingly *conscious* attempt by the ruling class to achieve its ends by orchestrating information flows and determining the content of television news. Thus:

The category of 'news' itself was a symptom of fundamental structural features of capitalism and consequent upon this, certain secondary formations and appropriate ideological systems exist to produce concrete news. In doing this they attempt to reproduce the general features of the society which sustains them. The mode of production itself is an historical formation which is subject to a continual process of internal re-structuring which can, and indeed does, lead to changes in the secondary structures and ideologies. (Sparks, 1977, p. 74)

Within this overall determination of the superstructure ('secondary formations and appropriate ideological systems') by the base ('mode of production') different modalities in the 'secondary formations' may exist as they respond to shifts in the primary formations – the mode of production.

His argument then is not, as it has widely been misrepresented as being, a conspiracy theory of the determination of TV news. Rather he argues that there are *conjunctures* (the present time being one such moment) in which the maintenance of the ruling class as the ruling class demands conscious organization (conspiracy), in the sphere of news content as in, doubtless, other spheres, by that class. But conspiracy may not *necessarily* be the mode whereby the *status quo* is maintained. Rather it is a mode of class rule necessitated by evident crisis in the base, the mode of production and the fissures that without management would yawn in the comprehensive explanation system of ideology that rationalizes and legitimizes class rule rooted in the social relations of production. It is notable that in Sparks's account the category 'state' is absent – the central category of the 'political' structure of social relations. His extreme integrationist view argues for a primacy of the economic which animates the totality of social relations – denying either the mediating institution of the state or the autonomy of the political. Rather than institutions charged with the role of reproducing the dominant relations of production, broadcasting and particularly TV news are conceived as agencies of capital with the state itself, viewed in terms of the classic formulation of the *Communist Manifesto*:

> The bourgeoisie has at last . . . conquered for itself in the modern representative state, exclusive political sway. The executive of the modern state is but a committee for managing the common affairs of the whole bourgeoisie. (Marx and Engels, 1848, p. 33)

Connell in his work (1978–9) is concerned to rebut not only the notions of bias propagated by the first generation of studies but also to assert that the concept of determination and the primacy of the economic are simply erroneous. His post-Althusser model of the social order is that of a system 'structured in dominance', insisting on the distinctiveness of the plurality of practices, institutions and relations within the social whole and deferring determination either to the 'last instance' (in which case the model is one of 'relative autonomy') or abandoning the primacy of the economic and the notion of determination and constituting the social whole out of the variety of political, economic and ideological practices thrown together in conjunctural relations.

Connell refers to Pateman's *Television and the 1974 General Election* (Pateman, 1974) as an example of a tendency which over-emphasizes the active role of TV in agenda-setting: 'The agenda of political issues, what I have called the "primary definitions" at a given moment in time, is not constituted by broadcasters, but rather by contending political forces and by economic forces that have pertinent effects for the conduct of the dominant parliamentary political practices. TV journalism takes its lead from political forces' (Connell, 1979, p. 90).

This critique of Pateman is reasonable but is a misleading statement of general theory. Let us consider an example from one of the most controversial fields for British news in recent years. In *The Press and the Peace People* (unsigned, in *Campaign for Free Speech in Ireland*, 1979) the then BBC Controller for Northern Ireland and later Director, News and Current Affairs BBC Richard Francis is quoted on the interviewing of the peace people's leaders eighteen times in January, February and March of 1977 and the 'balance' of eighteen interviews with leaders of paramilitary groups between October 1975 to October 1976: 'Maybe we have been guilty of under representing the forces which have had the most profound effect on everyday life in the province' (p. 40). Later in the same article reference is made to the conflict between the BBC account of the attendance at a People People's rally (40,000) and 'most other reports' of 'below 17,000' (p. 40). But it matters little whether or not the figure of 40,000 came from a BBC estimate (the BBC as dependent for its definitions on primary definers outside television). Consider the second of the alternatives and the choices facing reporter and newsroom over their primary definers. Whether they choose the police, the peace people, the army or whoever, they are only nominally dependent on that source and, paradoxically, autonomous of it in their choice of whether or not to go to it. Whichever choice is made one definition from a contested set of possible definitions has been chosen. A bargain has been struck and the BBC puts itself on the side of its information source by publicly granting its imprimatur to the source's account of events. TV news broadcasters are *autonomous* insofar as they may choose which primary definers to follow and thus offer (insofar as their own credibility permits it) their imprimatur to a legitimate and authoritative source. *Dependent* or *determined* insofar as certain sources, agencies and forces are within the realm of unproblematic acceptability. As these relationships of autonomy or determination shift they define, polemically, the edges of the spectrum between which the relations between broadcasting and the forces of state and capital are marked.

Connell's argument is, as he says, against the notion that:

> The pictures and definitions constructed by journalistic practices are said to provide 'biased' or 'distorted' accounts of independent and objective reality: they are 'biased' or 'distorted' because they are informed by a body of ruling and dominant ideas, which are said to 'belong' in a simple way, to ruling political or economic groups. In short television journalism is made to appear to be a kind of megaphone by which ruling ideas are amplified and generalised across all sections of the social formation. (Connell, 1979, p. 87)

He argues for the independence of the broadcasting organizations from 'ruling political or economic groups' and that the bias or distortion that is detected in their output is present in the world that TV news reports. In support of this argument he states that were there a conspiracy – 'a conscious use of the media by (the) ruling class, its servants or agents to achieve desired political social or economic ends' (Connell, 1979, p. 76) – then TV news would have no reporting that challenged the desired ends of the class controlling it. But this argument seems to imply an extreme lack of sophistication by a ruling class in the pursuit of its ends – the argument that 'repressive tolerance' is a more effective instrument of control than simple censorship is surely familiar enough to need explicit rejection. And 'conspiracy theorists' have not argued that *all* contradictory or oppositional reporting is suppressed but that those reports take place within an interpretative paradigm that enforces negative judgements. News, after all, has to engage with and represent to the audience the real world of their experience – no news programme during a war could retain its credibility and the legitimacy of the institutions its frame of reference supports by ignoring oppositional forces and activities. Rather the task of the conspiracy (if one there be) is to place the phenomena that are directly perceived by the audience/consumers into a paradigm that is harmonious with the dominant order. The processes of ideological management are most effective when they work by incorporation rather than exclusion.

However, this critique of conspiracy or integrationist theory is subordinate to Connell's main contention that the broadcasting organizations are secondary to the primary domains of political and economic struggle and 'amplify' through a 'megaphone' (his metaphor) meanings constituted in the primary domains. 'The practices of TV journalism reproduce accurately the way in which "public opinion" has already been formed in the primary domains of political and economic struggle, how it has been structured in dominance there (ibid, p. 88). This is a definition that would command little dissent in the newsrooms of Wells Street or White City. For example, the BBC in the constitutional section that regularly appears in its annual handbook defines its role similarly:

> The licence requires the BBC to refrain from editorialising; that is refrain from expressing a point of view of its own on any matter of public controversy or public policy. Careful safeguards have been erected within the BBC to prevent breaches of this rule. For the BBC to take sides in any controversial issue would in any case be contrary to its own long established policy which, unlike the rule on editorialising has always been self-imposed. The essence of impartiality is balance, and this element, so important to the proper handling of controversial subjects in fact helps the BBC to carry out its obligation to avoid expressions of editorial opinion. Careful attention to balance is one way by which the BBC seeks to ensure that it cannot justly be identified as a supporter of any particular 'line'. (BBC, 1974, p. 280)

There is, however, a crucial difference between Connell's and the BBC's conceptions of the broadcasting institution's subordination to the primary spheres. The BBC sees balance as something to be *constructed* rather than something that necessarily attends the reflection of the domains of political and economic struggle and that conscious human agency is involved in the constitution of meanings. The same handbook says:

> It has never been the policy of the BBC to try to 'balance' news bulletins internally. The content of bulletins is manifestly dependent on the uncontrolled succession of events which make the news, from hour to hour and from day to day. To attempt to balance it artificially would be to distort it. And in any case over a period of time the news tends to be self-balancing. Thus, there may be a day when the Prime Minister makes an important political speech, which is fully reported in the news, but there is nothing newsworthy to report from the opposition side; a day or two later the reverse may well be the case. (ibid, pp. 280–1)

Clearly the procedures indicated in this account of the way in which the 'uncontrolled succession of events' are constituted as news can only be believed by those who practise them to be neutral, impartial and balanced, if they take place within a larger framework of unquestionable political choices and definitions. Definitions of the place and relations of the individuals who operate the procedures of TV news and of the institutions that produce the news *vis-à-vis* the other individuals, institutions, classes and structures that make up the 'teeth gritting harmony' of the social whole. Connell goes on to say 'television actively and independently contributes to their dominance' (Connell, 1979, p. 88) (that is the dominance of the explanations of reality offered in the notionally primary spheres). I find this – and other similar statements elsewhere – difficult to reconcile with the main 'autonomist' thrust of his article but there is an overall clear unity of purpose in his argument: to realize the project of dissolving any impression of the determination of the discourse of TV news by pressure on the TV institutions. However, that thrust leaves a crucial absence – driving from the field a vulgar and erroneous theory leaves the necessary space for the articulation of a more sophisticated and adequate structure but Connell does not satisfactorily elaborate it. It is hard to know quite where to come to rest in his arguments – how to reconcile the hostility to bias and conspiracy theory with the conclusion that 'in and through the signifying practices specific to TV journalism, political economic antagonisms are contained and their development as antagonisms is neutralised' (ibid, p. 39). Except insofar as the agency whereby these reconciliations are performed is conceived as the abstract processes of 'the signifying practices specific to TV journalism' rather than the action of human beings his position is little different from Sparks.

The category that surely has to be inserted as a mediation between integrationist and autonomist models is that of the state. It is a category that Golding and Murdock – Connell's interlocutors in a debate in which his articles of 1978 and 1979 are important elements – consider, introduce and retreat from. They state:

> It is interesting that many writers have focused their attention on the BBC and have sought explanations for its output in terms of the complex relationship of the corporation to the state. This is to be expected since much of the work derives from a concern with the theory of the state. It does present major problems however when examining the news media as a whole the majority of course being in the private sector. (Golding and Murdock, 1979, p. 212)

Overall the impetus of their essay is to argue not that the state and state sector can be subsumed under the heads of the economic and of capital, as does Sparks, but rather that the relative importance of state and capital have been wrongly assessed in earlier studies and that the most important sector, the capitalist, has been neglected, and major problems of analysis stem from this mistaken emphasis.

Marxist sociology of culture in Britain remains remarkably parochial. This is a logical but none the less regrettable consequence of taking the relations between the media and the nation state, rather than those between the media and transnational corporate capitalism as the central focus for analysis. However it is not simply that the prevailing perspective contains important imbalances and hiatuses; it is also that it is unable to produce a convincing account of those areas and processes that it chooses to concentrate on. As we shall suggest with the case of news production, the failure to explore the nature and consequences of economic determination has produced a partial and truncated explanation. (ibid., p. 208)

However, the question of the relation of the state to the capitalist sector remains unresolved. Golding and Murdock's argument for the re-instatement of 'determination' and 'economistic' analytical procedures rightly leads them to stress the privacy of private capital, but the terms 'state' and 'capital' are unsatisfactorily articulated in their argument. Rather the evidently problematic fact of the BBC is forced into the Procrustean bed of economism with a reductive *coup de main*:

> The BBC remains the single significant exception to this emerging pattern of conglomerate dominance. It is however an exception. It is not paradigmatic. Indeed there is evidence that in key areas of its operations the Corporation's activities are increasingly governed by essentially capitalistic criteria. (ibid., p. 199)

It is unfortunate that Golding and Murdock's desire to assert the importance of the economic inhibits them from a proper sensitivity to the importance of the non-commercial nature of television news in the United Kingdom. Quantitatively they are right: the capitalist sector is larger and the BBC is increasingly governed by capitalistic criteria (and its sale of television news through Visnews is one of the best examples of this). But the BBC and ITN though not quantitatively predominant are for reasons very much to do with their non-capitalist status pre-eminent in British news. The BBC's Audience Research Report of 1971 *News Broadcasting & The Public in 1970* (the most recent substantial enquiry of its kind) noted the following percentages of respondents who considered each of five sources to be 'always trustworthy' or 'trustworthy most of the time'.

BBC TV	86 per cent
ITN	78 per cent
BBC Radio	74 per cent
Newspaper customarily read by respondant	40 per cent
All newspapers	30 per cent

These statistics (BBC, 1971, Table 14a) suggest some *a priori* grounds for scepticism about Golding and Murdock's downgrading of the importance of the category of the state and the assimilation of the BBC and ITN to the ranks of capitalist enterprises. The BBC and ITN are perceived by audiences as having a less direct connection to the interested party of capital than has the press. Their perceived independence earns their statements credence beyond that readers generally cede to newspapers. It is clear, at least to me, that the public sector 'state' news institutions are distinctively different in their effects and in other respects and cannot be assimilated simply to an economistic model.

But reintroducing the problematic and labile category of the state in itself advances us but little. For whilst there are, I believe, good grounds for dissatisfaction with the rival theoretical paradigms juxtaposed above – economic, conspiracy and autonomy – each bears a kind of truth, a substantial engagement with reality that must be integrated into a subsequent synthesis. How could the accounts of Connell, Golding and Murdock and Sparks not command at least partial assent coming as they do from knowledgeable, intelligent and perceptive commentators? My melancholy conclusion is that the problems of constructing a satisfactory analytical paradigm are not going to be solved by theoretical fiat. We will not arrive at a theory of the state and television news, capitalism and television news or the autonomy of television news because the reality that we are dealing with is constantly in movement. We should retire from the seductions of theory that, like the prospect that intoxicated Marlowe's Faustus, offer to 'resolve all ambiguities' to the more prosaic task of historical analysis from which hopefully one day may be constructed accounts that progress beyond description to real analysis. The second generation of news analysis has veered dangerously close to the walling of Germany with brass and the invention of 'stranger engines for the brunt of war than was the fiery keep at Antwerp's bridge' (Christopher Marlowe, *Doctor Faustus*, 1.1.77–96).

Rather than retreating into metatheoretical assessment of the competence of rival paradigms, considering whether there is an autonomy for the ideological, whether determination occurs in the first, last, or every instance let us consider the notion of differentiality. The relation of determination manifests itself differentially at different moments in the process of ideological reproduction.

Directly in the imperative for broadcasting organizations to maintain audience ratings and revenues secondarily at the level of what has been called the forms of representation. Further we may imagine conjunctures in which the ownership of ITN by the programme companies has not to date significantly differentiated its news values from those of the BBC. The *potential* power of private capital that is present in the ownership, organization and control of ITN is unexercised. A better theory is doubtless there to be constructed but none of the essays so far advanced carry us forward to a satisfactory general understanding. My modest proposal is then to refuse the seductions of theoretical ambition and consider a number of instances in which the determinations of television news were negotiated. Out of these instances come I suggest two modest conclusions: (1) that determination operates differentially: (2) that the relations between news producers and the (notionally) determining forces of state and capital are relationships of *bargaining*, the essence of a bargain being that the parties to it resolve the contradictions between their shared and antagonistic interests.

I want to consider some of the specificities of the relation in British broadcasting between TV news, the broadcasting institutions and the state and to suggest that it is in TV news that the relations between television, the state and people – or to use the categories in Grace Wyndham Goldie's very instructive book (Goldie, 1977) 'television, politics and nation' – are most clearly focused and negotiated.

Concepts of 'neutrality', 'impartiality' and 'balance' *are* so important in British broadcasting because the classic model of the press – the 'free market of ideas' – cannot apply to broadcasting. In broadcasting there can be no unlimited entry of voices competing in a market-place of ideas because the channel capacity of the radio spectrum available for broadcasting is limited, although the foundation of commercial broadcasting in the UK was rationalized in terms of the free market model and indeed the original status of the BBC as the British Broadcasting *Company*, a consortium of radio manufacturers, was invented as an organizational form to inhibit an anarchy of competition in the radio spectrum. Broadcasting, operating in a sphere where there are necessary limits on entry, has been given the role of *impartially reflecting and mediating the forces at work* in the world. The modes of organization and control of the broadcasting organizations in Britain have been devised in order to insulate these reflective bodies from external influence by separating their governance and income from governmental or commercial pressures. The conception of a body embedded within the social totality but operating neutrally within it to reflect the totality impartially to itself in a perfect undistorted, unblemished mimesis that, Narcissus-like, may be consumed nightly, is the governing theory of the relation of broadcasting to British society. Of course this conception of a body, an institution that is within society but which transcends it is not peculiar to broadcasting: it is a theory that has been used to characterize institutions as different, or similar, as the judiciary, the Civil Service or the Stock Exchange. And the *perceived neutrality* of the broadcasting institutions and these other institutions has been, I suggest, a very important factor in the legitimation of their output.

Now it is easy to demonstrate that the BBC and ITN are far from being as independent as my interpretation of the audience research report findings suggests. One can point to the mode of appointment of the governors, to the BBC's funding coming not direct from licence fees – 'clean' money untainted by government – but via the Treasury, and so on but rather than collapsing the specific modalities of the relation between state, broadcasting and public to a theory of *conspiracy to mystify*, it is instructive to look at how these relations have been negotiated.

Autonomy for the BBC came on 1 January 1927 when it metamorphosed from a confederation of radio manufacturers – the B.B.C(ompany) to the B.B.C(orporation) as we know it. What distinguished the programming of the new corporation from that of the old company was a qualitative and quantitative change in its news broadcasts. In the days of the company news broadcasting was confined to the reading at 7 p.m. of a bulletin composed and delivered by the news agencies at a time when it was assumed all newspapers would have been sold. The first charter of the new corporation authorized the BBC to:

> Collect news of an information relating to current events in any part of the world in any matter that may be thought fit and to establish and subscribe to news agencies (Briggs, 1961, p. 359)

The transition from an organization that simply relayed information to one that sought out and made its own news, from dependence on the news agencies to autonomy came at the time of the 1926 General Strike. Like Suez as apostrophized in Robert Dougall's autobiography this was not just a crisis for the whole nation but also for the BBC.

The strike intervened between the proceedings of the Crawford committee on broadcasting and the chartering of the corporation. During the strike the BBC emancipated itself for the first time from the news agencies *and* forestalled being taken over as a kind of voice of the *British Gazette* by composing its own news bulletins – in conjunction with J.C.C. Davidson the Deputy Chief Civil Commissioner – and transmitting them five times daily. The BBC's conduct during the strike, its 'responsibility' *vis-à-vis* news output, its deferred transmission of what was for the government an inopportune statement by the Archbishop of Canterbury leading to a warning in the *British Worker* that the BBC was an instrument of government (no. 4, 8 May) gave Reith the political weight to win two essential battles with the newspaper interests and the Post Office and have his organization constituted as an autonomous body 'within the constitution'. As Reith said in 1926: 'I do not welcome crises but admit to welcoming the opportunities crises bring.' Reith profited from the opportunity the crisis presented and in which the BBC maintained a formal independence of government to constitute it decisively as an organization that was wholly responsible for initiating and developing all its programme material. The relationship between government and BBC, the nature and limits of its independence are succinctly recorded in the letter to Baldwin in 1926 that Reith reproduces in his autobiography:

Assuming the BBC is for the people and that the government is for the people, it follows that the BBC must be for the government in this crisis too. It should be allowed to define its position to the country. It must assist in sustaining the essential services of the country, the preservation of law and order and the life and liberty of the individual and the community while it must broadcast orders and communications it should be consulted in the drafting. It must maintain with discretion its essential news service. Speaking with the authority of its own reputation for sincerity and impartiality it would emphasise and initiate statements likely to counteract a spirit of selfishness and hostility. In general it should be trusted by the government as it has been by the people; but it is necessary that cordial and constant liaison be in operation. (Reith, 1949, p. 109)

We have here the early articulation of the BBC's place as a 'body within the constitution' or as we might say an institution of state power. An institution which negotiates its relation to government and people and which at the time Reith wrote was engaged in the crucial battle for its identity and for the definition of its links to government and other news organizations. The relationship that Reith established between BBC and government guaranteed the success of the BBC's growth and its metamorphosis from company to corporation. Reith's prescriptions and the BBC's conduct during the strike therefore still enjoy a classic, exemplary status within the corporation.

The official BBC handbook that informs news values and newsrooms practice *Principles and Practice in News and Current Affairs* (BBC, updated) refers to the news practice during the strike as giving 'listeners authentic impartial news of the situation' and similar examples can be multiplied. Once a specific examination of the broadcasting institutions practice in news is performed it becomes evident that the autonomy or impartiality theory – broadcasting as a kind of Kantian transcendental subject – is fallacious.

Why should we not then adopt a conspiracy theory and interpret TV news as an expression of the conscious organization of the ruling class to achieve certain agreed class goals?

First of all a conspiracy theory of TV news does not correspond to how the practitioners perceive themselves. Grace Wyndham Goldie's autobiographical worryings in *Facing the Nation* are evidence of that. And if there were the perfect fit between state apparatuses (the subcommittee of the executive committee of the bourgeoisie) that conspiracy theory predicates then we would not, surely need a D notice committee, and we would not find ITN being subpoenaed to produce recordings of the 1974 Red Lion Square anti-fascist demonstration, the IBA banning Granada documentaries and so on.

The case of 1926 is one instance of that negotiated relationship. A more recent example may be found in the account of the siege of 22b Balcombe Street given by the foreign editor of

ITN. John Mahoney cites criticism of TV coverage of the police action.

> By the fourth day retired Major-Generals were writing to *The Times* complaining that the media were giving away vital information to the enemy and that the field should be left clear for the experts who know what they are doing. (Mahoney, 1976, p. 18)

He adds:

> The experts saw that TV and radio had a part to play in the action which could be combined with their normal duties of reporting and explaining the situation to the millions of non hostages. There were some misgivings within the ranks of the media too, for in spite of the successful close cooperation, indeed partnership between press and police on this type of story where hostages' lives are at stake, the terms of the *bargain* must be constantly reviewed. (ibid., p. 18)

The crucial metaphor here is that of the *bargain*. The term implies an agreed frame of reference within which negotiation takes place and the bargain is concluded. But it also implies an antagonistic, or potentially antagonistic relation between the parties to the bargain.

To point to a shared frame of reference between parties to an exchange is quite different to identifying conscious or conspiratorial collaboration to achieve a common end. Few suggest that the interests of capitalist and worker are common though their contradictory interests do not preclude negotiation of wage bargains.

In 1979 *The Leveller*, an independent socialist magazine, published the text of a procedural agreement between the BBC and the London Metropolitan Police (Appendix 1). This agreement was made following the transmission of the BBC Drama/Documentary series *Law and Order*, which aroused the sharp antagonism of the police. The memorandum was widely interpreted in left and libertarian circles in Britain as an indication of the BBC ceding *de facto* censorship powers to the Metropolitan Police. *The Leveller* itself chose to emphasize this interpretation:

They (i.e. the BBC) had agreed to a unique procedure of checks which would effectively give the police an infinitely greater editorial say than they had before. A new climate had been set which will dilute investigation in the most sensitive areas. Although the police hadn't got everything they wanted they had got more than any self-respecting independent broadcasting organisation should have allowed them to have. (*The Leveller*, 1979, p. 11)

But careful reading of the procedural memorandum shows that the crucial area, news, was excluded from the purview of the agreement and that the BBC preserved the freedom to proceed with coverage the Metropolitan Force found antipathetic.

Indeed, the necessity for a procedural agreement supports an argument that there exists a fundamental conflict of interests between the parties (albeit one that the parties agree they have a shared interest in mediating) as well as it does either a conspiracy theory or the autonomist argument that the news media simply adopt a pre-established agenda.

The year (1978) of the procedural agreement saw the publication of the memoirs of the recently retired Commissioner of the Metropolitan Police Sir Robert Mark. His book *In the Office of Constable* foregrounds three events in which police relations with the media were central: the Balcombe Street and Spaghetti House sieges, and the kidnap of a Greek Cypriot woman. One of these events (the Spaghetti House seige) was described by Mark as 'the most difficult and potentially explosive of all the various problems with which I have had to deal in my twenty years as a chief officer of police' (Mark, 1979, p. 197). In his account of these incidents Mark (1979) emphasizes the assistance afforded the police by the media. He refers to 'the help of the News media' (p. 194), states that 'it was possible to make clear to them (i.e. the Spaghetti House hostage takers RC) not only in shouted conversation but through the news broadcasts, that they were going nowhere except to a cell, or by implication, to a mortuary, if they preferred that' (p. 199). 'I have already thanked on behalf of the Force all those others, not least the news media and the Home Office, who gave such valuable support' (p. 203) that 'we could depend upon reasonable co-operation from Press, radio and television' (p. 204), and 'that there was no doubt in

the minds of the police who took part in the case that the Press
had played perhaps the most important part in making possible
the safe recovery of the girl' (p. 205). Now the predominant
interpretation of these events – relying principally on Mark's
account – has been to stress in a worried way the convergence of
interests of police and media and their co-operation: to see events
as exemplifying the harmonious collaboration of the ideological and
repressive state apparatuses. It is possible, *vide* Mahoney's account
discussed above, to see the police/media relations differently.
Indeed Mark's own account provides a basis for doing so. While
he principally discusses relations with the press (in particular the
instances of co-operation and antagonism experienced with the
Evening News and the *Daily Mail*), and prioritizes co-operation
rather than antagonism, there is clearly a perception of the
media as possessing interests antagonistic to those of the police:

> We did not relish the prospect of the 150 or so news and
> television cameras filming what might be a gory end to the
> siege. We knew only too well that Irish folklore would use the
> film to convert four seedy cowardly degenerates into martyrs,
> and that was the last thing we wanted. (Mark, 1979, p. 194)

and

> By this time, if the gunmen and their hostages were besieged,
> so were the police. Press, radio and television infiltrated the
> surrounding flats and other premises and every kind of listen-
> ing and watching device was employed to monitor the drama
> being played out in the small and suffocating basement. (ibid.,
> p. 199)

Evidence from the broadcasters' side that they bargain and do
not simply reflect in an impartial and balanced way ideologies
and politics defined outside their institutions comes in the ENCA
minutes of 1976 (a complete set of which have circulated in
samizdat format outside the BBC), some of which were published
by *The Leveller* in January 1978. ENCA is an acronym for Editor
News and Current Affairs and signifies a committee chaired by
ENCA and meeting weekly to review and make news policy.
The minutes are a very rich source of information which offer

fascinating material for detailed analysis. One minute, for example (390 of 30 April 1976) is concerned with the agreement between the BBC and police to embargo reporting of kidnappings. It states *inter alia*:

> Voluntary co-operation would be offered in connection with reasonable requests when it appeared that lives were at risk. Peter Wood underlined the point that co-operation was not obligatory saying that certain limited requests of this kind had in fact been turned down during the 1975 Spaghetti House siege.

More support for the propositions that the BBC bargains and does not simply accept or reject the agendas of other agencies in its news coverage is offered by the interesting example of relations with the Government of India which can be tracked in the ENCA minutes.

In order to achieve its aim of reporting Indian affairs in circumstances where the Indian government had withdrawn co-operation and expelled correspondents whom it deemed unfriendly, the BBC was compelled to review its relations with the Indian government and reflect on its bargaining strategy. The strategies canvassed spanned 'conspiracy'; lunching leading Indian officials, including 'scenic elements' in Indian coverage; making 'innocuous' programmes about India in order to restore good relations with the government of India; and confronting the Indian government 'head on'.

ENCA Minute 55: (23.1.1976)

> E.N.C.A. noted that the 'Guardian's' correspondent in Delhi for the last six months, Mr Lawrence Lifschultz, had been served with an expulsion order by the Indian Government (Later: D G said that he would like to know the circumstances).
>
> E.N.C.A. said that Mr Swraj Paul's lunch with himself and Mark Tully was due to take place on 26 January. Mr Paul would be returning to Delhi later that week.
>
> Noble Wilson (C.Int.R) suggested that it might be best to try out some comparatively innocuous programmes on the Indian government, as a means of restoring relations, before getting

back to hard current affairs reporting. A suitable opportunity might be a forthcoming Nature History Unit programme on the subject of elephant trails.

Chris Bell (H.P.P.(W.S.)) said that some fears had been expressed at Bush House about the apparent power of veto of the Indian government over what should be included in the Tony Mayer film. The BBC seemed to be faced with the unsatisfactory alternative of either showing something which the Indian government did not like or of providing what was virtually a party political broadcast for Mrs Gandhi. E.N.C.A. said that the BBC must of course ensure that the film as offered to it was editorially sensible and for the purpose specialists such as Mark Dodd (H.East.C.) and Mark Tully should view it in rough-cut. Desmond Wilcox agreed: those concerned should ring Tony Isaacs if they wanted to view the film. Once its content was settled the film would be presented as one which had been commissioned by the BBC. Chris Bell hoped that the proposed *Panorama* programme with Mrs Gandhi would take place before the Tony Mayer film was shown. E.N.C.A. was worried about the length of the original film and the possible Indian reaction to the huge amount of cutting which would be required. Desmond Wilcox thought that Mrs Gandhi would raise no objections: she fully understood that it had been Tony Mayer's intention not just to provide a soft film, and she had been co-operative throughout, even during sessions of tough questioning.

Later: D G said that he would be lunching with the High Commissioner on 23 March. On hearing the suggestion that it might be best initially to make some innocuous films, and that Mark Tully might go to Delhi to discuss them, D G said he would prefer a head-on approach to the subject in which the BBC's conditions for Mark Tully's return would be clearly stated to the Indian government.

Peter Wood said that, if Mark Tully was to return, there should be a decision about his title – whether he should be called Delhi Representative or Correspondent. He would prefer the latter as more truly descriptive of his rôle. D G said that Mark Tully had been withdrawn in his rôle as Correspondent but he was bound to be doing both jobs if he returned to Delhi.

Referring to Chris Bell's fears about the Tony Mayer film, D G said that it was up to the BBC to decide whether to accept the film in the form in which it was eventually offered. If the film was not fully acceptable it would not be shown. He accepted Desmond Wilcox's view that, once the film had been fully seen and approved, it should be presented as a film for which the BBC would take full editorial responsibility. Desmond Wilcox explained that Tony Mayer would be going back shortly to India to tidy up the film and update it. All being well it was intended to transmit it between the middle of February and the middle of March. It would be about 50–60 minutes long and would not be confined to interview material but would include a scenic element.

Essentially this minute records a review of negotiating strategy in which the BBC wishes to regain freedom to report Indian affairs as it judges fit, but recognizes that a *quid pro quo* has to be offered to the Indian government in order to advance this end. Neither conspiracy nor the broadcasts accepting and reproducing agendas established elsewhere seem appropriate to defining this process.

Until the South Atlantic war of 1982 and the publication of the first of what will surely be a tide of academic studies of news management (one commissioned by the Ministry of Defence, and one from the Glasgow University Media Group among them) the Mark autobiography and *The Leveller* publications were the best material in the public domain on which to construct a theory of the relations of state and media, police and broadcasting, repressive and ideological state apparatuses. The evidence, I suggest, lends little credence to any of the dominant theoretical paradigms. Rather it suggests that the relationship between the agencies in question is a shifting negotiated relationship dependent on circumstances, the nature of the crises in question and the power disposed of by the parties in question. If determination is an appropriate theoretical category then determination manifests itself differentially and in a negotiated settlement of antagonistic bargainers reluctantly securing a 'teeth-gritting harmony'.

The South Atlantic war was a formidable stimulus to the UK Information economy. Of the plethora of publications that rapidly followed the ceasefire *Gotcha! The Media, the Government and the Falklands Crisis* by Robert Harris (a BBC journalist writing in his personal capacity) and the *The Military & The Media* by serving Royal marine officer Alan Hooper – a general discussion of media/military relations but including a section on the Falklands crisis – are the most interesting so far available.

Harris's book takes for its title the headlines from *The Sun* that reported the sinking of the Argentine cruiser *General Belgrano* and the loss of many of her crew. Although Harris focuses on the press there are sections that describe and analyse the role of broadcasting in the South Atlantic war. His account suggests there was no 'conspiracy' between the media and government in reporting the Falklands crisis. Rather that reporting expressed both enormous antagonism between the state and its agencies and the British news media resulting from the bungled and inadequate arrangements made by government for fighting an 'information war' and the substantial assent given to the government's war policy by the British and by the media. The general assent of the media to the task the government prescribed for them of promoting national solidarity and support for the war and the media's exasperation with the incompetence of government waging of the information war is epitomized by the remark of a senior BBC official, Richard Francis (previously Head of News and Current Affairs) that: 'We had no opportunity to condition the mass audience' (Harris, 1983, p. 67). The mass audience, though, did not require the conditioning Francis contemptuously enjoined for it; disquieting though the sinkings of *Sheffield* and the *General Belgrano* were, no crisis of popular assent to the war and failure of national nerve ensued. Perhaps because the news management and delay in flow of information blunted the people of Britain's vicarious experience of the war, but I speculate most importantly because a national character formed over centuries for the successful prosecution of war was experiencing again the successful execution of its national military purpose. After decades of national decline, introspection and despair the South Atlantic war fed the national imagination with a positive self-image.

Harris's book offers the elements of a fascinating case study of a process whereby journalists identified themselves with the military units to which they were attached and whose doings they reported. It becomes clear from his account how that process of identification and attachment was necessary for personal, physical and psychological survival. In war conditions the journalists' personal survival was conditional, to a large extent, on the competence and success of the unit to which he was attached. Psychological survival also depended on journalists' ability to attach themselves to the military – for their peers, other journalists, were competitors, not allies:

> After the war, Surgeon Commander Morgan O'Connell, a psychiatrist sailing with the task force, described in the *Guardian* the symptoms of battle stress that he noticed in the men under his care: 'emotional tension, hypersensitivity to noise, explosive rage, a feeling of helplessness, amnesia and regression to childish behaviour.' Of all the groups during the war he found that the journalists fared the worst: 'They had no group cohesiveness. They were in competition with each other all the time, so they couldn't draw the same security from the group.' (ibid., p. 144)

But convergence between the values and aims of the military and the government on one side and broadcasters on the other was not confined to the hazardous and stressed conditions of combat.

> When the collected coverage of the campaign was eventually broadcast after the Argentine surrender, it included some harrowing shots of badly burned faces and blown off limbs. But the worst material was never shown. It was weeded out by the television companies themselves. Major General Sir Jeremy Moore the commander of the British land forces, afterwards wanted 'to pay tribute to the good taste of our journalists that they did not show anything as unpleasant as could have been available'. (ibid., p. 60)

The metaphor of the 'information war' was the means whereby journalists and the broadcasting institutions managed the contradiction between their identification with the successful prosecution of the war and their self-image as independent, non-partisan reporters.

The information war was on one hand a war that the media was convinced it could fight very much more effectively than the bungling ill considered and ill coordinated attempts of the government and military agencies to command the assent of the

international community and the British public to the exercise of
armed force.

In its retrospective *Panorama* documentary *The Media War* on
the war and its reporting, the BBC attempted to justify its activities
in the face of government antagonism by arguing that winning the
information war imposed different priorities to those of winning
the military campaign. The argument essentially was about the
best means of achieving the goals defined by Mrs Thatcher. But
as Harris says:

> One of the features of the so-called Information War was that
> everyone fought everyone else; Whitehall fought the Navy, the
> Government fought Whitehall, all three fought the Media and
> the Media fought among themselves. (ibid., p. 31)

It is clear that the government was extremely dissatisfied with the
BBC's lack of patriotism in reporting the war. Another of Richard
Francis's statements

> To report the resilient reaction of the Argentine people to the
> losses among the armed forces provides an important element
> of the picture for the British people. The widow of Portsmouth
> is no different from the widow of Buenos Aires. (ibid., p. 83)

followed BBC programmes on the World Service and the main
evening television news in which a senior journalist from *The
Sunday Times* was interviewed and asked how much credence
could be given to information reaching the public from the South
Atlantic. He suggested that since the information was passing
through two levels of military censorship audiences would be
well advised to treat it with scepticism. The principal occasion
for government displeasure was the *Panorama* of 10 May which
interviewed a number of the major dissenters from the government
war policy (including Conservative members of parliament). Mrs
Thatcher's response, made to the House of Commons, is quoted
by Harris:

> I share the deep concern that has been expressed on many sides,
> particularly about the content of yesterday evening's Panorama
> programme. I know how strongly many people feel that the case

for our country is not being put with sufficient vigour on certain – I do not say all – BBC programmes. The chairman of the BBC has assured us, and has said in vigorous terms, that the BBC is not neutral on this point. (ibid., p. 80)

Her statement is in a sense emblematic of this essay's theme, for it is open to a variety of contradictory interpretations. Delete the last sentence and there is good grist for the mill producing under the BBC independent of government defining its own news values label; retain only the last sentence and the millers of conspiracy theory appropriate it as raw material. It is the nature of the operations of the powerful that the mechanisms whereby their power is exercised are rarely apparent. Mrs Thatcher and her government have made no explicit moves against the BBC in punishment for its lack of patriotism in 1982 and its refusal to conform to the norm implied later in the Prime Minister's statement:

It is our great pride that the British media are free. We ask them, when the lives of some of our people may be at stake through information or through discussions that can be of use to the enemy to take that into account on their programmes. It is our pride that we have no censorship. That is the essence of a free country. But we expect the case for freedom to be put by those who are responsible for doing so. (ibid., p. 80)

But the same chairman who 'assured us' of non-neutrality and who was savaged by a Conservative Party media committee frightened by the sinking of the *Sheffield was* replaced. And since then the government has backed the launch of competitive (notably cable) information and entertainment services. Before Mrs Thatcher's re-election *The Times* reported (26 April 1983) that 'the case for dismemberment or even abolition of the BBC is gaining ground among the Prime Minister's advisers' and that 'if Mrs Thatcher has a second term there will be a radical reappraisal of public service broadcasting'. It seems that the circle begun by John Reith with good behaviour in 1926 earning the BBC its independent status has been closed in 1983 with the BBC's independent status under serious threat following its insufficiently zealous support of 'our boys'.

Hooper's *The Military and the Media* complements Harris's *Gotcha*. Like Harris, Hooper addresses the processes whereby dominance and subordination are negotiated, informed by experience of the other, military, side of the relationship. The overt intention of his work is to promote convergence or 'understanding' between what he identifies as similar professions. The book offers considerable evidence of long-standing and well established convergence and, like many of the other texts taken by previous analysts of bias in the news, offers ample material for selective appropriation and support of antithetical theses. It can therefore be mined both for evidence to support a conspiracy thesis or the reverse. *The Military and the Media* can be seen as an attempt to promote the information policy enjoined by General Kitson in *Low Intensity Operations* and as evidence that the processes Kitson proposed were well advanced.

> The next area in which the army can make a contribution before the outbreak of violence lies in the field of psychological operations and propaganda, where the Government not only has to counter the steps which the enemy are taking to get their case across to the population, but also has to put its own programme in an attractive way. There are three aspects to this business. In the first place careful assessments and appreciations have to be made by trained men and presented to the government leadership at the various levels so that policy can be laid down. This policy then had to be turned into specific propaganda material such as films, broadcast programmes, newspaper articles, leaflets and so on. Finally, the material has to be disseminated by mechanical means, that is to say by broadcasting, printing or by the projection of films on the screens. (Kitson,, 1971, p. 77)

The quotation above is also used by Sparks (1976). It serves his conspiracy argument well. There is ample evidence in Hooper's account of *co-operation* between broadcasters and the British armed forces in the production of television series to sustain Sparks's argument with a plethora of case studies. Similarly there is substantial anecdotal and case study evidence to support a thesis of *antagonistic* relations between military and media and the maintenance of a scrupulous independence by broadcasters from their informants and the subjects of their stories. Support from Hooper for the convergence and conspiracy thesis (or as Hooper says the 'affinity' of soldiers and journalists) may be neatly apostrophized by Alan Protheroe's (the Assistant Director General of the BBC) foreword in which he states *inter alia*: 'There is no need for journalists and military men to be at loggerheads' and

> Major Alan Hooper is a distinguished Royal Marines officer who has demonstrated his academic capabilities. His book shows perception, understanding and substantial reporting skills. The greatest compliment I can pay him is that if he wasn't a Marine he'd make a very fine journalist. (Hooper, 1973, p. xi)

The antagonism and conflict of interest thesis is represented in Hooper's cherished list of disparaging remarks by irascible military gents about journalists of which the following is perhaps the most temperate and intelligent:

> It may well be that between press and officials there is an inherent, built-in conflict of interest. There is something to be said for both sides, but when the nation is at war the men's lives are at stake, there should be no ambiguity. (General W C Westmoreland, quoted in Hooper, 1973, p. 6)

But the bargain is the metaphor to which Hooper has continuous recourse, and is the ideal relationship between military and media that he recommends to his readers and fellow officers. To be sure the nature of the something for something relationship will shift with the relative power of the two sides engaged in negotiating a bargain. The bargain relationship will span all points on a spectrum bounded by conspiracy at one end and antagonism at the other. The power enjoyed by the parties to the bargain will similarly shift with time and circumstances. When both parties share a set of aims (and for such major agencies in the social formation not to assent to most of the same aims for most of the time is equivalent to a state of social disintegration) then the bargains struck will be ones that lend credence to analyses asserting convergence or conspiracy relations. When they refuse to bargain and act as independent agencies a certain danger for each party grows – the media actually and potentially are excluded

from doing their job of reporting the doings of major social actors
– the military of fostering public assent for their actions. But for
each party to the bargain to express and advance shared interests,
there are other interests that are threatened in tthe bargain and are
opposed to those of the other party. Hooper in his accounts of the
making of television series and single dramas about military life
surveys a range of cases. His most interesting comments on the
bargain are in relation to a single play *Vanishing Army*, where,
in his view, a bargain was wrongly refused by the army.

> What would the Army have achieved by agreeing to co-operate?
> They would not have been able to demand changes in the
> script but they would have been in a good bargaining position
> to influence certain alterations in exchange for the loan of
> a modern barracks for location shots . . . The military would
> have lost nothing by meeting the producer, offering advice on
> the script, providing a technical adviser and making available
> the facilities requested by the BBC. At the same time this
> would have enabled them to advise on the accurate portrayal
> of service life. The point about this particular play was that the
> Northern Ireland scenes were depicted so realistically that one
> naturally accepted the whole of the play as being authentic. The
> failure to develop any kind of liaison was a mistake. (Hooper,
> 1982, p. 101)

To argue, as I have done here, that determination is exercised
differentially and that the metaphor of the bargain is the best
route to understanding the nature of news bias and the power
relationships that shape the values of television news is a somewhat
melancholy activity. For it is tantamount to a retreat from theory
and the search for theoretical accounts that will 'adequate the real'
and a return to conjunctural analysis. None the less I think that
retreat has to be made from the intoxication with theory that in
the seventies led us to believe that something was there to be
found that would perform a Faustian alchemy and resolve all
ambiguities. My hope is that this scepticism and the return to
that most enduring of the peculiarities of the English, conjectural
analysis, is but a *reculer pour mieux sauter*.

This chapter was first published in 1984 in *Media, Culture and
Society*, vol. 6, no. 1.

Note

1 Though ITN is owned by the customers for its products and in the last analysis producing for capital it is shielded by its arm's-length relation to the advertising sales department of the ITCA companies and its production for a public service television system from the naked imperatives of profit maximization and commodity production. See Collins (1976) pp. 11–13.

References

Althusser, L. (1969), 'Ideology & ideological state apparatuses', in *Lenin and Philosophy & Other Essays* (London: New Left Books), 1971.

Baggaley, J. and Duck, S. (1976), *The Dynamics of Television* (Farnborough: Saxon House).

BBC (1971), *Audience Research Report: News Broadcasting and the Public in 1970*, London.

BBC (1974), *Handbook*, London.

BBC (undated memo). *Principles and Practice in News and Current Affairs*, London.

Briggs, A. (1961), *The Birth of Broadcasting*, Oxford.

Campaign for Free Speech on Ireland (1979), *The British Media & Ireland*, London.

Cohen, S. and Young, J. (1973), *The Manufacture of News* (London: Constable).

Collins, R. (1976), *Television News* (London: British Film Institue).

Connell, I. (1978), 'Monopoly Capitalism and the Media' in Hibbin (ed.), *Politics, Ideology & The State* (London: Lawrence & Wishart).

Connell, I. (1979), 'Television news & the social contract' in *Screen*, vol. 20, no. 1.

Glasgow University Media Group (1976), *Bad News* (London: Routledge & Kegan Paul).

Glasgow University Media Group (1980), *More Bad News* (London: Routledge & Kegan Paul).

Goldie, G. W. (1977), *Facing the Nation. Television and Politics 1936-1976* (London: Bodley Head).

Golding, P. and Murdock, G. (1978), 'Ideology & the mass media: The question of determination', in Barrett, Corrigan, Kuhn & Wolff (eds.) *Ideology and Cultural Production* (London: Croom Helm).

Harris, R. (1983), *Gotcha! The Media, the Government and the Falklands Crisis* (London: Faber).

Holloway, J. and Piccotto, S. (eds.) (1978), *State & Capital* (London: Arnold).

Hooper, A. (1982), *The Military and the Media* (Aldershot: Gower).

Lang, K. and Lang, G. (1952), 'The unique perspective of television and its effects', in W. Schramm (ed.) (1960), *Mass Communications* (Urbana: Illinois).

Kitson, F. (1971), *Low intensity operations* (London: Faber).

Mahoney, J. (1976), '22b Balcombe Street London. The Television Siege', *European Broadcasting Review,* vol 27, March 1976 pp. 16–18.

Mark, R. (1979), *In the Office of Constable* (London: Fontana).

Marlowe, C. (1924), *The Tragical History of the Life and Death of Doctor Faustus*, R. Gill (ed.) (1965), (London).

Marx, K. and Engels, F. ([1848] 1970), *Manifesto of the communist party*, trans (1888), S. Moore (Peking: Foreign Language Press).

Miliband, R. (1969), *The state in capitalist society* (London: Weidenfeld).

Miliband, R. (1972), 'Reply to Nicos Poulantzas' in R. Blackburn (ed.), *Ideology in Social Science* (London: Fontana).

Pateman, T. (1974), *Television and the February 1974 General Election* (London: British Film Institute).

Poulantzas, N. (1972), 'The problem of the capitalist state', in R. Blackburn (ed.) *Ideology and Social Science* (London: Fontana).

Reith, J. (1949), *Into the Wind* (London: Hodder).

Schlesinger, P. (1978), *Putting Reality Together* (London: Constable).

Smith, A. (1977), 'Telecommunications & the Press' Long Range Research Group Report no. 15. (Cambridge: Post Office Telecommunications).

Sparks, C. (1976), 'Review', *Screen Education* no. 21.

Sparks, C. (1977), 'Reply', *Screen Education*, no. 22.

Appendix

Procedural arrangements with the Metropolitan Police

1 These points are only for cases which the Metropolitan Police consider delicate, affecting privacy, 'sub-judice', national security and such areas. They are not for news items or straightforward current affairs features on police work – for example the opening of new police stations, the introduction of new vehicles and equipment, etc.

2 When embarking on a potentially sensitive programme, a BBC producer would meet with somebody from 'P' Department to talk over the subject and the area the BBC wished to portray, as well as the facilities they considered necessary to do this. The programme area would be defined as clearly as is possible at this stage. Afterwards, the BBC producer would send a letter to the Metropolitan Police setting out what had been agreed.

3 The Metropolitan Police would then agree the letter's contents and acknowledge that it covered the necessary points.

4 The Metropolitan Police would be kept informed of any subsequent change of plan and, if necessary, a further meeting
   would be convened to agree any alterations. Similar talks
   would be held between the Police and the BBC to sort out
   any disagreement.
5 It would be open to the Metropolitan Police to write to the
   BBC outlining anything they thought went against one agreement between them. The BBC would then look into the matter
   and report their findings to the Metropolitan Police.
6 If the Police were not satisfied, they could register a formal
   complaint with the BBC's Director-General.

Chapter 11

Seeing is Believing: The Ideology of Naturalism

All broadcasting systems however organized and controlled have to command the assent of their audiences to their messages. The problem clearly becomes most pressing in relation to messages – the programmes – that are explicitly concerned with presenting reality; the informational programmes of which news, current affairs and documentaries are the most important.

Successive audience research reports mark the decline in confidence of UK television viewers in the trustworthiness of television news. In 1971 the BBC's audience research report noted these percentages of respondents who considered each of five sources to be 'always trustworthy' or 'trustworthy most of the time': BBC TV 86%; ITN 78%; BBC Radio 74%; Respondents own newspaper 40%; All newspapers 30%. These 'scores' mark a decline in the credence ceded to television's informational programming since the 1950s and a further decline is marked by the 1984 report commissioned by the BBC, *Perception of Bias in Television News* (Collins, 1984). The 1984 bias study is not directly comparable to previous reports: it asks different questions and documents different answers and yields results from which it is difficult to generalize confidently. However the following conclusions can, plausibly, be drawn: that the BBC remains the most trusted of television information channels and that audience confidence in the impartiality of television as an information source has declined.

Perception of Bias in Television News attempted to determine whether viewers perceived television news and current affairs as biased. Respondents regarded television as the most accurate and

255

detailed source of information (they were asked about coverage of three issues: the police, Common Market, unemployment).

	TV	Press	Radio	None/ Don't know
Most accurate source	41	17	7	36
Most detailed source	41	25	6	28

There seems no reason to doubt that television remains the information source in which UK consumers have most confidence. Of TV channels:

	BBC1	ITV	BBC2	Channel 4
Most accurate	57	26	15	2

The by-channel 'scores' are curious because the four news and current affairs sources are, essentially, only two. The BBC channels 1 and 2 emanate from the same organization and newsroom (though there are differences in personnel, format and content in BBC 1 and 2 news and more marked differences in the two channels' other informational programming it is essentially the same personnel and apparatus that speaks on the two channels). And Channel 4's news is originated by Independent Television News (ITN) as is that of ITV. Here though there are more marked differences in the two channels' other information programming. The report suggests, plausibly, that 'The view of Channel 4 is unlikely to be based on consideration of its news and current affairs . . . the perception is based on the general image of Channel 4' (Collins, 1984, p. 5).

The trust in the BBC (or at least in BBC 1) coexists with a perception of the BBC as the channel most biased in favour of the government. Of the 25 per cent of respondents who thought any channel was likely to represent the government view (i.e. about half thought somewhere in UK television a pro-government bias existed) most thought the BBC to be the most pro-government.

BBC 1	BBC 2	ITV	Channel 4
44	23	25	8

Though again we find the curious differences in the perception of the BBC's two channels. We have then a contradictory set of perceptions of television as a source of information: of it as more accurate than other media, of the most accurate channel also being that most likely to be biased in favour of government and of different evaluations of the accuracy and bias of information distributed on different channels by the same organization.

The decline (from the 1950s to the 1980s) in trust in television and in the impartiality of the message sources will doubtless have been accelerated by the wider circulation of knowledge about security vetting of personnel and the method of appointment of Governors following the BBC's Board of Governors prohibition of the transmission of the *Real Lives* documentary *State of the Union*. But television remains the preferred source of information and its message sources – notably ITN and the BBC – are generally perceived as preferable to the available alternatives.

In Britain the products of the domestic mass media are the only readily available source of an interpretative paradigm that enables an individual to relate his or her direct experience to the social totality, to the world at large. Whether or not this paradigm and the relations it assigns are believed or not, it remains the only framework in which the day-to-day experience of an individual can be related to the whole. Either its agenda is accepted or the refuser remains in a state of, at best, sceptical agnosticism. Of these domestic mass media the BBC and ITN are correctly perceived as having a less direct connection to one interested party, to capital, than the press (though recent events and the decline in public trust in television suggests that the suzerainty of the state is becoming more apparent and more regularly exercised than before). Hence, I suggest the perceived relative independence of the BBC and ITV earns their statements a degree of trust and credence beyond that generally accorded the press. Secondly, I suggest the aesthetic, or style, of naturalism that governs information programmes earns assent to the programmes' messages. The accumulations of still and moving images in television news, for example, are rhetorical devices that, on the basis of seeing is believing, the camera cannot lie, sustain and authenticate the verbal narrative that alone gives these images coherence. To show an event is to demonstrate its authenticity and the authenticity of the governing voice-over of narration – whether of newsreader, anchor man or woman or interviewer/interviewee. It is the trust invested in the image, the idea that seeing is believing that accounts for the greater degree of trust in television news than in radio news.

This problematic, that of trust invested in the image and the conditions on which that trust is ceded, can be productively considered by examining the work of the most thoughtful and self-conscious of the practitioners of television's dominant mode of informational representation, Roger Graef. Graef is an American documentary film-maker long resident in the UK and is now a member of the board of Channel 4 who defines his own project as that of 'observational cinema' or '*ciné verité*' ('we were observers, not participants, not intruding to control the action as we might have in a conventional documentary'). He has worked consistently with a small group of colleagues who, like Graef, are unusually ready to reflect on and make explicit the bases and procedures of their work, though their characterizations are sometimes interestingly contradictory (see Vaughan, 1976, and Wyver, 1982). Charles Stewart, one of Graef's regular camera operators, pulls the rug from under Graef's customary self-presentation as a practitioner of 'observational cinema'. He states:

When we start to shoot, much of Roger's work is finished.

that is, Graef's work is in the planning and organization of that which is to be 'observed', and Stewart further states:

Any time we think there's going to be something happening, then we start filming, and when we know it's not going to be interesting we stop filming.

The style of observational cinema or *ciné verité* within which Graef works and of which he is a notably skilled and serious exponent dates from its development by Drew and Leacock, sponsored by NBC and Time – Life in the late 1950s and early 1960s to produce a distinctive new product for US network television, and it has its archaeology in the *ciné verité* monuments of Vertov and Flaherty and its varied practices in France, the USA, Britain and Canada (Charles Stewart worked with Terence McCartney Filgate, one of the leading documentarists of the National Film Board of Canada.) Graef's work is then a distinctive 'ideolect' within a shared international language.

This truth telling of 'observational cinema' is, I suggest, no less chimerical than the independence of broadcasting institutions. Just as the BBC's independence has a reality, though tightly bounded by unacknowledged constraints like the Treasury's control of the purse strings and the Prime Minister's influence in the appointment of the Governors, so observational cinema's capacity to tell the truth is real but considerably more closely circumscribed than its practitioners believe.

This ideological practice of legitimation has, properly, been the object of attack in an important (dominant in the 1970s) tradition of film criticism and film practice. However the attacks on the 'classic realist text', the naturalization of the status quo and the demand for a modernist cinema in which the device was foregrounded and a critique of the sign mounted, did not customarily make differentiations *within* the practice of what was loosely termed bourgeois realism. Distinctions are there to be made and the central tradition in Marxist aesthetics, initiated by Engels and carried on by Lenin and most importantly Lukacs, distinguishes within an apparently undifferentiated mimetic tradition, two epistemologies of representation.

For Lukacs, mimetic representations required categorization under two heads: realism and naturalism. Naturalism was simply ideological (and open to the critiques mounted by the anti-realists in British film culture). However, realism was a mode of cognition and representation that could enlighten, liberate and 'adequate the real'. For Lukacs, naturalism, whatever its actual historical productivity (which in the case of Zola or Strindberg could be argued to have been progressive), was based on a false epistemology and thus offered no adequate basis for cognition, no way of satisfactorily knowing the world. Naturalism is distinguished by scrupulous fidelity to the here and now, to the immediate and the apparent. It is an aesthetic that seeks to minimize the mediation through consciousness of the real, in perception and representation. In film theory the classic site of a naturalist aesthetic is in Bazin. In his 'Ontology of the Photographic Image' Bazin states:

> The aesthetic qualities of photography are to be sought in its power to lay bare the realities. It is not for me to separate off, in the complex fabric of the objective world, here a reflection on a damp sidewalk, there the gesture of a child. Only the

impassive lens, stripping the object of all those ways of seeing it, those piled up pre-conceptions, that spiritual dust and grime with which my eyes have covered it, is able to present it in all its virginal purity to my attention and consequently to my love. (Bazin, 1967, p. 15)

This strict naturalism is often contradicted in Bazin's critical writings, which approach at times a conception of representation closer to Lukacsian realism than the strict naturalism of his explicitly theoretical essays as exemplified above. Lukacs, though, argues that scrupulous fidelity to the here and now, the immediate and the apparent, is an inadequate mode of knowing. Events, objects, phenomena are chimerical, caught in a process of change and a network of causal relations that require representation if the real is to be fully adequated and understood. Therefore some analytical and constructive activity of human consciousness is necessary for the real to be produced for representation.

> The artistic correctness of a detail thus has nothing to do with whether the detail corresponds to any similar detail in reality. The detail in a work of art is an accurate reflection of life when it is a necessary aspect of the accurate reflection of the total process of objective reality, no matter whether it was observed by the artist in life or created through imagination out of direct or indirect experience. (Lukacs, 1970, p. 43)

Whether a particular mimesis is realist or naturalist cannot be determined by the presence or absence of particular formal qualities; rather the criterion is the degree to which the major determining forces in the social totality which fix and produce particular phenomena are represented.

> The work of art must therefore reflect correctly and in proper proportion all important factors objectively determining the area of life it represents. It must so reflect these that this area of life becomes comprehensible from within and from without, re-experienceable, that it appears as a totality of life. This does not mean that every work of art must strive to reflect the objective, extensive totality of life. On the contrary, the extensive totality of reality necessarily is beyond the possible

scope of any artistic creation; the totality of reality can only be reproduced intellectually in ever-increasing approximation through the infinite process of science. The totality of the work of art is rather intensive; the circumscribed and self-contained ordering of those factors which objectively are of decisive significance for the portion of life depicted, which determine its existence and motion, its specific quality and its place in the total life process. In this sense the briefest song is as much an intensive totality as the mightiest epic. The objective character of the area of life represented determines the quantity, quality, proportion, etc. of the factors that emerge in interaction with the specific laws of the literary form appropriate for the representation of this portion of life. (Lukacs, 1970, p. 3)

For Lukacs, the extensive totality of the material world required ordering in the intensive totality of the artistic representation, and the major agency whereby this process of transformation and representation was to be performed was that of 'typicality':

The typical is not to be confused with the average (though there are cases where this holds true), nor with the eccentric (though the typical does as a rule go beyond the normal). A character is typical, in this technical sense, when his innermost being is determined by objective forces at work in society. Vautrin or Julien Sorel, superficially eccentric, are typical in their behaviour: the determining factors of a particular historical phase are found in them in concentrated form. Yet, though typical, they are never crudely 'illustrative'. (Lukacs, 1967, p. 122)

Both realism and naturalism are mimetic systems or practices of representation but are based on different epistemologies and this distinction between realism and naturalism within the category of mimesis is of great use in exploring the competence of documentary in adequating the real.

I have suggested earlier that if the first of the ideologies that legitimize informational television is that of the apparent neutrality of the originating institutions then the second is that of 'seeing is believing'. Consider the operation of the images in a television news programme: the succession of stills, interviews to camera, location film or video footage that have the rhetorical function of authenticating the governing narrative of the newsreader. The images are unintelligible without commentary and generally consist of no more than public figures entering or leaving buildings, cars or aeroplanes or reporters standing outside factory gates or government offices. The images' significance comes from the context and interpretation provided by speech, yet their presence, the visible evidence they offer of an event, authenticates the carrier of the meaning – the commentary.

Within broadcasting there has been a consistent push towards the refinement of technical equipment so as to minimize the transformation of 'reality' in the process of recording; to reduce what the BBC's *Principles and Practice in Documentary Programmes* (the institution's guide to programme makers, equivalent to a newspaper's style book) describes as the 'constant obstruction between the producer and his subject'.

'The documentary producer can only create his programme with the aid of a mass of equipment and a whole team of people. Indeed, the equipment is a constant obstruction between the producer and his subject, and a great deal of his skill is devoted to presenting his subject matter as if the equipment and the technical processes were not there' (BBC, 1972, p. 7). The techniques and technologies pioneered in British broadcasting in radio features and in the areas that Norman Swallow (1966) called 'Personal documentaries' have become normative over informational (or factual) television.

These technological and stylistic characteristics of television programme-making are symptoms of the passive project implicit in the word 'documentary' or 'recording'. These working practices, the trajectory of technological development and the vocabulary and ideas of informational television, are manifestations of the ideology of naturalism. The conception is of a perfect mimesis, an unstructured recording of an immanent apprehensible reality that is to be achieved by minimizing the interventions and transformations specific to the recording process. This ideology that reality is passively reflected rather than actively constituted in the process of programme-making is the ideology that legitimizes the constituted reality that is transmitted in informational programmes and the chimera that resolves the paradox experienced by TV workers between their active crafts of programme-making – their creation of a spectacle – and their conception of their role as one of non-intervention. *Principles and Practice in Documentary Programmes* uneasily manages the contradiction, insisting alternately on the 'creativity' of the documentary project and the necessity for the accounts of events and relations recounted in informational TV to be an impartial, balanced record. Indeed *Principles and Practice* recognizes that for the desired simulacrum to be achieved a certain active, structuring, creative activity on the part of the programme makers is not only necessary and unavoidable but desirable. The intriguing standard term of TV or film production, 'cheating' (the practice of amending an 'unreal' appearance in things in the recorded format by performing a reorganization of their real relations so that 'unreal' appearance is avoided), does not appear in *Principles and Practice* but the necessary practices involved in constituting the recorded reality are set out. The 'innocent eye' of the researcher sees 'What really happens when people go about their daily lives without the knowledge that a television audience is watching. He sees how a man really behaves when he is not putting on a show for the camera', and from that notional reality the producer 'carries out the first of a series of selection processes. He decides broadly what to include and what not to include; he undertakes his "casting" – as vital in a documentary as in a work of fiction, he decides which individuals should take part and which should not. If the subject is a contentious one, he must decide which arguments should be included and which are too trivial to warrant a place.'

He (or she) then directs the shooting stage – 'The director is in fact directing two quite separate things: his camera and his art. On the one hand he is telling cameramen and soundmen exactly what he wants to see and hear. On the other, he is assuming that what he wants to see and hear takes place in front of his camera . . . In practice, most of the things he needs to show are not going to happen in front of the camera of their own accord.'

It is Graef's work that most nearly approximates to the naturalistic ideal that governs the injunctions of *Principles and Practice* and that offers the most serious challenge to the arguments that I am developing in this paper and to the related argument of Robert Tyrell (1972). Addressing the ambiguous zone opened up by the contradictions of naturalist ideology, in a section on 'problems of the documentary' Tyrell argues that informational programmes are governed by contradictions:

> It is not that documentary film-makers are dishonest, they are usually the most earnest and conscientious of men: it is the form itself that is flawed by its own internal contradictions. It purports to show us reality; but what we see is inevitably an illusion. A documentary has to be constructed and contrived. Things have to be included and excluded, time has to be telescoped, space shrunk or stretched, action specially performed. The camera must be there to make the film and its presence must affect the subject in all but the most desperate of circumstances and yet the film-maker is at pains to conceal this fact from the audience. (Tyrell, 1972, pp. 27–8)

Graef's film-making, his practice of *ciné verité* or what he prefers to call 'observational cinema' is contrive to transcend the contradictions that Tyrell points to in the documentarists' project and that surface so evidently in *Principles and Practice*:

> The standard procedure for many film-makers seems to be, 'Forget it'. The BBC Green Book on documentaries suggests that you go along, spend a day or two watching what happens, and then you are suddenly an expert on what's typical. And then you stage what's typical. It implies that you know more about what's typical than the participants do. And what we're saying is that we know all along that we don't. (Graef, 1976a, p. 4)

Graef's claim to respect the internal natural logic of the subject was formulated to resist the suggestion by one of his usual co-workers, Terence Twigg, that their practice was one of: 'Proceeding in part to structure your material as is general practice in informational TV. Producing "films of record".' Elsewhere he describes his practice as one of producing

> Films of record – unstaged. Filmed without lights or interviews and using a minimum amount of apparatus. Our goal is to produce an account of a decision that matters to the people involved and to the public at large, and which is condensed in a manner that the participants will confirm is accurate. To

that extent we suggest these films are 'objective' – dangerous a word as that is. (Graef, 1976b, p. 8)

Of the four stages in constituting a documentary itemized in *Principles and Practice* – preparation, shooting, editing and finishing – Graef's practice can be differentiated from the norm in two stages of the construction of the programme.

In 'preparation' Graef's procedure is, as specified above, to eschew the positive and conscious structuring of the programme concept: he does *not* do what *Principles and Practice* enjoins of the director, namely that

> He decides broadly what to include: he undertakes his 'casting', as vital in a documentary as in a work of fiction: he decides which individuals should take part and which should not. If the subject is a contentious one he must decide which arguments should be included and which are too trivial to warrant a place.

Rather, Graef's decisions as to inclusions and exclusions, of dramatis personae and argument come principally in the third stage – in editing. *Principles and Practice* specifies that editing ratios:

> may be anything from 5 to 25 times the length of the finished film. A shooting ratio of 11:1 or 12:1 would be quite normal for a major documentary.

Accounts of Graef's editing ratios vary but cluster around 30:1 to 33:1. Beyond the ratio of film shot to film used there is little discussion of editing in the published statements or interviews of the Graef team. This suggests, I think, that there is little in this process of constituting the final text to differentiate Graef's work from that of other film-makers in informational TV – an impression that is borne out in viewing the programmes. Vaughan in his 'The space between shots' says:

> Despite his infatuation with the 'real time' experience – and hence with the eventual extinction of his office – the editor finds himself willy nilly making cuts; firstly to overcome camera run-outs and wobbles, then to eliminate longeurs and repetitions; next to clarify points of confusion created by the earlier cuts;

and finally with resignation, to allow the film to take on the form to which it seems to aspire . . . . The way in which 'a slice of life' takes on the quality of being 'about' something. (Vaughan, 1974, p. 80)

In the realm of editing the differences between Graef's programmes and the normative practice are differences of degree rather than of kind. Graef's films have a 'dramatic form'; the choice implied in the title of his series *Decision* constitutes a beginning, middle and end to the process with which the films concern themselves and this is so too in his earlier series *Space Between Words*. 'Work' is ended with a mass meeting of workers outside the factory at which the narrative that has been presented up until then is resumed in the account of negotiations given by a shop steward to the shop floor workers. The shift in location from the previous footage shot inside to an outside location clearly signals an end to an episode and the use of the steward's speech to close the narrative is an employment of one of the classic conventions of mystery or detective stories in which the resolving and explanatory function is given to a character and signals the end of the narrative.

So, whilst Graef's cinema does not use many of the familiar techniques of the familiar documentary, for example counterpoint montage, the creation of mood by means of music or sound effects, the film's material *is* ordered, it constructs its meaning through familiar formal practices. As Vaughan says:

> The 'Space Between Words' films can be analysed with much the same critical vocabulary as can other films. The differences quarantine themselves in the area where moral uncertainty resides – that of the film-maker's subjectivity. The problems are in one respect worse than those which the BBC booklet evades, for the Mitchell style (*the man not the camera* ed.) left no-one in doubt that what he was seeing was poetry. (ibid., p. 81)

It is clear that the procedures involved in producing this effect are no less creative than those of Godard or TV pioneers like Denis Mitchell.

Principles and Practice states that shooting ratios of between 5:1 and 25:1 are the parameters of normal usage. Graef customarily exceeds a ratio of 30:1. His prodigality in the use of film stock enables him to deny himself a number of the established practices in constituting a film and eschew most of the injunctions in *Principles and Practice*. Instead of preconceiving the material to be shot, acted or reconstructed and adding commentary or interviews to explicate any matters that are unclear in the photography, Graef is able to postpone some of his process of selection and constitution of a narrative until shooting and the interaction between subjects and film-makers begins. Once again, his remarks on the Green Book's ideas on typicality, briefly commented on earlier, are relevant:

> The BBC Green Book on documentaries suggests that you go along, spend a day or two watching what happens, and then you are suddenly an expert on what's typical. And then you stage what's typical. It implies that we know more about what's typical than the participants do, and what we're saying is that we know all along that we don't. But we're going to try to pay some sort of respect all the way through the process to what is actually happening and what it tells us. (Graef, 1975a, p. 4).

Here Graef is arguing *against* a recurrent practice of dressing experience in one of a restricted set of off-the-peg professional paradigms and *for* a discovery procedure in constituting the film's subject (and Graef's sensitivity to the specificities of experience is one of the major elements in his work that differentiates it from the familiar management of subject matter in shooting television documentary).

But Graef's argument implies that it is the participants' perception of the film's concern that is authentic. It is to be sure an implication, not a necessary conclusion to the argument, but Graef's characterizations of his work are rich in implication rather than unambiguous in their conclusions. I will return to this characteristic, but suggest here that the implied authority ceded to the participants' perception does not stand examination. How is the validating perception of the participants formulated and recognized? It is in the nature of Graef's method (and here he's at one with standard practice where conscious reflection and construction of the film's content is the prerogative of the recording crew not of the film's subjects) that an orchestrated performance is not mounted for the camera. The subjects – the 'participants' as Graef names them – of the film do not discuss together what is the problem – what is the film's subject or concern. They have no means of formulating a collective view, for often Graef has chosen to depict a relation of antagonism – management and union in 'Work', the two sides in the Korf contract negotiations, the family that has developed no collective harmony in its own interactions, let alone in its self-presentation to the television film crew and the television audience. The only viewpoint that embraces the situation of the participants is that of Graef for he constitutes that situation, defines its bounds in time and space, peoples it with Mr X and Mrs Y but not Mr Z and witnesses the reflections, negotiations and self-presentations of X apart from Y; Y apart from X, as well as their interactions.

Graef's procedures differ from the normative professional practice he abhors in degree not in kind. His method of constituting a film, his scrupulous endeavour to live out the implications of the documentary-project, differentiate his work from, say, *World in Action, Panorama,* or the news, but the difference is one of style, of achieving a distinctive personal articulation of the same recurrent elements and relations. Graef's project is one of scrupulously performing the naturalist imperatives that govern informational programming, clearly framing *Steel, Rates,* or *Work* by titles, commentary and introduction by anchor man rather than integrating these elements, alien to strict naturalism, with the location-shot, direct-sound kernel of the film. As Dai Vaughan says: 'What we are doing is closer to the nineteenth-century novel. We're treating it as naturalism.'

The limits of this approach become evident in the great baggy, three-decker work on the 35th congress of the Communist Party of Great Britain, *Decision: British Communism* (Granada TV, 1978). Here the viewer was lost among a variety of personae and arguments without adequate 'cueing' by narrator or introduction – the spectacle embraces so much that it becomes incomprehensible.

And a number of the 'invisible' natural rhetorical devices of naturalistic diegetic construction spring to the sceptical eye in Graef's best work, for example the framing of the diegesis with an internal narrator/interpreter in *School,* choosing a 'natural' armature for the narrative organization – the nuclear family – in *Family,* the recurrent annual ritual of the local authority budget

in *Rates* and so on. It is clear that the central claim of naturalist aesthetic practice to offer a perfect mimesis, to achieve an
unmediated 'impartial' representation is impossible to sustain.
Graef, though within this tradition and more scrupulous in the
practice of its norms than others who rest more confidently on
its ideology, does *not* claim with André Bazin that:

> Only the impassive lens, stripping its object of all those ways
> of seeing it, those piled up preconceptions, that spiritual dust
> and grime with which my eyes have covered it, is able to pres-
> ent it in all its virginal purity to my attention. (Bazin, 1967,
> p. 15)

Rather, he claims that structuring and intervention are minimized
and that the light of events is permitted to shine through when
artifice and the processes of constitution and mediation of the
subject are stripped away:

> How much we affect the scenes we film is hard to say, but we
> have never claimed to be filming reality as it would be without
> us there. All we have endeavoured to do, in devising a unique
> set of procedures in our film-making – no lights, no interviews,
> no staging and showing the main protagonists the edited film
> before transmission – is to attempt to minimize the effect of
> our presence. (Graef, 1977, p. 285)

The question is how adequate a basis for cognition, for understanding the world, is naturalism – whether that of Bazin, Graef's more
modest aspiration of minimizing mediation so that truth may be
recorded and fairly represented, or the strategies of nineteenth-
century naturalist prose invoked by Vaughan?

The prospect of an extended comparison of Zola and Graef's
aesthetic and a few reflections on the Second Empire and Britain's
contemporary post-imperial state is seductive indeed, but that *tour
de force* can await another writer. But both Zola and Leacock
have a shared positivistic fascination with scientific method and
discuss their representations in terms of scientific enquiry, and
Zola and Graef share a concern with detail. The more than
30 documentaries that Roger Graef has made for British and
non-British broadcasting organizations are classic instances of

this style and, certainly in the UK, his best known works, the five *Space Between Words* programmes made for the BBC in 1972, the six-part *Decision* for Granada between 1975 and 1978 and the thirteen-part *Police* series for the BBC in 1981 are the best known examples of the observational cinema style.

Graef is the most scrupulous practitioner of the imperatives of the BBC's *Principles and Practice* who is currently working in British television – Graef more consistently, consciously and thoroughly attempts to reduce the mediations between the subject of his films and their audiences than does any other British television documentarist. Other film-makers like Paul Watson or Angela Pope work in the same manner but not with the same lacerating commitment to a scrupulous recording of events as Graef. To appropriate a category from an aesthetic (and intellectual) tradition to which Graef is firmly opposed he is the 'typical' instance of British television documentary. The aesthetic which has typicality as one of its central categories is realism – an aesthetic which, like Graef's asserts the primacy of the real but, unlike Graef's, asserts that apprehension and representation of the real is a matter of active selection and organization. 'Realism', as Friedrich Engels said in a formulation on which Lukacs's work and much of Marxist aesthetics has been constructed, 'implies, besides truth of detail, the truth in reproduction of typical characters under typical circumstances.' Implicitly, every documentary whether 'observational' or not presents itself as 'typical'. If it did not, what claim would it have on the attention of its viewers? Unless there is a general representative quality to representations their significance can only be of extremely parochial interest. The chief interest of Graef's work is the spectacle it offers of time, intelligence and considerable resources devoted to squaring the circle. It is an exemplary site for the study of the major aesthetic mode of ideological management performed by British television (and, it has to be said, by most other television systems).

Note

An invaluable source of information about Graef's film-making is *Nothing But The Truth* (ICA/BFI, 1982) edited by John Wyver.

This chapter was first published in *Documentary and Mass Media* J. Corner (ed.) (London: Edward Arnold, 1986). It is based on a review of *Nothing but the Truth* which appeared in *Media Culture and Society* (Vol. 5, no 2) in 1983 and also draws on my discussion of Lukacs and the ideology of realism in *WDR and the Arbeiterfilm* (BFI, 1981) which, in turn, was pre-echoed in my remarks on Graef's *Decision: British Communism* project in the pages of *Comment* in 1978 (themselves cited in *Nothing but the Truth*). However this bibliographical etymology does not adequately indicate my debt to *Nothing but the Truth* and I am pleased to acknowledge here more than the usual reviewer's debt to the work that occasioned the review.

Filmography

One of Them is Brett, Dir/writer R. Graef, Society for Thalidomide Children, 1964. *The Man From Sotheby's*, Prod/Dir/Writer R. Graef, CBC 1964. *To The Manner Born*, Prod/Dir/Writer R. Graef, CBC, 1965. *Gunter Grass's Germany*, Prod/Dir/Writer R. Graef, CBC/BBC, 1965. *The Life and Times Of John Huston, Esq*, Prod/Dir/Writer R. Graef, CBC/BBC/NET, 1965. *Who Is?* (13 episodes), Exec Prod R. Graef, 5 episodes Dir R. Graef, CBC/BBC/NET/BR, 1966–67. *Why Save Florence?*, Prod/Dir/Writer R. Graef, CBC/BBC/NET/BR, 1969. *In The Name of Allah*, Prod/Dir/Writer R. Graef, CBC/BBC/NET/BR, 1970. *The Space Between Words* (5 episodes), Prod/Dir R. Graef, BBC/KCET, 1972. *The State of The Nation: a Law In the Making*, Prod/Dir R. Graef, Granada, 1973. *Is this The Way To Save A City?*, Prod/Writer R. Graef & M. Dibb, Dir R. Graef, BBC, 1974. *The State Of The Nation: Inside The Brussels HQ*, Prod/Dir R. Graef, Granada, 1975. *Decision* (3 episodes), Prod/Dir R. Graef, Granada, 1976. *Pleasure At Her Majesty's*, Prod/Dir R. Graef, Amnesty International, 1976. *Decision: British Communism* (3 episodes), Prod/Dir R. Graef, Granada, 1978. *The Mermaid's Frolics*, Prod R. Graef, Amnesty International, 1978. *Inside Europe* (5 episodes), Coordinator and series editor R. Graef, Dir (episode 5) R. Graef, Granada/RTB/DR/NOS/SR/WGBH/ZDF, 1977–79. *The Secret Policeman's Ball*, Co-prod/Dir R. Graef, Films of Record for Amnesty International, 1979. *Police* aka *Police: Operation Carter*, (13 episodes), Prod/co-dir R. Graef, BBC, 1982. *Nagging Doubt*, Dir R. Graef, Limehouse/Channel 4, 1985. *Fifty Minute*

Hour, Dir R. Graef, Limehouse/Channel 4, forthcoming. *Maybe Baby*, Dir R. Graef, Limehouse/BBC, forthcoming. (Filmography 1964–1982 from *Nothing But The Truth*, ed. J. Wyver, ICA/BFI, 1982.) BBC = British Broadcasting Corporation, BR = Bayerische Rundfunk, CBC = Canadian Broadcasting Corporation, DR = Danmarks Radio, NET = National Education Television, NOS = Nederlandse Oemrop Stichting, SR = Sveriges Radio, ZDF = Zweites Deutsches Fernsehen. KCET and WGBH are the identifying letters of two major Public Broadcasting Service stations in the United States of America. The letters are not initials.

References

Bazin, A. (1967), 'The ontology of the photographic image', in *What is Cinema?* Volume 1 H. Gray (ed.) (Berkeley: University of California Press).

BBC (1972), *Principles and Practice in Documentary* (London: BBC).

Collins, M. (1984), *Perceptions of Bias in Television News* (London: Social and Community Planning Research).

Graef, R. (1976a), 'Decisions Decisions', in *Sight and Sound* vol. 25, no. 1.

Graef, R. (1976b), *Decision. Granada and Political Broadcasting* no 6 (Manchester: Granada Television)

Graef, R. (1977), 'The decision programme', *Comment* 6 August 1977.

Lukacs, G. (1967), *The Meaning of Contemporary Realism* (London: Merlin).

Lukacs, G. (1970), *Writer and Critic* (London: Merlin).

Swallow, N. (1966), *Factual Television* (London: Focal Press).

Tyrell, R. (1972), *The Work of the Television Journalist* (London: Focal Press).

Vaughan, D. (1974), 'The space between shots', *Screen* vol. 15, no. 1.

Vaughan, D. (1976), *Television Documentary Usage* (London: British Film Institute).

Wyver, J. (ed.) (1982), *Nothing but the Truth: Cinema Verite and the Films of the Roger Graef Team* (London: Institute of Contemporary Arts and British Film Institute).

Index